The Progressive Century

The Progressive Century
The Future of the Centre-Left in Britain

Edited by

Neal Lawson

and

Neil Sherlock

Foreword by Roy Jenkins

palgrave

Editorial matter, selection and Introduction © Neal Lawson
and Neil Sherlock 2001
Foreword © Roy Jenkins 2001
Chapter 23 (Endpiece) © Peter Mandelson 2001
Remaining chapters © Palgrave Publishers Ltd 2001

First published 2001 by
PALGRAVE
Houndmills, Basingstoke, Hampshire RG21 6XS and
175 Fifth Avenue, New York, N. Y. 10010
Companies and representatives throughout the world

PALGRAVE is the new global academic imprint of
St. Martin's Press LLC Scholarly and Reference Division and
Palgrave Publishers Ltd (formerly Macmillan Press Ltd).

ISBN 0–333–94961–7 hardback
ISBN 0–333–94962–5 paperback

This book is printed on paper suitable for recycling and
made from fully managed and sustained forest sources.

A catalogue record for this book is available
from the British Library.

Library of Congress Cataloging-in-Publication Data
The progressive century : the future of the centre-left in Britain /
[edited by] Neal Lawson and Neil Sherlock.
        p. cm.
    Includes bibliographical references and index.
    ISBN 0–333–94961–7
        1. Great Britain—Politics and government—1997– 2. Right
    and left (Political science) I. Lawson, Neal, 1963– II. Sherlock,
    Neil, 1963–

    JN231 .P76 2001
    320.51'3'0941—dc21
                                            2001019445

10   9   8   7   6   5   4   3   2   1
10   09 08 07 06 05 04 03 02 01

Printed in Great Britain by Antony Rowe Ltd, Chippenham, Wiltshire

Contents

Preface

This book was written in the months before a likely spring 2001 general election and will be published shortly after. So in terms of a result we are writing blind. We believe that the forces of progress will have triumphed over the forces of conservatism. We hope that swathes of the electorate will have voted tactically against William Hague's swing to the right. But we fear that turnout will have plummeted as growing alienation from the old politics spreads like an unchecked cancer through our body politic (this is a huge concern that only a commitment to new politics will rectify) and that any new mandate for Labour will only have been given less than enthusiastically.

But while majorities clearly matter they are of secondary importance to the ideas and movements that drive political progress. The first term of Labour's administration has by historic party standards been a managerial success with the ghosts of Wilson and Callaghan finally laid to rest. But Labour still looks unable or unwilling to build moral legitimacy for its project and recognise the limits of central managerialism. Even with the prospect of another clear majority New Labour already looks in danger of running into the sand before we reach a third term. Meanwhile the Liberal Democrats need to keep their eyes firmly on the big prizes that a dynamic relationship of co-operation and competition with Labour could deliver.

The lesson of the first Labour term is that the pattern of the whole administration is largely established within the first twelve months. After that the course is set. So we do not have much time to influence hearts and minds and build the forces of progressive change. Another lesson is that people and events change quickly. We have lost count of the times that the prospects of a progressive century have been written up and just as suddenly dismissed. Two facts suggest we should hold our nerve. The first is the strength of our opponents. Writing in the *Financial Times* Philip Stephens reminds us that 'The iron law of British politics has not changed. The destiny of the centre-left remains to provide the brief interludes that separate long periods of Conservative rule' (2 February 2001). Second, we have seen the political climate change as advocates and opponents of this progressive agenda come and go. But the underlying logic, for social democrats to be more liberal and for liberals to be more collectivist, grows more compelling by the day. Labour ministers are at last learning that delivery from the centre has its limits – they are finding out that pluralism rather than centralism is 'what works'. Liberal Democrats recognise that the best guarantee of individual liberty is increasingly communal action. The prospects for a progressive century may ebb and flow – but the need will not go away.

On publication of the book the landscape of British politics may have changed somewhat but the underlying contours – the essential strengths and weaknesses of the centre-left – will remain as they were. Two different players, who may stubbornly refuse to play them together, will still hold the cards of a winning progressive hand. Regardless of who won and by how much, the challenge for the centre-left remains the same – how to unite the strands of social democracy and liberalism and give voice to a new social democratic liberalism that can dominate the twenty-first century.

Foreword

Roy Jenkins

Politics at the beginning of the year 2001 are in a state at once partisan and becalmed. Everyone can hear the noise of the leading politicians grinding their sword-sharpeners for the coming electoral battle. Yet few feel exhilarated by the sound. Political interest is at a low ebb, and while the greatest danger of the general election, that of it propelling Mr Hague and his peculiarly unprepossessing Shadow Cabinet into office seems unlikely, the second greatest danger, that of a depressingly low turnout, looms ominously.

The first Labour government for nearly 20 years should therefore achieve what has often seemed to be its main objective, its re-election for a second term, and it will on the whole deserve it. But what then is going to be its next central objective? The cautious fostering of a third term, with the avoidance of such dangerous diversions as referenda on the euro and electoral reform, will hardly inspire.

Part of the government's problem has been that, despite its vast and somewhat deadening parliamentary majority, it did not secure more than 43.2 per cent of the vote, which left it only 1.3 per cent more popularly backed than was Mr Major's ill-fated administration of 1992. The hope was that Lib-Labery would transform the position by bringing an auxiliary force of another 17 per cent of the vote and giving the government a confidence and a moral authority which no other post-war government had enjoyed.

In a purely electoral sense this was achieved in 1997. Tactical anti-Conservative voting probably gave the Labour Party nearly 60 seats they would not otherwise have won, and it gave the Liberal Democrats a good half of its total of 46. But despite endless discussions and some bravery on the part of Tony Blair and Paddy Ashdown it did not produce a remoulding of the sadly sclerotic shape of British politics. And it left the Labour government at once cautious and nervous of dissent.

One of the discussions which, five or six years ago, gave me great hope, in politics generally and in Tony Blair personally, was that we were both thinking in the same terms about healing the split on the centre-left and making the twenty-first century, in contrast with the essentially Conservative twentieth century, a 'progressive century', which is the title of this book. I cannot now remember which of us first used the key phrases which have since become something of clichés. Probably, as with most useful meetings of mind, they just emerged.

I do not believe that Mr Blair has resiled from that intention, which would itself leave a great impact on British politics, and which would also give him the freedom to make his second term much more adventurous and historically productive than his first. This is what this admirable book is about. It makes the valid point that, as the Ashdown/Blair conversations foundered, or at least failed to produce dramatic results, on the conservative of forces within the Labour Party and to a lesser extent the Liberal Democrat Party, it is desirable in future to work towards increasing collaboration at grassroots as well as at leadership level.

Notes on the Contributors

Rt Hon Sir **Paddy Ashdown** KBE MP served in the Royal Marines for twelve years and was First Secretary to the UK Mission to the UN in Geneva. He was elected MP for Yeovil in 1983, and before being elected leader of the Liberal Democrats in 1988 he was spokesman on Trade and Industry and then Education and Science. Under his leadership the Liberal Democrats enjoyed a period of unprecedented growth, becoming the second party of local government, winning 46 seats at the 1997 general election and forming an administration with Labour in Scotland.

Menzies Campbell is the Liberal Democrat Spokesperson on Foreign Affairs and Defence.

Philip Collins is the Director of the Social Market Foundation.

Robin Cook is Foreign Secretary.

Anna Coote is Director of the Public Health Programme at the King's Fund, London. She was formerly Deputy Director of the Institute for Public Policy Research, consultant to the Minister for Women, Senior Lecturer in Media and Communications at Goldsmiths' College, London Univerity, a producer and editor of current affairs and documentaries for Channel Four TV, Deputy Editor of the *New Statesman*, and a journalist and broadcaster.

David Cowling is a political analyst who formerly worked for ITN and prior to that in local government and Westminster.

Philip Dodd is Director of the Institute of Contemporary Arts. The co-curator of the Hayward's 1996 art and film exhibition, 'Spellbound', an award-winning broadcaster and author, he was an academic for 13 years, deputy editor of the *New Statesman*, founding editor of the BFI's award-winning *Sight and Sound* and a consultant to Alan Yentob (1986/89) at BBC Music and Arts. Among his books are studies of art and value and of autobiography, as well as two influential arguments on British national identity, *Englishness: Politics*

& *Culture* (1986) and *The Battle Over Britain* for the think tank Demos. He is Visiting Professor, South Bank University.

Don Foster – a former teacher, university lecturer and author of science resources for schools – has been the Liberal Democrat MP for Bath since 1992. After several years as his party's education spokesman, he now speaks on the Environment, Transport, regions and Social Justice.

Pam Giddy is the Director of Charter 88.

Olly Grender is a public affairs consultant who was Director of Communications at Shelter and before that the Liberal Democrats. She also worked as Paddy Ashdown's researcher and speechwriter.

Harriet Harman is Labour MP for Camberwell and Peckham.

Chris Huhne MEP, former City economist and award-winning *Guardian* and *Independent* Economics Editor, is economics spokesman of the European Liberal Democrat and Reformist group in the European Parliament.

Will Hutton is CEO of the Industrial Society. After starting his career at stockbrokers Phillips & Drew, he pursued a media career, fulfilling roles as Producer/Director of *The Money Programme*, Economics Editor of *Newsnight* and reporter for *Panorama*. In 1990 he joined Guardian Newspapers as Economics Editor and became Editor in Chief of the *Observer* in 1998. He has written five books, including the best-selling *The State We're In* and has presented several topical television and radio series.

Ruth Kelly is MP for Bolton West and became parliamentary private secretary to Agriculture Minister Nick Brown after serving on the Treasury Select Committee. Previously an economics writer for the *Guardian*, she has also worked for the Bank of England.

Neal Lawson is the Managing Editor of the Labour journal *Renewal*. He is a former researcher for the TGWU and for Gordon Brown. He worked for Peter Mandelson during the 1997 election. He is a member of the management committee of Make Votes Count, and is a council member of Charter 88.

Roger Levett is a Director of CAG Consultants who specialise in sustainable development policy and management. He has recently advised DETR on sustainability in planning guidance and appraisal of sustainable communities, the Countryside Agency on quality of life capital and sustainable settlements, the UK Round Table on Sustainable Development on indicators, and the Royal Commission on Environmental Pollution on energy and planning. He was formerly a Department of Energy civil servant, and studied philosophy and politics.

Ruth Lister CBE is Professor of Social Policy at Loughborough University. She is a former Director of the Child Poverty Action Group and served on the Commission on Social Justice, the Opsahl Commission into the Future of Northern Ireland and the Commission of Inquiry into Poverty, Participation and Power. She is a founding Academician of the new Academy for Learned Societies for the Social Sciences. She has published widely around poverty, income maintenance and women's citizenship. Her latest book is *Citizenship: Feminist Perspectives* (Macmillan 1997).

Calum Macdonald is Labour MP for the Western Isles.

Donald Macintyre is Chief Political Commentator at the *Independent* and is author of *Mandelson and the Making of New Labour*.

David Marquand was MP for Ashfield from 1966 to 1977, and a Chief Adviser in the European Commission from 1977 to 1978. He was Professor of Politics and Contemporary History at the University of Salford and then Professor of Politics and founder-director of the Political Economy Research Centre at the University of Sheffield. From 1987 to 1997 he was joint editor of the *Political Quarterly*. He is now Principal of Mansfield College Oxford. His books include, *Ramsay MacDonald* (2nd edn) (1997), *The Unprincipled Society* (1988), *The Progressive Dilemma* (1991; 2nd revised edn 1997), *The New Reckoning: Capitalism, States and Citizens* (1997).

Kirsty Milne has been a columnist and political commentator for the *Scotsman* since the first elections for the Scottish Parliament in May 1999. She has also worked for the *New Statesman*, *New Society* and the BBC.

Mark Oaten MP is PPS to Charles Kennedy and is spokesman on Europe for the party. He is Chair of the All-Party Parliamentary Prisoners-of-War Group. He is a member of the Public Administration

Committee and is on the political board of Britain in Europe. He was elected twice in 1997 for the Winchester constituency.

Andrew Pakes is Director of the New Politics Network, an independent network whose aim is to develop an open debate on the future of centre-left politics, and previously President of the National Union of Students; outside work he has been an active member of the Labour Party for eleven years.

Kate Parminter was appointed director of the CPRE in 1998. She was a district councillor for eight years in West Sussex. Kate worked for the RSPCA where she led a number of high-profile campaigns including wildlife protection and the abolition of hunting with dogs.

Greg Power is Director of the Hansard Society's Parliament and Government Programme. Previously Head of Campaigns at Charter 88, he has written widely on politics, politicians and Parliament. He is currently writing a book for Palgrave on MPs' constituency work.

Steve Richards was a BBC Political Correspondent for four years. In 1996 he became Political Editor of the *New Statesman*. He has been the Chief Political Commentator at the *Independent on Sunday* since September 2000. Steve Richards also presents BBC2's *Despatch Box* and Radio 4's *Week in Westminster*.

Peter Riddell is political columnist and commentator of *The Times*. He has written several books on the British political system, most recently *Parliament under Blair*. He is a member of the council of the Hansard Society and is vice-chairman of its Commission on the Scrutiny of Parliament. He is Visiting Professor of Political History at Queen Mary College, University of London.

Michael Rustin is Professor of Sociology at the University of East London. He is the author of *Towards a Pluralist Socialism* (1985) and *The Good Society and the Inner World* (1991), and is co-editor of *Soundings* magazine.

Neil Sherlock is a partner at KPMG. A former President of the Oxford Union Society, he was an adviser to Paddy Ashdown. He is a member of the management committee of Make Votes Count, and is a council member of Charter 88, New Local Government Network and the

Hansard Society. Neil fought the 1992 and 1997 general elections for the Liberal Democrats.

Andrew Stevens is Labour's Political Assistant for the London Borough of Lewisham. He was educated at the University of Teesside and Goldsmiths' College, University of London. He is a regular contributor to a wide range of labour movement publications and was a contributor to *Beyond Good Governance*, published by the New Politics Network.

Dave Sullivan is Mayor for Lewisham, having been elected leader of the London Borough of Lewisham in 1998 (and 1985–88). He was educated at Ruskin College and the University of Kent at Canterbury. He has been a Lewisham councillor for 20 years.

Matthew Taylor is Director of the Institute for Public Policy Research, Britain's leading centre-left think tank. Until December 1998 he was Assistant General Secretary for the Labour Party. During the 1997 general election he was Labour's Director of Policy and a member of the party's central election strategy team. Amongst other areas, Matthew Taylor is interested in the renewal of civil society and modernisation of government.

Polly Toynbee is a columnist on the *Guardian* and *Radio Times* and was previously Social Affairs Editor of the BBC.

Stephen Twigg was elected MP for Enfield Southgate in May 1997. He was previously General Secretary of the Fabian Society and has been an active member of the Labour Party for 19 years.

Tony Wright is the Labour MP for Cannock Chase. He is also Honorary Professor of Politics at the University of Birmingham, joint editor of the *Political Quarterly* and author of many books including *Citizens and Subjects* (1994), *Socialisms Old and New* (1996) and *The British Political Process* (2000).

Acknowledgements

Neal Lawson

I am largely what society made me. From that social democratic premise to trying to narrow down a list of heartfelt thank yous is an impossible task. But there are some people I cannot miss out. Neil Sherlock was the first to show me that party labels mean much less than the values and beliefs that underpin them – most notably the desire for a more equal society. It has been a joy to work with him. For political friendship, encouragement and opportunity I am especially grateful to Scarlett MccGwire, Paul Thompson, Lindsay Thomas, Peter Hyman, Pam Giddy, Simon Buckby, Sion Simon, Ben Lucas, Matthew Taylor, Gordon Brown, Peter Mandelson and John Joynson. For political inspiration I have turned again and again to Noberto Bobbio (*Left and Right*) and David Marquand (*The Unprincipled Society* and *The Progressive Dilemma*). My parents and my sister have shown me how to be compassionate and caring and provided me with much love and support. There are other special people and I can only hope you know who you are. Finally, my love and thanks go to Caroline, Buddy and Joe, whose tolerance of an always-busy husband and father I have stretched by at least a century. They will hopefully be compensated in part by the fact that it may still be a progressive century.

Blackheath
London

Neil Sherlock

I first met Neal Lawson as Tony Blair was beginning the process of modernising the Labour Party. It soon became clear that although we were passionate and active members of different political parties, we shared a commitment to progressive values, principles and policies – not least on electoral reform and Europe. The book stems from that commitment and a desire to demonstrate that this century can be a progressive century in marked contrast to the last Conservative century. My inspiration has been the speeches and writings of Roy Jenkins, the leadership of Paddy Ashdown, the wonderful Liberal Democrats in South West Surrey and the practical liberalism of my father and late mother. Two friends in particular, Ian Wright and Nick Harvey, have provided guidance and wisdom which has been invaluable in shaping my thoughts – my thanks, as ever, to them both. Above all, I have had the incalculable blessings from the friendship, tolerance and love of Kate, who, despite being pregnant and then bringing our Rose into the world, found time not only to write a chapter for this book but also to encourage and guide me. My hope is that Rose grows up in a more progressive Britain than her parents, and my part of *The Progressive Century* is dedicated to her.

Farncombe
Surrey

Both editors would like to express their thanks to the contributors to this book, all of whom moved with speed and enthusiasm to make the venture possible; to Stuart Thompson and Barbara Gunnell for comments and assistance with editing; to Laura Shepherd-Robinson for setting up the roundtable, and to Alison Howson at Palgrave for her support and enthusiasm.

In particular, we would like to thank the Trustees of the Joseph Rowntree Reform Trust – Archy Kirkwood, David Currie, Christine Day, Pam Giddy, Christopher Greenfield, Diana Scott, David Shutt, Trevor Smith – as well as Tony Flower whose generosity and support made the book possible.

1
Introduction
The Progressive Century: Ours to Make

Neal Lawson and Neil Sherlock

This book is based on three important propositions. The first is that neither the social democratic nor the liberal tradition can deliver a 'progressive' century by themselves. The second is that progressive politics in Britain cannot rely on the whims of senior politicians, no matter how well intentioned. The third is that without the right combination of leaders, ideas and movements, the next shift in political power in Britain is more likely to be towards the forces of 'conservatism' than the forces of progress. We face a choice: to create the conditions for a progressive century out of the joint strengths of liberalism and social democracy, or to witness another hundred years of Tory hegemony.

The Blair paradox

Four years ago, it felt as if that choice had been made. On the night of 1 May 1997 the hearts of progressives soared. How could they not? For the first time since 1974 the Conservatives had lost a general election – and they had not just lost, they had been thrashed. In particular, hopes had been raised by the fact that people had voted intelligently to inflict damage on a party that had done so much damage to the country over the previous 18 years. For a fleeting moment there was the promise of a new dawn – not just a new government but a new way of doing politics. At its heart was 'the project' – an approach that promised to be non-tribal and pluralist through a realignment of the centre-left. It was epitomised by the pre-election deal struck between Tony Blair and Paddy Ashdown, which would have seen Liberal Democrats in government for the first time since the early part of the century.

The 'project' to realign British politics had been prepared in advance. Blair and Ashdown were unusually close for leaders of competing parties. Blair had also come to rely on the wisdom of Lord Jenkins, the doyen of British liberal/social democracy. Playing Obi Wan to Blair's Luke Skywalker, Jenkins had instilled in his apprentice a belief that the great rupture of radicals at the turn of the twentieth century was unnecessary and unwarranted. The divorce of Liberal and Labour had served only as handmaiden to a Conservative century.

The pre-election manifesto of the 'project' was the Robin Cook/Robert MacLennan agreement on constitutional reform that established parameters for far-reaching change in the political system if the Tories were kept out. Deep behind the scenes, election organisers from both parties were identifying the seats that could be targeted to maximum effect. Explicitly, both parties fought every seat; implicitly, resources were targeted and blind eyes turned to tactical campaigning. The results were spectacular, none more so than Enfield Southgate where Stephen Twigg replaced Michael Portillo on the basis of unprecedented tactical voting.

But it was an illusion to think that a new politics could be delivered from the top down. The commitment to it was probably sincere enough but was confined to too few leaders. It had never been sufficiently grounded in a deep-rooted account of the repeated failure of the centre-left in Britain. Meaningful and lasting political advance is only ever secured when the ambition and capability of leaders chimes with ideas and movements outside of Westminster. A progressive century will be created from the bottom up or it will not be created at all.

The illusion is revealed in contemporary accounts of the Blair–Ashdown courtship,[1] which identified a level of misunderstanding and a lack of nerve at the crucial moment. Despite the failure to reach a deal, advances have since been made, primarily in the field of constitutional reform where the devolution of power to a Scottish

Parliament and a Welsh Assembly has seen the biggest shock for more than 150 years to the UK's sclerotic political system. The Scottish coalition was able to introduce a number of progressive measures such as free tuition for university students and better freedom of information legislation. At the time of writing, a new Welsh coalition also offers a ray of hope to progressives. Charles Kennedy has rightly refused to shut the door left open by Paddy Ashdown's departure and there has been some extension to the work of the Joint Cabinet Committee into European defence and security policy, as well as United Nations reform. Nick Harvey, Liberal Democrat Spokesman on Health, made important contributions to the NHS plan launched in summer 2000 by the Prime Minister and Health Secretary. But given the promise of Blair's implied deal with the Liberal Democrats, progress has been disappointing. Ashdown has left the stage. Lord Jenkins' elegant report on electoral reform gathers dust on the shelf. The hopes of electoral reformers became channelled into the lesser campaign of seeing the referendum pledge make a reappearance in the 2001 election manifesto. Vitally, Blair has failed to muster support among Cabinet colleagues and in the rest of Labour. Even more importantly, there has been a failure to 'do' politics differently. The opportunities of 1 May 1997 were slipping through the fingers of the centre-left.

It is easy to feel frustrated and demoralised by the lack of progress and the timidity of party leaders. But crying 'betrayal' only takes progressives down a political cul-de-sac that has proved a desolate haven for the centre-left over the past century. Leaders will play a pivotal role and their visions, hopes and fears will be crucial, but they are frequently constrained by their respective parties, by the media and by the intellectual community that supports them. Paddy Ashdown was driven to ask whether Blair was a 'control freak' or a 'pluralist'. The real answer is that he is a complex and fluid mixture of both. But the narrowness of the question shows that there is much work to do before a broad base of support can be built for a decade – let alone a century – of progressive politics. The drive and enthusiasm of the leaders of both parties is a necessary but not insufficient condition for a new progressive politics of the twenty-first century. It is the world beyond Westminster to which progressives must appeal and from which they must draw strength if the promise is to be realised.

Progressive principles

A progressive century will not come about just because the Tories lost in 1997, even by a landslide. Indeed, it will not come into being just because they lose again. It will not come about because one or two leaders will it, or because electoral arithmetic demands it. It will not happen without the recognition that the traditions of liberalism and social democracy are two sides of the same progressive coin. The task of progressives is to create the context – the analysis, ideas, policies and forces – in which leaders, parties and other social forces can play their part in delivering a progressive century.

Roy Jenkins once made a famous call for the strengthening of the 'radical centre'. This is at the heart of the progressive cause and his historical analysis is the inspiration for this book. But it is inspired, too, by our own experiences working alongside politicians and activists in both parties and by the potential for reform that we believe remains under the lock and key of tribalism.

The dictionary definition of progress is 'to move forward or bring nearer to completion or perfection'. By definition, then, progressive politics identifies restlessness and dissatisfaction with the world as it is. It is the opposite of conservatism. Progressives look around them and see levels of inequality that should not be tolerated in a decent, affluent society. They see vital public services such as health and education choked by years of underfunding and creeping marketisation. They look back to J.K. Galbraith's sense of 'private affluence and public squalor' and see the challenges still to be faced. They share a sense of outrage at a political system that permits a 'culture of contentment' for some and denies a decent living for so many. They feel the lifeblood drain from the body politic, as a system invented for the nineteenth century struggles to contend with the demands of the twenty-first. They share the anxiety of environmentalists that the current rate of growth is unsustainable. They believe that their own parties are still run by the few rather than the many. They are temperamentally internationalist and proudly European. They know that, left untamed, capitalism will deny for the majority the life chances and opportunity that should be every citizen's right.

Social democrats and liberals share, as Polly Toynbee has argued, certain fundamental positions: a presumption in favour of the underdog; a belief that things can always get better; a trust in reason;

taxing as much as you dare; tolerating almost anything except intolerance; striving for a more equal society; siding with the consumer; celebrating diversity; and regarding sex and family life as no business of the state. Above all, they both believe that all humans are redeemable.

The obstacles to reform

All of this begs the obvious question, if social democrats and liberals share such strong values, why the split in their organisational forces, and what are the themes that will unite them in working towards a progressive century?

Over the past hundred years unnecessary divisions left radicals weaker and paved the way for the 'Conservative century'. The roots of the division go back to the turn of the last century when the Liberal Party was groping for a way to humanise and moralise the market. The emerging forces of labour, both inside and outside of Parliament, saw this task as unnecessary. The newly industrialised workers, and intellectuals and politicians who represented their workerist interests, believed history was on their side and would ultimately sweep away the whole capitalist system. Why try to tame a beast that was already condemned to the dustbin of history? It was an assumption without foundation that with hindsight was to prove costly to both parties.

The Liberals were to be proved right. Capitalism was not going to be swept away but the divisions remained, enforced by tribalism and cultural animosity. Tribalism, in particular from Labour, saw interest take precedent over ideas and a defined identity in which adversarialism became an inherent part of the party's practice and ethos. Cut off from their radical roots in the emerging industrialised society, the Liberals lost their sense of purpose, compounded by the schism between Lloyd George and Asquith. During much of their wilderness years the social liberalism of T.H. Green was relegated to the margins. It was Jo Grimond who laid the groundwork for the party to embrace the progressive cause once again. During the 1960s, Grimond revived the modern Liberal Party as the gathering point for local action and national realignment. His successors, from Jeremy Thorpe to Charles Kennedy, have built on that.

Labour had to wait for Tony Blair to explicitly force the party to recognise that replacing capitalism with state-driven socialism was neither achievable nor desirable. The problem is that, in ditching the party's former anti-capitalist stance in favour of a 'humanising' approach, Labour appeared to swallow the demands of global capitalism hook, line and sinker in order to win in 1997. This is not to criticise New Labour's path to power. Electoral pragmatism was essential to deny the Conservatives a fifth election victory. After the 1992 defeat it was time to do or say almost anything to win. Nearly all on the left and centre-left felt that enormous pressure to win and shared the relief when it was achieved. But the victory was secured at a high price. In effect, it was a short-cut to power secured through a ruthless repositioning of Labour in order to destroy a Conservative enemy desperately clinging to power. The price was that Labour failed to develop a progressive philosophy of governance that would underpin and direct the new government through good times and bad. In New Labour's rush to power, fundamental ideological issues were glossed over. Cracks in the thinking of the centre-left were papered over.

The reality of New Labour

Paradoxically, the very success of the landslide victory in May 1997 constrained the potential for progressive politics. First, the majority was too big. New Labour was left defending constituencies and people who had little in common with the goals of the centre-left, let alone any aspirations for a progressive century. The fragile collective psychology of New Labour seemed to lead them to believe that the electorate was a pack of regimented dominoes – if one vote or one seat tumbled, they all would. A party that had become the 'It girl' of modern British politics, successful because it was successful, was unable to countenance any failure. In the pursuit of a bogus 'one-nation' politics, New Labour painted itself into a corner by trying to be all things to all people. But satisfying no one for fear of offending anyone would prove to be unsustainable. Worse, Labour was made timid by the fear that Britain really was a 'Conservative country' and was reluctant to engage with the public and win the case for policies on tax-and-spend and electoral reform. Where it has been essential for Labour to look at the big issues necessary to build a progressive country, short-termism has always won out. The most striking example is over the single European currency. If the vote had been held in the first year of the new government it could have been won. We have lost count of the number of times advisers have whispered in our ears that in the second term it will be 'different'. But ends have a habit of being shaped by means. The tap of radicalism cannot just be turned off and on at the whim of party leaders. Radical politics requires support within civil society, the voluntary sector and local communities, support that needs to be built, nurtured and encouraged.

Second, despite the rhetoric, Labour did not win as 'New Labour'. It won as 'not the Tories'. There is no shame in that. The old adage that it is governments that lose elections not oppositions that win them, became a maxim because it is largely true. New Labour, to its credit, made itself safe by identifying what it wasn't, but not by defining what it was. So the mantra 'we won as New Labour and we will govern as New Labour' imposed constraints that were simply unnecessary. As long as they didn't govern like the Tories, anyone winning the 1997 election had the opportunity to create a new vision for Britain. And governing in terms of 'what you are not' has obvious limitations. New Labour had moved beyond the neo-liberal worship of the market but had failed to define an alternative. The slogan 'Opportunity for All' spoke to a still live social democratic instinct to provide a level playing field, but the field turned out to be rampant global capitalism. But the government never questioned the notion that there would be deserving winners and undeserving losers. The very concept of taming the beast of capitalism had become strangely alien to a party that still contained the word 'Labour' in its title. New Labour became a permanent balancing act, courting Middle England but with an instinctive impulse to help the 'failures' in a marketplace defined by a zero sum game. Redistribution was a feature of budget decisions, but is was practised by stealth for fear of offending those with something to lose. Liberal Democrats have been braver. Charles Kennedy advanced the idea that those earning more than £100 000 should pay 50 per cent tax and that the money would go to improving pensions. Despite the fact that even at 50 per cent the rate is lower than it was for the bulk of Lady Thatcher's premiership, it was not received warmly by the government. Yet progressive income tax has always been at the heart of a progressive society and must remain so if growing social inequality is going to be reversed and public services rebuilt. This has been the case since Lloyd George's

'People's Budget'. Politics had come full circle. The Liberals were still trying to humanise capitalism, but now Labour was trying to appease it. New Labour has managed to invert the traditional social democratic model, fitting people to the needs of capitalism not capitalism to the needs of the people.

In many ways New Labour was simply a more pragmatic and smarter version of traditional labourism. It challenged and changed some issues such as Clause IV, uncosted tax-and-spend policies and its party structures. What it ducked, either through lack of time or inclination, was the difficult stuff, the culture of labourism. What was never 'modernised' was the notion that there was only one party, one history and one future – that Labour knew it all and could do it all. The winner-takes-all approach embedded in our adversarial politics was never questioned. It was still assumed that the institutions of the state could simply be inhabited by the left and redirected to deliver 'what works' from the top down. As such, New Labour was always going to be constrained by a view of its own uniqueness. Even where decentralisation was enacted, in Scotland, London and Wales, it was grudging and preceded in two cases by heavy-handed and ultimately unsuccessful attempts to impose candidates from the centre.

In reality, New Labour's leaders recognised the shallow nature of the power they held and that there was still little positive support for what the party in its heart of hearts really stood for – a more equal society. They were right. But, crucially, the lessons they drew were the wrong ones. Their answer was to circle the wagons even tighter, to demand even greater control over Ministers, the party and MPs. The courtship of a sceptical media intensified and Labour sacrificed progressive values like liberty, equality and fraternity rather than take on the searing scorn of a right-wing press. A command and control regime was instilled across all Whitehall departments right down to the local delivery of key public services such as education and health. Targets became sacrosanct and, despite devolution of power to the nations, local authorities were further undermined, bypassed and castigated. Like all army generals, they were guilty of fighting the previous war, doing in the late 1990s what they felt should have been done in the late 1970s. All of this was bound up with the most dispiriting issue of all, the fact that if you had asked any senior Labour politician what the goal of a first term in office was, the honest answer of most would have been 'a second term'. Through excessive electoral pragmatism New Labour made a virtue of perceived necessity by elevating the desire for a second term into a principle. In so doing it denied opportunities to lay firmer foundations for a third or fourth term, the catalysts of a progressive century.

Instead of its fixation on short-termism, New Labour should have recognised that you can't cheat history for long. You have to do things properly or you get found out. That requires a theory of modern capitalism (and its failures), the state and democracy. By the autumn of 2000 New Labour was being found out. The fiasco that engulfed the Millennium Dome confirmed nationwide suspicion that Labour's modernisation-without-purpose was merely vacuous. A crisis over pensions identified the failure to make, let alone win, the redistributive case for tax-and-spend. The 'fuel protests' in the autumn of 2000 sent shock-waves throughout the political system for a government that looked out of touch. In three years, politics had returned to 'normal', with New Labour saved only by retaining the benefits of the electorate's doubt and the poverty of the Opposition it faced. This was a government, and in particular a leader, full of good intentions, but as John Major might have told us, 'fine words butter no parsnips'. With the Clinton era squandered in the US, the limits of a managerial approach to politics, on both sides of the Atlantic, were being heavily felt.

New democracy, new politics

What the social democrats had failed to learn and what liberals could teach them was that a purely mechanical reform has its limits. The statist tendency inherited from Old Labour is a conservative creed. It is akin to the Tory faith in a natural order and in settled hierarchies. Within Labour's modernising ranks there were two competing views of how a progressive century could be realised. The still dominant position around the Cabinet table was that an inclusive new Labour Party could be the home for all anti-Tory progressives. We don't believe this is the case. If the shift to a new politics is to be made, the DNA of labourism needs an infusion of diversity and pluralism that comes, not from merely absorbing (and suffocating) diverse political strands, but from co-operating with others outside the confines of the party and drawing strength from difference.

A modern and progressive nation will thrive only on the basis of real inclusion, autonomy and empowerment. As Charles Kennedy wrote in *The Future of Politics*, 'the challenge is to build a truly civic Britain, where power has been devolved, where people no longer expect changes to come slowly and inefficiently from Westminster, but have power within their own communities and exercise it themselves'.[2]

Yet New Labour made a pact with the forces of conservatism over the implementation of public service change. They knew that in education and health in particular they had to deliver a step-change in public services and decided this could only be done quickly through greater centralisation. This may work, but only in some areas and only for a while. Only local empowerment, participation and autonomy will really transform the way in which our health service operates. Political, social and economic systems are just too complex to be 'run' from an all-knowing, all-powerful centre. By the end of Labour's first administration in almost two decades, it was becoming clear that instead of active modernisation, we were seeing passive managerialism that neither worked sufficiently nor inspired the institutions and agents for change.

Most frustrating is the fact that the mind-set of single-party hegemony now fails to win even on its own terms. New Labour sat on a 178-seat majority after 1997; king of its parliamentary castle, but unable to deflect the tides of globalism and populism that swept against it. Power is now diffuse. It resides in the media, with consumers and pressure groups. The genie has left the Westminster bottle and swirls around in new sites; in Brussels, in the regions, on the internet, on the talk shows and down the mobile phone. Parliamentary majorities of any size are worthless unless they are energised and endorsed by the legitimacy of public accountability. But democracy without ideology becomes a meaningless choice. If political institutions refuse to reflect the real choices and interests of society then it is no surprise that they are increasingly ignored or bypassed. Indeed, the growth of rootless opportunist politics outside of Westminster is reinforced by the way in which politicians behave.

The world we live in has an increasingly complex social order that is multilayered and multifaceted. In this dense web of identities, cultures and habits, getting things done means winning and renewing the consent of the electorate. Failure to do this will create in Britain an American-style politics where comfortable conservatives dominate and the disadvantaged opt out. More money will be spent on negative politics to encourage fewer and fewer to vote. Progressive politics is ultimately about empowerment; it is about helping people to help themselves. The clever approach is to go with the grain, to make people want what you want – not to use the mechanical might of the state to force people against their will. The simple fable of the bet between the sun and the wind over who could get the coat off a man explains it best. The wind blew and blew and tried to force the coat off, but all the man did was to button his coat up tighter. The sun then beamed down, and with the rising temperature the man took his coat off.

Progressive politics is about letting go and allowing people to make their own decisions. There is a risk that people will make the wrong decisions, but the biggest risk lies in thinking that the centralised state can do it all. To cite one example: has the sky fallen in because the Scottish Lib-Lab coalition has abolished university tuition fees? To give another, surely it would have been far better to allow a national debate on the conclusions of the Jenkins Commission on electoral reform than keep it to a few senior figures in both Labour and the Liberal Democrats? There are few more important debates than how we elect our parliamentary representatives. This debate should not have been 'managed' and shelved, it should have been encouraged.

The process of politics must be about interpretation, negotiation, empowerment, autonomy, risk, mutualism and tolerance. The process is as political as the policy. Pluralism is not the easy answer; it is the most difficult. But it is the right answer. It is about leading and having a vision but also having the confidence for that vision to be tested and negotiated. Pluralism makes delivery possible. But it also builds moral legitimacy and support for a set of progressive values and outcomes. If it is 'their' political system, not 'ours', and 'their' public services, not 'ours', then the electorate is much more likely to abandon the institutions of social solidarity when the going gets tough during an economic downturn. This means going beyond the instrumental value of collective action towards an understanding that there is an intrinsic value in solidaristic activity. We are social animals, able to understand ourselves only through our interaction with each other. Without institutions and mechanisms to mediate our need to socialise, we deny a key facet of our identity.

Even within the progressive camp there is much to debate. We should welcome the ongoing tension between equality and liberty, solidarity and diversity, and efficiency and empowerment. To negotiate these and other debates the revival and reform of Parliament is crucial, but so too is that of local government. At the same time, the media, civil society and the opportunities presented by the dot.com age for democratic dialogue need to be recognised and encouraged as spaces for engagement, debate and interaction.

A progressive agenda

The contours of a progressive politics are rough but ready. David Marquand sketched them out in his insightful *Progressive Dilemma*[3] and they are themes that have run through the pages of *Renewal* and *Reformer*, in the work of the IPPR, the Fabians, Demos and the Centre for Reform as well as the speeches of leading progressive politicians and commentators:

1. Its economic goal is egalitarian and therefore essentially social democratic.
2. The means of achieving it are politically pluralist and therefore essentially liberal.
3. Its instincts are socially liberal and anti-establishment.
4. It is for capitalism but recognises the collective constraints necessary on powerful corporate interests – as such, there is a broad acceptance of the stakeholder model.
5. It has learnt the value of political professionalism from the US Democrats, but its heart and future lie with the political and moral economy of Europe.

Blair and New Labour have the propensity to embrace or reject all these key facets of a progressive reform agenda not short on priorities. They include embedding democratic reform; winning the case for redistributive tax-and-spend policies; building support for Europe; reforming welfare; making the case for sustainability, and being passionate about the need for women and people from ethnic minorities to play a greater role in the running of Britain. But while the theory and policy of progressivism is crucial, so to is the practice. The Conservatives created their own hegemony. They shaped the political contours of Britain through a series of political values, rewards and institutions. The centre-left has always been too timid and too reactive, trying to fit its values to the world rather than the world to its values. As this was always an essentially capitalistic world then the grounds for meaningful reform were always limited. There now needs to be some sense of what constitutes progressive institutions. This should be centred above all on the role of civil society as the space between the market, the state and the family where individuals can create their own opportunities for empowerment. There also need to be progressive agents for change that act as outriders for a new social order, prefiguring the politics and practice of a radical century. They should be encouraged and facilitated in civic institutions, progressive business, and the third sector as well as the mutual and co-operative movements.

The goal of a progressive century starts in the here and now. It begins with the realisation that 'conservatives' are not just found in the Conservative Party. They lurk in Labour's undergrowth, eager to fix their way to power. They can be found, too, among Liberal Democrats, vainly rejecting power and the compromises necessary to achieve it. The Pavlovian response of those unable to see beyond tomorrow's headlines or who are suspicious of the new politics is to distract the debate from why to how. They ask, 'Do you mean a pact, a deal or a merger?' This misses the point. Form follows function. The crucial issue and the real political point is a discussion on function – the creation of a philosophy of governance that is progressive and enduring. What form it takes can only be a question of secondary order.

The options on political form are as wide as our imagination. At this point in our political history we need to be the champions of 'co-opetition', a mixture of co-operation and competition. In areas where Labour and the Liberal Democrats agree they should co-operate, even if this goes beyond Europe and constitutional reform. But where Labour and the Liberal Democrats disagree, that should be equally clear. Of course, this does not fit the old Westminster model – and nor should it, because that is the mould we need to break. But, by definition, the sweep of agreement must be pluralist, empowering and decentralised. We have talked in the past not of one 'big tent' for progressives, but of a 'camp site' where values are shared and defined but where there is space for constructive differences to be aired. What is important is that the desire for a progressive century is not driven by political arithmetic or jobs for the boys (although more jobs for the girls would be a welcome part of a more progressive politics).

Where do we go from here?

The journey to a new politics will only be possible if we challenge some of the key assumptions that underpin British politics. The adversarial nature of our Parliament must go, and along with it the short-term pragmatism it inspires. Here we get to that old chestnut of fair votes and electoral reform. If we put aside the fact that 'first past the post' (FPTP) has been the mechanism that delivered a Conservative century, the real issue is moral. The debate about electoral reform speaks volumes for a moral as opposed to a mechanical view of politics. Electoral systems are too often seen as a zero sum game between effectiveness and fairness. More of one means less of the other. But a system that lacks legitimacy increasingly cannot function efficiently as its power is usurped and bypassed. Politics is ultimately about different concepts of morality and, for liberal and social democrats, ends often cannot justify means. If we live by a rigged and unjust system then it will be rigged and unjust to us. If we proclaim a mandate in 1997 for Blair, how could we deny one for Major in 1992 or Thatcher in 1987 or Heath in 1970? In the meantime the rotten core of the system infects the rest of the body politic. It turns people off. Why vote when your vote doesn't count? Why shout if no one is listening? If you're a woman or black, then what do rows of white men indicate to you? Disillusionment and cynicism are the corrosive forces that are slowly draining the life out of 'democracy'. The way we cast our votes for representation at Westminster is not the only reason for the cynical turn-off from politics but it is a crucial cog in the wheel. As turnouts continue to decline we should recognise that the problem is with our democracy and not with the people.

For progressives, the problems of FPTP are made worse by its distorting effect. As things stand, the wants, hopes and dreams of a few mainly middle-class people in a few mainly Middle England seats outweigh the wants, hopes and dreams of millions of people in hundreds of seats across the whole of the country. The fact that general elections are now decided by swing votes in swing seats by around 100 000 people brings into question the very term 'general'.

A pledge to hold a referendum on electoral reform, just like a vote on the euro, is a vital staging post for progressives. The embrace of electoral reform and the acceptance of Europe as our ideological home will help make or break the prospects for a progressive century. It is therefore inconceivable for the referendums on the euro and electoral reform to be prolonged beyond the next Parliament. The government and wider progressive forces need to make the weather on these key issues – not just float on populist tides.

Party reform

The strongest objections in Labour's ranks, not just to greater collaboration with the Liberal Democrats but more importantly to an embrace of pluralism, comes from both the old right and, ironically, the traditionalist left. The old right epitomises the doomed politics of command and control and is the natural opponent of a liberal and pluralist approach to political process. But the animosity of the traditional left is harder to fathom given the Liberal Democrats' essentially radical policies on tax, civil liberties, public services and the environment. And yet what we know is that views among Labour and Liberal Democrat rank and file members towards each other are far from cold. Consider the work of Paul Whiteley and Patrick Seyd from Sheffield University, who set out to measure party members' affiliation to left–right ideological views. Scoring interviewees along a nine-point scale where 0 is extreme left and 9 extreme right, the two researchers found the mean score for Labour members was 3.5 and that for Liberal Democrats was 4.1. This contrasted with a mean score for the Conservatives of 6.7.

The fact that members share basic values is one reason why both parties should address the issue of internal reform, to allow such ideological proximity to find expression. While in opposition, Blair staked his claim as the leading moderniser through his tough stance on 'one member one vote', but in government he has allowed the party fixers and block votes to win elections against the wider views of the party in London and Wales. The Liberal Democrats need to ensure that the wider membership is involved in key policy decisions and internal elections. Charles Kennedy was brave to raise this early in his leadership. He should not allow the voices that argue for an activist 'democracy' to prevail. Such reforms are not only right in themselves but they reduce the impact of tribalists on the culture of our parties and open the way for progressive advance.

From the Liberal Democrat standpoint, 1997 was the best Liberal result since Lloyd George. It was bolstered by the Ashdown move away from 'equidistance' to explicitly support Labour over the Conservatives. This was the message of his Chard speech in 1992 when he said that the Liberal Democrats 'must be less exclusive in our approach to politics ... more inclusive to others'. Those voices in the Liberal Democrats who call for a return to equidistance and the ending of any co-operation with New Labour should be clear who would benefit – Hague, Portillo and Widdecombe. An all-out war between Liberal Democrats and Labour would most put at risk the very seats that Liberal Democrats won in 1997 and hope to win again. While such fighting talk may go down well with some party activists, the great causes that the Liberal Democrats desire – electoral reform and euro entry – would be put off for a further generation if the Conservatives reclaim their traditional place in government. Indeed, even a modest Conservative recovery could delay for another four or five years the referendums on electoral reform and the euro. Tactical voting and the bounty of seats it brings has made its mark. It is not unimportant in the grand scheme of things that almost half the Liberal Democrats' seats at the 1997 election and one in seven of Labour's were won on the spoils of tactical votes. At the next election, if the tactical vote fails to materialise, Labour's majority could be cut to 60 even if the Tories fail to get one extra vote.

A time to dream again

Against the many obstacles outlined above, the call for a progressive century is a tall order. But the time is ripe for tall orders. Free from the constraints of guilt by association with communism and the electoral domination of neo-liberalism, the centre-left can dream and be inspired again. Labour needs to step out of the shadows of its own failures and the political trauma of Thatcherism. Liberals need to move beyond old glories. Meaningful political advance requires sacrifice, but sacrifices are made for crusades not managerialism. The far-reaching benefits of proactive collaborative and pluralist politics are there for all to see. We are demonstrably made stronger when the strands of progressivism come together. Think of the early part of the last century when the Liberal government, encouraged and supported by the new Labour Party, reformed trade union law and began to look after the disadvantaged. Think of Labour's post-war construction of the welfare state, inspired by the Liberal minds of Keynes and Beveridge. We do not pretend that there aren't substantial differences between social democracy and liberalism. But those differences are both bridgeable and pale into insignificance against the values and threat of the right.

One of us sees himself as a new social democratic, forging a link between the goal of a more equal society but achieved through the new politics: the heart of Roy Hattersley and the head of Charter 88, if you like. The other is looking for the rebirth of the New Liberalism that threatened hegemonic rule in the early part of the last century but was thwarted by the division of the radicals as the Labour power base grew. Although we stand under different banners, we believe in virtually the same things. We are not alone in recognising the potential of finally mending the false division among progressive radicals. Tony Blair is fully aware of what can still be achieved:

> When it was formed, out of the dissent from the Liberal Party ... the Labour Party suffered as a result. It was narrower in its base, it was more doctrinaire in its views, and it lost an essential Liberal strand of radical thought. And the truth of the matter is that people like myself in the Labour party today and people like Charles Kennedy and the Liberal Democrats, we are basically driven by the same value systems. There may be differences of policy but that's almost the accident of being inside different political parties than some great division of ideas. So I think it's important that we move closer together. I've never given up on that goal.[4]

Charles Kennedy, in his speech to his party conference in September 2000, said the Liberal Democrats were not to the left of Labour, not to the right of Labour, but ahead of New Labour. This suggests that he believes that the two parties are on the same kind of trajectory. Indeed, he has made clear a number of times that 'Labour is the competition and the Tories are the enemy', while emphasising that he and Tony Blair can do business together. But, as we have stated from the outset, the attitude of leaders is a necessary but insufficient ingredient of progressive success. It is behaviour that matters, and wider forces than the personal intent of leaders govern behaviour.

Labour reinvented itself to move from opposition to power. It now needs to reinvent itself again and accept that a progressive century cannot be built inside an inclusive New Labour tent. Liberal Democrats have to accept that the constructive part of 'constructive opposition' is as important as the opposition part.

Philip Gould, in his post-election analysis of the march of the modernisers, recognised that in 1997 New Labour had won an election, not a century.[5] Now that historic rupture with Labour's radical stablemate has to be mended. We refuse to be constrained by the intellectual and political limitations imposed on us by a century-old rift of progressive forces. We are both deeply rooted in our respective parties but our attachment to a set of values and goals, which transcend party loyalty, go much deeper and are much stronger.

We do not yet live in a progressive land. People are still tired of the Tories but they are already growing tired of New Labour. The case for a progressive politics has not yet been put. It won't just happen. We live in a country that can face both ways – conservative or progressive. Centre-left politicians need to be confident that they can appeal to the progressive side of the nation rather than timidly ameliorate the conservative tendencies. The challenge in politics is to strike the right balance between power and principle. A coalition of radical forces allows the balance to be struck for a popular and progressive politics. It is time to have faith in the people and believe that given a meaningful choice they will opt for a progressive over a conservative path.

This book is an attempt to bring together some of the important strands of progressive thinking. It does not attempt to cover all the policy bases. It is structured into four parts. Part 1 analyses the philo-sophical foundation of 'liberal socialism', the historic and contemporary relations between Labour and the Liberals, the lessons from abroad about collaboration and the state of the electorate. Part 2 examines the structures, institutions and culture necessary for progressive politics to flower. Parliament, the reforms in Scotland, local government, the wider constitution, the third sector and the sociological foundation of pluralistic politics are all scrutinised. Part 3 looks at policy. From the economy to welfare reform, from globalisation and the environment, to health and family policy the central themes of progressive politics are examined. The final part of the book consists of a roundtable discussion in which a group of commentators, thinkers and politicians committed to progressive politics outline what they consider to be the key issues before us.

There are tough words in this book for our colleagues on both Labour and Liberal Democrat benches. But we hope the emphasis is on constructive criticism. For the reality is that without a new politics, the next most likely shift of power will be to a Conservative majority. We do not want to see another period of Conservative rule before members of both parties agree to learn the lessons of the historic failures of progressives. Now is the time for a truce in the hundred-year war between progressives, with the combined fire turned on the real enemy – the forces of conservatism.

Notes

1. See in particular Andrew Rawnsley's *Servants of the People*, London: Hamish Hamilton, 2000; and Sir Paddy Ashdown's first volume of diaries, *The Ashdown Diaries, Volume One, 1988–1997*, Harmondsworth: Penguin 2000.
2. Charles Kennedy, *The Future of Politics*, London: HarperCollins, 2000.
3. David Marquand, *The Progressive Dilemma: From Lloyd George to Blair*, (2nd edition), London: Phoenix, 1999.
4. Quoted in the *Guardian*, 23 May 2000, and taken from the unpublished parts of an interview with Robert Harris which appeared in the US in *Talk Magazine* in early 2000.
5. Philip Gould, *The Unfinished Revolution*, London: Little Brown, 1998.

Part 1

The Case and the Prospects for Progressive Politics

2
Liberal Socialism: Then and Now

Tony Wright

Progressive movements need progressive ideas. Those who think that a progressive century can be secured by political fixes of various kinds (even by a fix of the electoral system) are wrong. Such devices and contrivances may be desirable, or useful, or both, but they do not go to the heart of the 'progressive dilemma' (Marquand 1992) that made the centre-left weaker than it should have been for much of the last century. If this next century is really to be different in this respect, the centre-left has to win the battle of ideas.

It took the Blair government some time to understand this, which was curious in view of the central role of ideological revision in the renewal of the party. Only when backs were to the wall, suddenly and unexpectedly, did the government discover its authentic voice, arguing rather than accommodating, and confronting people with fundamental political choices. What had previously seemed politically risky had now become a political necessity. The big tent might have become somewhat smaller, but it had also become a good deal stronger. Instead of the suffocating assumption that everybody was already inside it, there was a bracing invitation to enter. Policy particulars were reconnected with the big picture and the grand narrative.

This is a reminder that a progressive movement requires a pros-elytising mission. When William Morris used to insist, against the mechanical Marxists and the no less mechanical Fabians, that the real

23

task was to 'make socialists', this was his message. It is still worth listening to. A focus group makes no converts. That requires a continuing enterprise of argument and persuasion. Paradoxically, all the modern complexities and blurring of old ideological dividing lines make this task more rather than less necessary. The fragmentation of traditional certainties may mean that the joining up of analysis and argument is more difficult, but it is also even more of an imperative. In a world without reliable maps, compass points become more essential. Without them we are liable to wander all over the place, radiating uncertainty about who, what and where we are.

Again, the experience of the Blair government offers an instructive lesson here. For much of its life, the government seemed preoccupied with demonstrating what Labour was not. It was not a party that screwed up the economy, or taxed people until the pips squeaked, or waged war on business, or gave in to the unions, or was soft on crime – and so on. Much of this was quite understandable, in view of the party's recent past and the political price that had been paid for it. There were many ghosts to be laid. But for as long as this remained a reckoning with the past rather than an engagement with the future, so it was harder to forge a positive identity. Ghost-busting only takes you so far.

This suggests a further point, of a more far-reaching kind. To compress a long story, much of the recent history of the left has involved a process of adjustment, adaptation and accommodation to individualism and market liberalism. On tax, ownership, welfare, regulation and much else, old territory has been abandoned in order that new positions can be occupied. Far from being a distinctively British phenomenon, the British experience sits squarely within the general trajectory of parties of the centre-left across Europe (Sassoon 1999). We might describe this process in the simplest terms as going with the flow, a response to the social and economic currents that seemed to be reshaping the political landscape.

Yet such going with the flow, necessary as it may be for political adaptation and ideological repositioning, has also to be combined with efforts to staunch the flow and redirect it into new channels. This requires a robust engagement with the battle of ideas, often of a fundamental kind. The more clamorous the welter of private interests, the more pressing the task of defining a public interest. The more rampant individualism is, the more necessary it becomes to resolve its contradictions. The more differentiated society becomes, the more important it is to strengthen the conditions of social unity.

Nor are these abstract propositions, for they make themselves felt on all sides. The failure to provide everybody with a stake in society leaves many to kick over the traces. We demand the right to drive our cars until gridlock descends, then realise we should have developed a high-quality public transport system. Many of the things we need most in this age of individualism – not least, a decent environment – are obtainable only by collective action. We resist paying taxes to the state, but then discover that what we most want for ourselves and our families – such as excellent schools, good health and social care – is not available when we need it.

These are elementary propositions, but it is the continuing duty of the centre-left to propound them. They do not impede the proper and necessary revisionism that should be a permanent feature of progressive politics, but they do constitute a standing reminder of some basic linkages and connections. The neo-liberal right has a mission to show that collective action fails. The left has to show that it is indispensable for a good society, which includes enabling individuals to secure what they want. The forms and mechanisms of collective action should change and develop as circumstances require; but its point and purpose is a durable truth. The socialist (or even social-ist) argument has always been both moral and empirical: fairness is morally right, but a fair society will also work better. This is another linkage that has constantly to be argued, and given practical illustration.

The progressive failure of the last century, which needs to be remedied in the next, was an inability to mobilise such propositions into a politically serviceable public philosophy capable of winning support over an extended period. This would have required the labour movement to become more than a labour movement. It would have required the left to see its mission as empowering people rather than making them supplicants of a central (and centralised) state. It would have involved new relationships between individual endeavour and collective action. It would have fostered a social market in which economic competition was combined with social obligation. For all its huge achievements, Labour in the twentieth century failed to assemble a progressive coalition of this kind and eventually paid a heavy price for not having done so.

Yet the materials for it were there at hand, right at the beginning of the last century. When Tony Blair, commemorating the fiftieth anniversary of the 1945 Labour government, invoked the heritage of 'liberal socialism' (Blair 1995), this was his reference point. His immediate political message was about the electoral cost of the fragmentation of progressive forces, and the need to rectify this if the next century was to be different from the last, but the reference point involves more than this. It means putting progressive liberals alongside progressive socialists (Hobhouse and Tawney, Keynes and Cole, Beveridge and Attlee ...), not to show that they inhabit the same tradition – which they do not – but to demonstrate that there is an intermingling of progressive traditions that is capable of producing something richer and more vital than the constituent parts. In simplest terms, they need each other.

In this sense liberal socialism represents the original Third Way. Its source is the meeting between 'new' liberalism and ethical socialism in the early years of the twentieth century. It was a peculiarly British encounter, involving an intermingled progressivism that has good claim to be regarded as the richest repository of applied social thinking that modern Britain has produced. 'Liberalism has passed through its Slough of Despond,' declared the liberal theorist L.T. Hobhouse in 1911, 'and in the give and take of ideas with Socialism has learnt, and taught, more than one lesson. The result is a broader and deeper movement in which the cooler and clearer minds recognise below the differences of party names and in spite of certain real cross-currents a genuine unity of purpose' (Hobhouse 1911, p. 226). Here was the basis for a broad progressivism beyond the confines of party.

Both traditions were the product of internal revisionism. The new liberalism was a break from the *laissez-faire* individualism of the old, having discovered that individual freedom could often be enhanced rather than diminished by collective action. Ethical socialism was a rupture from an economic determinism that repudiated bourgeois democracy and moral choice. These twin revisionisms found much common ground; but this is less interesting than the nature of their dialogue. For it was out of this dialogue, with its different perspectives and preoccupations, that a richer body of ideas was nourished that fed into progressive politics in Britain. If it failed to be organised into a coherent governing force, this was not because the theoretical ingredients were unavailable.

The conversation between new liberals and ethical socialists ranged widely. The socialists thought that liberalism was still too soft on capitalism; the liberals thought that socialism was too trusting of the state. Socialists pressed for equality, while liberals cautioned about the effects on liberty and enterprise of pressing too far. Liberals wanted to diffuse power in the name of diversity and citizenship; socialists thought that an equity of common citizenship demanded central provision. Liberals worried about the dangers of bureaucratic collectivism, socialists about the perils of leaving people unprotected. Socialists talked of communal duties, liberals of individual rights. The liberal emphasis on political and civic freedom was countered by the socialist emphasis on economic and social freedom. Liberals thought that socialists were too preoccupied with class; while socialists believed that liberals were too in thrall to individualism.

This is a bald summary of dense arguments. The point is not that the protagonists were lined up on opposing sides but that the dialogue produced a body of social thinking, fusing and mingling its constituent strands, that informed progressive politics in Britain. At least that was the promise. Hobhouse wrote:

> If, then, there be such a thing as a Liberal Socialism – and whether there be is still a subject for inquiry – it must clearly fulfil two conditions. In the first place, it must be democratic. It must come from below, not from above. Or rather, it must emerge from the efforts of society as a whole to secure a fuller measure of justice, and a better organisation of mutual aid. It must engage the efforts and respond to the genuine desires not of a handful of superior beings, but of great masses of men. And, secondly, and for that very reason, it must make its account with the human individual. It must give the average man free play in the personal life for which he really cares. It must be founded on liberty, and must make not for the suppression but for the development of personality. (Hobhouse 1911, pp. 172–3)

In other words, it required a genuine synthesis of liberalism and socialism as the creative product of a process of mutual learning.

The ideological battleground of the twentieth century left little political space for a synthesis of this kind. Yet it was there to be drawn on when imaginative minds tried to think their way out of the ideological impasse in which they found themselves. For example, G.D.H. Cole responded to the totalitarian experience by explicitly invoking a 'liberal socialism' as the basis upon which the left could be reconstructed after the Second World War, with democratic freedom at its centre. This was grounded in the Western liberal tradition, of which the socialist view of freedom was a natural extension and complement. It valued tolerance and diversity, hated bureaucratic monoliths, and was fiercely libertarian and democratic. The only kind of socialism that was worth having was one that incorporated the best of liberalism. The direction of the contemporary world

> should make even Socialists wary by now of tearing up by the roots any small man's refuge that is left in a world so ridden as ours by hugeness. It should make them regard the farmer, the shopkeeper, the small manufacturer, not as obstacles in the way of universal centralisation, but as valuable checks upon a dangerous agglomerative tendency. Politically, this opens up the possibility of immense innovations ... (Cole 1942, p. 12)

So much for the pedigree of liberal socialism. Its ingredients were assembled at the beginning of the twentieth century, as ethical socialists met new liberals. Although the meeting shaped much subsequent progressive thought in Britain (for example, the way in which R.H. Tawney famously tied together equality and freedom, and tied both to an idea of community), the twentieth century was brutally hostile to such nice synthesis. It was an age of polarities – capitalism versus communism, class against class, equality or liberty, state or individual – and social democrats struggled to find convincing third ways between competing positions. British labourism, despite its practical achievements, was notably unsuccessful in the task of theoretical construction. Yet the materials were at hand, in rich abundance, once the collapse of the old polarities opened up a space where a public philosophy of liberal socialism could flourish.

That space now exists. Having promised so much at the start of the twentieth century, liberal socialism might finally deliver that promise at the start of the twenty-first century. The conditions are propitious.

There is an openness and interchange among progressive forces of an unprecedented kind, as old tribalisms and sectarianisms collapse, and in the face of issues and alignments that do not fit neatly (or, in some cases, do not fit at all) into traditional ideological categories. In this sense the new politics is not a glib phrase but an accurate description of the need for politics to be conducted differently. There are two main reasons why this provides an opportunity for the liberal socialist synthesis to come into its own. The first is rather general and theoretical; the second more particular and practical.

In general terms, liberal socialism provides a basis upon which a progressive approach to politics can be constructed. Some of its elements can be briefly sketched. A market economy is distinguished from a market society. Both state and markets need to be made to work in the public interest. The balance between rights and duties should be carefully weighed. Citizenship is about empowerment and not just about provision. Collective action nourishes a good society, but it is not for the state to tell people how to live their lives. Enterprise should be encouraged, while security is guaranteed. There can be too much regulation, and too little. The demands of equity need balancing against the claims of diversity. Unjustified inequalities should be removed while cherishing individual liberties. Economic dynamism and social justice are conjoined.

Such liberal socialist propositions, wholly unexceptional in their nature, define the territory of contemporary political debate. Yet their real test – and opportunity – comes in their ability to open up innovative policy thinking. Once the old categories and polarities are escaped from, it should become easier to follow policy ideas where they lead. It is not difficult to identify some areas and issues where this is required. Once choices are extended beyond state or market, other providers of services become possible, thereby extending experiment and diversity. Traditional battles about levels of taxation become less significant to the extent that it becomes possible to construct more direct and transparent connections between taxes paid and services delivered. Redistribution that confers endowments upon individuals to improve their lives and advance their careers offers a practical liberty. Sponsoring new forms of bottom-up community provision in place of top-down statism strengthens the frayed bonds of citizenship. Extending democracy to new areas lifts the curse of centralism. Finding a version of Europe that has democratic resonance replaces a version that conspicuously lacks it.

There is much here for liberal socialists to do. Out of that original meeting between the new liberals and the ethical socialists, there came a connecting tradition that integrated equality and liberty, community and individual, solidarity and individuality, enterprise and justice, state and market, centralism and localism, responsibilities and rights, collectivism and citizenship, into a rich synthesis that has informed progressive politics in Britain. It also carried with it innovative policy implications. Yet, in the last century, its political promise was not fulfilled. If the next century is really to be a progressive one, liberal socialism will have to come into its own.

References

Blair, T. (1995) 'Let Us Face the Future – the 1945 anniversary lecture', Fabian pamphlet 571 (lecture given by Tony Blair to mark the fiftieth anniversary of the election of the 1945 Labour government, 5 July 1995, London). London: Fabian Society.

Cole, G.D.H. (1942) *Great Britain in the Post-War World*. London: Gollancz.

Hobhouse, L.T. (1911) *Liberalism*. London: Williams and Norgate.

Marquand, D. (1992) *The Progressive Dilemma*. London: Heinemann.

Sassoon, D. (1999) 'European Social Democracy and New Labour: Unity in Diversity?', in A. Gamble and T. Wright (eds), *The New Social Democracy*. Oxford: Blackwell.

3
The Threat of the Right

Stephen Twigg and Andrew Pakes

There is something of the optimistic gambler in the eyes of many of today's Labour activists. After 18 years drinking away at the edge of the card table they are finally dealt a winning hand, yet instead of calling it quits they are still willing to gamble success on the turn of the electorate. In any other walk of life the odds stacked against continued success at the polls, combined with a steady headed look through the history books, would certainly convince most people of the need to change their ways. Nearly all Labour governments have been plagued by economic difficulties, internal inertia or lack of unity, and whilst Tony Blair continues to present a coherent and innovative case for his administration, it is still unproven at the ballot box a second time around.

The stakes are somewhat higher for the politician than the lone gambler and the perils of losing are not just about personal ruin, family tension and living life as a washout. In offering all the gains of office up to the highest bidder then Labour's potential losses become the rich takings of the Conservative Party. There is an intoxicating substance in politics and the lure of power and authority seem to create an amnesia against the threat posed by the right in British politics. The bitter social division portrayed in television dramas like *Boys from the Blackstuff* or films like *Brassed Off* and *Billy Elliot* appear a world apart from most people's lives today. Eighteen years of mismanagement and attacks on the social fabric of Britain are put aside,

31

with the rhetoric of 'Never Again!' and 'Down with the Tories', in favour of the winner-takes-all gamble in our current electoral system.

The purpose of this chapter is to make the argument that Labour has a historic opportunity to forge a new progressive political agenda with the Liberal Democrats, and some of the enlightened Greens and other social actors, to create a fluid and powerful combination of ideals and values willing and able to stand up to the pervasive electoral force of the Conservatives. Despite the current failure of William Hague to provide leadership to his cause, it is wrong of the centre and left in British politics to consign his party to the electoral graveyard. Of all parties in British history, the Conservatives have proved themselves to be the most durable and successful in elections. Recent political history offers the example of the Labour Party recovering its position from the disastrous routing at the 1983 general election; similarly, the Conservative Party recovered rapidly following sizeable victories by Labour in 1945 and 1966.

This new consensus on the centre-left has its roots in the early collaboration between trade union MPs and the Liberal Party, where joint interest was utilised to make inroads into conservative electoral territory; and more recently in Tony Blair's and Charles Kennedy's commitment to a progressive century. By drawing on the notions of a well managed economy, investment in public services and a plural political culture, there is space to reassess the dividing lines on the centre-left and construct a more durable progressive political tradition.

The opportunity for a new centre-left consensus in British politics is timebound and will not last indefinitely. Labour and the Liberal Democrats may be forced into co-operation due to electoral fortunes but that may only result in a narrowly defined concept of shared values. Charles Kennedy has already spelt out the Liberal Democrats' opposition to the Conservatives and how he would be unwilling to work in conjunction with the right should the election produce a hung Parliament. Paradoxically, whilst Labour are in their strongest parliamentary position for many decades, it is the time for us and the Liberal Democrats to reach accommodation on the breadth and shape of the new politics. If the leadership of both parties cannot transcend their traditional electoral appeal and tribal loyalties, at the period of their greatest political authority, then the danger is of further electoral division and public cynicism towards the political system. This is not an argument for a merger between the two political parties – such a move would be inappropriate and damaging, but rather for a renewed narrative on the enduring relevance of the social democratic model. Alongside this particular message is the opportunity to remove the historical root of conservative hegemony, the fear of insecurity and division amongst the left and centre in politics. The opportunity for progressive-minded politicians, at the end of 18 years' continuous rule by a party which is still struggling to find its equilibrium in the political landscape, is historic.

Across the whole spectrum of public policy there is now a proximity between Labour and the Liberal Democrats that has not been seen since the emergence of the Labour Representation Committee at the start of the twentieth century. Whereas in the years of its birth Labour evolved out of a frustration with the then existing political system, and the inability of the Liberal and Conservative establishment, to reflect the aspirations and hopes of a newly enfranchised male working class, this time the position of Labour and the Liberal Democrats is defined by a fundamental cleavage against the Conservatives. In both instances there is a desire to establish a politics that addresses the concerns of a new meritocratic and inclusive society. The political opportunity to address the symbolic divide between liberalism and labourism is understood best through joint opposition to contemporary developments on the right of British politics.

The division of the two mainstream British parties of the centre and left has only served to perpetuate the electoral advantage of the Conservatives. Between the two points from historical divide to historic opportunity is the story of the ongoing success and dominance of British politics by the Conservative Party. The backdrop to this tale is the opportunism and pragmatism that the right have been able to exploit in the name of retaining power. Unencumbered by the values of the left or aspirations of the disenfranchised, their branding as the natural party of the elite and 'those who ruled the Empire' has been remarkably adept at switching leaders, policies and language to ensure their triumph at the ballot box.

This durable and loose coalition was perfected through trial and error during the heady days of industrial expansion and imperial growth. The advance of international influences was kept in check by the polarisation of foreign development during the Cold War. However, once the false protection of the Soviet threat had been erased, the floodgates opened to the impact of globalisation; not just in the economy and means of production, but significantly also through the immediacy and images of culture. The Conservative Party that had invested so much of its decency and values in the imagery of 'One Nation' and the British people was now open to the same threats and insecurity that had previously challenged socialism.

Whilst the concepts of the nation-state and sovereignty have become subject to reassessment, the Conservatives have continued to wrestle the traditional tension between the free market and British interest. The globalisation of wealth, power and information has altered the boundaries and assumptions of existing political ideologies to an extent that has caught conservatism, usually the most flexible of the ideologies despite its title, off guard. The preoccupation of Conservative policy with the defence of family values, asylum and outright hostility to Europe indicates a populist strand that is desperately searching for the security of past glories.

Whereas the Liberals had faced their day in the first part of the twentieth century where individualism was unable to capture the hopes of a working class newly enfranchised and toiling within industrial capitalism, socialism had become destabilised by the energy of the market economy in matching production and entrepreneurship with public desire for better living conditions. Arguably, the battle for supremacy in the Cold War took its first victim in the collapse of state-based socialism and the related crisis of traditional Western socialism, yet it is only now that conservatism and the advocates of the free market are facing the impact of the new global politics.

The inability of the 'wet' brand of conservatism to add a credible alternative to the emerging knowledge economy and regional role for Britain has given the zealous right the opportunity to take hold of the main body politic of Conservative thought. It is not surprising that the failure of the last Conservative government found it roots in the emerging debate on Europe following the demise of the East–West split. The media and political commentators focused on the sleaze and corruption of a tired old government that had simply been in power too long which were symptomatic of the seismic impact globalisation had made on a self-assured but now challenged ideology. The victors in this battle were the right-wing tendency characterised by a strict line on law and order, immigration and welfare and a siege mentality for the English identity.

By the late 1990s the struggle for supremacy had clearly been won by a more cynical right-wing element, less concerned with dismantling socialism and the trade unions, rather than with protecting its own role as defender of England. An early casualty in this shifting dominance within the right were the values of compassion and tradition associated with the 'One Nation' brigade. In consequence, key figures like Ken Clarke and Michael Heseltine have found themselves increasingly left jilted at the altar whilst others, such as Alan Howarth, Peter Temple-Morris and Emma Nicholson, have been pushed into changing party allegiance.

There is a new ideological debate within the Conservative Party in which the traditional Tory left fails to register as a significant interest. The most visible illustration of this shift has been in the selection process for parliamentary candidates in preparation for the general election. Despite public statements from Steve Norris about attracting high-calibre candidates from all walks of life, there has been a clear shift to the right. 'Essex Man' might be on the verge of extinction but the policy approach heralded by his introduction to the parliamentary party in the early 1980s has not been abandoned. Symbolically, right-wing candidates have been selected to replace both John Major and Michael Heseltine. At the time of writing, all the seats being vacated by the retirement of Conservative MPs have selected white men almost exclusively from the right of the party.

There is a combination, then, between the historical domination of British politics by the Conservatives, and an ideological challenge to the basic assumptions of traditional conservatism and subsequent shift to the right by key personnel in the party. The convergence of these events has dual significance. First, there is now a common opposition for both Labour and the Liberal Democrats (despite a few inner-city and parliamentary battlegrounds) which has transferred from political co-operation at a national level to a comprehension amongst the electorate. Unlike the early period of the Thatcher government there is an identification between Labour and Liberal Democrat voters that the real divide is with the right. The use of tactical voting saw both Labour and the Liberal Democrats make great gains in the 1997 general election which then re-emerged in the Romsey by-election in May 2000 where the voters entered into their own ad hoc coalition to capture a previous Conservative stronghold. This co-operation is not necessarily replicated within the tribal environment of party activists, but it is a key condition of forging a new centre-left agenda.

Second, the emergence of the new ideological balance within the Conservative Party has created a diversion in which progressive politicians can nurture and develop a proactive policy agenda based on shared values and interest beyond party boundaries. The constitutional agenda co-ordinated through the Joint Cabinet Committee, and then joint health policy thinking, has been cemented by the coalition arrangements in Scotland and Wales. This dual impact can be illustrated in the main policy debates of the contemporary political landscape, with Europe, employment rights and questions of diversity as prime examples.

The debate on Europe, with honourable exceptions, has been sterile and removed from the bread and butter questions concerning much of the British public. Attempts to reduce the single currency to a debate on economic conditions, as in the Danish example, have failed to address concerns about identity and accountability in the European Union. Politicians need to face Europe as a political project, and those on the centre-left need to be prepared to enter into a defence of the European social model. Although the Conservatives have adopted a short-term and confusing policy agenda, ruling out the single currency but only until the end of the next Parliament, there is an obvious division between their enthusiastic and robust support for sterling and the almost timid response from the pro-camp.

There are common values between Liberal Democrat views on Europe and the response of mainstream Labour thinking. The Conservatives are committed to a renegotiation of the British position, whilst the progressive left embraces the notion of a social Europe capable of producing environmental and public policy rather than simply free movement of commerce and trade. John Monks, General Secretary of the TUC, illustrated the point in his ground-breaking address to the annual Liberal Democrat Conference in September 2000 (the first address by the leadership of the trade union movement at the Liberal Conference):

the fundamental choice is now about what kind of capitalism we want. Is it the deregulated wild-west devil take the hindmost style of the US? This is clearly the Conservative option. Or is it the European approach? This combines productive economies with good welfare states, rights for people at work and environmental protection. (Monks 2000)

The challenge for pro-Europeans on the centre-left is to regain an initiative which was lost almost a decade ago. The gap between the Conservatives and the other two main parties is very wide indeed. The Conservatives' hardline stance resonates well with many, but is a major reason for their loss of credibility in the business world. Whatever happens on the euro, there can be little doubt that the UK's economic future lies in the European Union. The growing influence of Conservative rejectionists could be exploited by a pragmatic pro-European agenda that recognises the need for real reform to connect the EU with its citizens.

Similarly, on rights in the workplace there are two clear policy approaches. Interestingly, the Liberal Democrats used the legislative agenda under Labour to move closer to longstanding trade union demands. Traditional support for individual rights were accommo-dated alongside collective rights such as the national minimum wage to bring liberalism and the left closer than for many years. However, whilst the Conservatives have publicly stated they will not repeal the minimum wage, they have consistently opposed Labour moves to introduce greater social protection, scaremongering on the financial implications of equalising rights for part-time employees and opposing parental leave. Much of this criticism is linked to the enthusiasm by which Labour has adopted European guidance, yet there is also basic hostility to the role of trade unions witnessed in their continued opposition to legislation on union recognition. Whereas in the 1970s and 1980s the Liberals were generally closer to the Conservatives on employment rights and trade union reform, today it would be very rare to see disagreement between Labour and the Liberal Democrats.

Finally, on diversity, there is a massive gulf in Conservative thought between Ann Widdecombe advocating a socially authoritarian approach and Michael Portillo recasting himself as the champion of social acceptance. Dr Liam Fox's statement on why foreign-born doctors should face 'English tests' to prove they can understand our language follows in the rich vein of prejudice represented by Norman

Tebbit's infamous comments on cricket tests for immigration cases. So whilst Steven Norris and Michael Portillo claim that the Conservative Party should become more inclusive and open, the official position from the leadership continued to fight a bitter campaign to retain Section 28 and urged tougher restrictions on immigration and asylum. William Hague has abandoned his 1997 rhetoric of inclusion and has seemed closer to the Widdecombe view than that of Portillo. Whatever his private views, Hague has been content to pander to prejudice for possible electoral gain. It was these contradictions that forced former Conservative hopeful for Mayor of London, Ivan Massow, to join a growing list of high-profile defections. Labour and the Liberal Democrats still have a considerable distance to travel in addressing equality issues and questions of identity, but there is an easily identifiable agenda that contrasts with the right.

The political proximity of Labour and the Liberal Democrats, and the historic opportunity afforded by the current state of the right, are balanced against the political expediency of poll ratings and elections. Modern media-managed politics does not encourage broader thinking within party traditions. For Labour, the promised land of claiming a second term, complete with working majority in the House of Commons, commands the attention of most politicians. Compared to the failure of previous Labour administrations to deliver a second decisive election victory, it is a legitimate and necessary objective. However, there are also many latchkey modernisers using the language of modernisation and democratic reform to mask more tribal aspirations so that it is difficult to determine where New Labour ends and self-interest starts. Similarly, there is great pressure on the Liberal Democrats to pursue an oppositionist strategy and exploit frustration at the pace of change for electoral advantage over Labour.

Electoral opportunism could be the greatest threat to forging a new progressive political agenda. The politics of power runs through the calculations of all three mainstream parties and creates the conditions in which there could be a return to the usual divides and fortunes of the politics of the last century. The central question, then, is: Have Labour and the Liberal Democrats learnt from their mistakes, or is there a predestined organisational divide on the centre-left? Tony Blair started to address that conundrum in building New Labour and the election campaign in 1997. As David Marquand summarises: 'Blair's achievement was to mobilise and lead a tacit anti-conservative electoral coalition, centred on the Labour Party, but extending well beyond its confines. And that coalition won' (Marquand 1999, p. vii). At the next general election it will probably win again, but it would be foolhardy to ignore the Conservative threat at the election after next.

Despite the ideological shift to the right, Conservative strategists are also aware of the opportunity for a broad-based coalition. It is the ability of the Conservative Party to adapt and mould itself to the prevailing political conditions that has characterised its durability as a political force. The populist campaigns on asylum seekers, fuel duty and sterling are matched with other initiatives to move into the political centre. Conservative speakers now talk of social entrepreneurship, the plight of inner-city deprivation and renewing civic society in an attempt to secure a niche in the centre ground of political debate. It is in these moves that the historic opportunity for Labour and the Liberal Democrats could be challenged. To return to the saloon bar and casino table at the start of this chapter, Labour now has its rich winnings from the 1997 general election, but where is it prepared to gamble next? Even with an unprecedented majority, and the contradictions in the Conservative Party, the odds are still stacked against the progressive century. The wisest gamble would be to invest in ending the century-long divide between labourism and liberalism; the Conservative Party will be watching with keen interest.

References

Marquand, D. (1999) *The Progressive Dilemma*. London: Heinemann.
Monks, J. (2000) Speech to Liberal Democrat Conference, Bournemouth, Tuesday 19 September.

4
Do Two Tribes Have to War?

Don Macintyre

Michael Meadowcroft, who founded his own Liberal Party after refusing to accept the formation of the Liberal Democrats, once described at a party fringe meeting how he had asked an elderly and lifelong Liberal activist how it was that the flame of liberalism was kept alive during those – for the party – dark days of the late 1940s and the 1950s when its General Election percentage vote share was consistently in single figures. 'We couldn't stand the Tories', the old man replied. 'And we didn't trust the state.'

This describes accurately, if brutally, one of the important ideological differences which maintained the distance between Labour and liberalism for more than a generation after the Second World War. While the Labour Party had long been a coalition between socialists and social democrats, its positioning up to the 1970s as a statist, mixed economy party, committed to the public ownership of at least some industries in practice – and all of them in theory until Clause IV was replaced in 1995 – made it inimical to the truly liberal strand in British politics.

Of course, it had been two Liberals, Keynes and Beveridge, who had been the intellectual architects of much that was best and most enduring – and, indeed, most cherished within the Labour Party – in the post-war transformation wrought by the Attlee Government. That fact alone goes, or should have gone, a long way to demolishing Labour's tribalist belief that it enjoys, on the left, a monopoly of wisdom; indeed, as Sherlock and Lawson have argued, it demonstrates that 'progressive politics are demonstrably stronger when the strands of progressivism come together' (Sherlock and Lawson 2000).

Nevertheless, almost all the rhetoric, and much of the practice, of the Labour Party in the post-war period militated against that lesson being learned. Even as late as the two Wilson governments Labour was driven in part by a belief in a model of a centrally planned command economy which Liberals naturally distrusted. All this helped to explain why at certain periods – for example, after the first general election of 1974 – the Liberal leadership was at least prepared to contemplate coalition with the Conservatives, even if this did not actually happen. That in turn fuelled Labour suspicion of the Liberals.

True, in the shock inflicted by Hugh Gaitskell's comprehensive general election defeat in 1959, there were subterranean mutterings within Labour about the need to join forces with the Liberals. But any such project would only have attracted at best a small fraction on the social democratic right of the party, with the bulk of the Labour Party remaining in being as a competing force, just as it would so remain, however damaged in the short term, after the creation of the SDP in the arguably much more propitious circumstances of 20 years later. These, then, were the certainties which sustained the familiar three-party model from 1945 until – despite the relative success of the SDP – after the 1987 election. It is almost impossible to overstate the gradual reshaping of the electoral landscape which has occurred, sometimes falteringly, but still unstoppably, since then.

One seldom-discussed factor in that process is the end of the Cold War, or rather the collapse of the communist world. A minor consequence was that it accelerated the demise of the British Communist Party which had long exercised a disproportionate influence through its presence in the trade union left on the Labour Party itself. Much more profoundly, it demonstrated the invalidity of the state socialist goals which had continued for so long to influence the Labour left, and through it the coalition of forces which any Labour leader, whatever his personal preferences, was obliged to reconcile. Any Labour leader might justly say, as one by one the socialist experiments were seen to fail across Europe, that we are all, if not liberals, at least social democrats now.

It would take another five years after the fall of the Berlin Wall for Labour formally to abandon its utterly obsolete adherence to 'common ownership of the means of production, distribution and exchange', but the emergence of the new pluralist and embryonically capitalist democracies in Eastern Europe helped to make it achievable by Tony Blair without any of the concerted internal opposition which had finally derailed Hugh Gaitskell's attempts to do the same thing almost 25 years earlier.

Against this background, first Neil Kinnock, then John Smith – who was himself a lifelong member of the social democratic, Atlanticist, pro-European right of the Labour Party – and finally, and most dramatically, the party's two leading 'modernisers', Gordon Brown and Tony Blair, were able to reposition Labour on the non-statist, pro-enterprise, fiscally responsible, centre-left. This was a position which leading figures in both Labour and the Liberal Democrats were quite quick to see eroded by most of the fundamental differences which had long existed between the two parties. Even before the abandonment of Clause IV, Paddy Ashdown had used his famous Chard speech after the 1992 election – to the irritation of many in his own party – to pave the way towards ending Liberal Democrat 'equidistance' between the two main parties.

At the same time some leading Labour figures were privately drawing attention to the convergence between some of the main elements in the manifestos on which the two parties had fought that election. But, after John Smith's death and Tony Blair's accession to the Labour leadership, that became, at least in private, much more explicit. According to Ashdown, Gordon Brown, then Shadow Chancellor, told him in a private conversation in December 1996:

> I reviewed the situation after 1992 and discovered that you lot were right. In all the economic policies you've been trying to pursue, especially competition, and enterprise and equality of opportunity, you have been leading the agenda. I have decided that what we have to do is basically adopt the classic Liberal agenda, in favour of competition, in favour of enterprise, and centred round equality of opportunity. (Ashdown 2000, pp. 484–5)

This is not to gloss over the strong resistance in both parties at the time to institutional links between the Liberal Democrats and Labour up to and including coalition; resistance which helped to ensure that coalition did not happen after the 1997 landslide. Brown himself, for example, had clear – and far from empty – reservations about whether beyond leading figures like Ashdown and Menzies Campbell, the Liberal Democrats had the cohesion and will required to be in power. Ashdown also reports Brown expressing his grave doubts about PR; citing, for example, some of those in his own party who 'push for PR because they believe it will enable them to push Labour back on to a conventional left wing agenda'.

But that is not the real significance of the Brown–Ashdown exchange. Instead, it is the ready recognition that ideologically the two parties had converged, perhaps more fully than at any time since the Edwardian era. And that is without mentioning the speed with which the new Labour government have enacted some long-sought constitutional goals of Liberal Democrats: the Scottish Parliament and the Welsh Assembly, both elected under a PR system; abolition of hereditary peerages with a joint Lib-Lab committee meeting to discuss the Lords' future under Robin Cook, the Labour politician who, apart from Blair himself, has most zealously promoted co-operation between the two parties; and PR for the European Parliament, the objective denied the Liberals in the 1970s when they were propping up the Callaghan government.

It is in this context that those in each party have to confront the question of whether the parties' individual identities and separateness are so prized that they must be preserved at all costs – including the cost of facilitating Tory victories, as the schism between the two parties repeatedly did during the twentieth century. Of course, there are differences between the two parties; but almost invariably, they are now differences which also exist within the parties as well. To take a single, if important, example: many of the liberal objections to some of the more draconian aspects of the government's law and order legislation – like the Mode of Trial Bill which narrows the scope of jury trial – are shared by those in the Labour Party who reflect the long tradition on the left of protecting the rights of defendants.

This isn't the place to debate the merits of either argument, or to underestimate the strength of feeling that exists among many Labour voters in favour of tough policies on crime. What the example instead illustrates is a peculiar anomaly at the heart of many Labour objections to closer links with the Liberal Democrats, which is that they are based on obsolete grounds. Many Labour MPs argue against a co-operative relationship with the Liberal Democrats in terms which have failed to catch up with the changes in the landscape. They speak as if the true soul of labourism would be contaminated by the centrist aspirations of the Liberal Democrats, when the reality is that on many issues dear to the Labour left, from public spending to civil liberties, the Liberal Democrats have policies which are more congenial to them. True, there are more orthodox Liberal criticisms to be made of Labour; it may still be too statist and regulatory for some Liberal Democrat tastes. But these are not the unbridgeable differences they were from the 1940s to the 1980s. And most of those on the left would actually like the Labour Party to be more liberal. Because, in several respects, coalition did not happen immediately after the general election of May 1997, or in the months following in which the *Ashdown Diaries* show that it continued to be discussed, it is tempting to think that the moment has now passed.

First, the question remains as to how serious Tony Blair really was in securing such an outcome, particularly if it required the Prime Minister to commit himself personally to electoral reform. Second, it is clear that this was the last period when the parties could have been brought together in government from a position of strength and – if Blair was prepared to go that far – on the high-minded grounds that such a coalition government would have more truly reflected the anti-Tory vote share of over 60 per cent than a one-party government elected by no more than just over 43 per cent of the electorate. In addition, it is clear that within Labour there is strong opposition to electoral reform, supposedly a *sine qua non* of permanent co-operation, or at least there is within the party conference, the Cabinet, and the Parliamentary Labour Party, which is not quite the same thing since it ignores a substantial body of support for reform among individual party members.

But none of this alters the less high-minded imperatives of mutual self-interest between the parties. Sooner or later Labour will face an election it cannot be confident, or even optimistic, about winning. The prospect of sustained co-operation between the parties then offers a concrete alternative prospect to defeat. It could even mean a clear choice between a Lib-Lab coalition government on the one hand, or a Conservative one on the other. At that point electoral reform becomes, or should become, more attractive to those MPs who currently resist it. Even those who continue to resist it because it might threaten their own individual seats would, if they persist in their resistance, be exposed in such circumstances as preferring to save their own parliamentary skins to seeing the continuation of a Labour-led government.

Of course, some of those who recognise that such a dilemma could at some point be a real one, argue that there is no need to advance the cause of inter-party co-operation now. Much better simply to wait until the parliamentary arithmetic dictates a solution. If Labour wins an overall parliamentary majority, so be it. But if there is a hung Parliament then that is the moment to start negotiations with the Liberal Democrats. And given that the electorate proved in 1997 a willingness to vote tactically to keep the Tories out, there is no need for a formal compact between the parties to ensure the maximisation of the anti-Tory vote.

This ignores two important points. The first is that waiting for a hung Parliament is about as sensible for opponents of the Tories as waiting for an asteroid to fall on Conservative Central Office. In every circumstance that a hung Parliament is likely, a Conservative majority is likelier. To plan for a hung Parliament carries with it the risk that the Conservatives will accede to power and the whole business of trying to achieve the long-sought realignment of British politics has to start afresh. The second point about this fatalistic analysis is that tactical voting can't be treated as a permanently guaranteed outcome. Even now, it isn't quite as certain as it was that the Lib Dem vote will as automatically gravitate to Labour as vice versa.

There is some evidence, for example, that in the Romsey by-election Labour support gravitated to the Lib Dems not for simple tactical reasons but because Labour supporters were disappointed with the performance of the government. If, for example, Labour becomes unpopular in the middle of a second term – and there is still no sign, say, of a winnable referendum on electoral reform – then Charles Kennedy could well come under irresistible pressure to jump clear of any co-operation with Labour and start opposing the government with clarity and determination. Given, too, that Kennedy has so far failed in his plan to make the main committees of the party subject to election by the whole membership rather than by the activists who dominate the party conference, that course is all the likelier.

In other words, there is everything to be said for both parties beginning to face up to the need for maintaining and enhancing co-operation. And this may require a greater proactivity by the leaderships of both parties in conditioning their members to the advantages of a closer relationship. In his *Diaries*, Paddy Ashdown compares the different possible levels of co-operation with 'casual sex', an 'affair' and 'marriage'. In the end, the relationship was an affair. Unfortunately, however, it was also, at least at its height, a largely secret affair. While Ashdown may have taken more of his colleagues into his confidence about the process than did Tony Blair, it was hardly conducted openly on either side. The Joint Cabinet Committee, which was its principal outcome, was of course public. But the scope and range of the discussions was not.

But leaders have to lead; if Kennedy is as keen on serious power as he looks, and if Blair is as serious about co-operation, then they may have to do more to persuade their own supporters. For all Ashdown's courage as a politician he never risked dividing his conference by confronting them with the choices – including, perhaps, an electoral system which falls short of the party's ideals – they may have to make if they are serious about power.

It now falls to Charles Kennedy, an instinctively more consensual figure, to do just that at some point in the post-election. Equally, Blair may need, after the election, to use his formidable powers of persuasion to mobilise support for what was once assumed to be a central part of his project – ending the schism on the left which helped to make the last century a Conservative one. Even those in the Labour Party who support that goal have very different views about what compromises the party would in turn have to make. Would it be Roy Jenkins' recommended system of electoral reform? Would it be the Alternative Vote system which would institutionalise tactical voting but might quite easily be presented as a Lib-Lab stitch-up in a referendum? Or would it simply be a matter, as some Blairites continue to believe, of an electoral pact in which candidates of either party are somehow persuaded to stand down in constituencies where their presence threatens to let in a Conservative.

These are huge issues, but they are less fundamental than the delivery of the common elements of the programmes in which both parties believe. By first reminding the parties what is truly at stake in the attempt to reunite the centre-left, the leaders of each may be in a better position to secure the practical accommodations needed to achieve it. In turn, this may mean compromises, and therefore seems to some to be a cynical prescription. Yet the true cynics are surely those for whom names, labels and tribes are more important than realising the aspirations and ideals which brought them into politics in the first place.

References

Ashdown, P. (2000) *The Ashdown Diaries, Volume One, 1988–1997.* Harmondsworth: Penguin, 2000.
Sherlock, N. and Lawson, N. (2000) 'We must sink our differences', *New Statesman*, 26 May.

5
Blair's Progressive Paradox

Steve Richards

Take two wildly differing snapshots from recent political history. One comes shortly after Labour's lowest point in its undistinguished electoral history. The other represents the party's triumphant peak. Together they form the backdrop to the elusive, enigmatic 'project'.

Consider, first, the Sunday evening of the Labour Party Conference in October 1983. To excited, optimistic cheers which thundered around Brighton's Conference Centre, a youthful Neil Kinnock was elected Labour leader. Kinnock leapt on to the stage, with members of the party's National Executive Committee sitting behind him, and improvised a victory speech with one central message. To wild acclaim he told the delegates not to forget, ever, what had happened in the election three months before. 'June 9th, 1983, never, never again!', he proclaimed. The activists cheered, but they were not listening. At the end of the week they headed off home and quickly forgot about the grimmest political night of their lives. They had more battles to fight, more internal victories to win. The views of the wider electorate were not to get a look in for another decade or so.

More than 17 years later and Kinnock's message still applies. Let us not forget 9 June 1983, the election which produced a landslide for the Conservatives and nearly wiped out Labour as a political force. In terms of votes cast, the SDP/Liberal Alliance came within a whisker of Michael Foot's party. With only a small number of seats, the Alliance did not do well enough to give it fresh momentum; Labour did not do badly enough to fade away and die. Instead, two confused, demoralised forces were left to fight it out.

Let us not forget 9 June 1983 for another reason. This was the election in which Tony Blair was elected to the Commons. To understand the Blair paradox, the control freak who seeks sometimes to give away or share power, this is the key. Blair became an MP at a time when it was widely assumed that Labour would never govern again.

Fast-forward to May 1997. 'A new political dawn has arrived!' Those were Blair's words as the sun rose over the Royal Festival Hall, greeting the new Labour government. The new dawn brought a landslide for Labour of undreamed proportions, much higher than Thatcher's in 1983. The new political landscape was Blair's to do with what he liked. He began by appointing a Labour Cabinet without a Liberal Democrat in sight, and by insisting that the campaign for the next election began right away. There was no complacency in New Labour.

On the surface these two landmarks are miles apart, almost polar opposites. But one feeds the other. 1983 is as significant a moment for Blair, still, as 1997. 1983, and the elections in 1987 and 1992, explain why Blair has led a cautious government. Labour is used to losing elections, not winning them. They do not believe that governing is really their right. They are the impostors until the Tories resume their rightful place as our governors, reigning over us again. That is one of the reasons why William Hague is so calm against seemingly appalling odds. He leads the party that tends to win elections.

Those election results explain Blair's interest in creating and maintaining a relationship with the Liberal Democrats before the 1997 election and why he was right to do so. The 1983 election result was calamitous for the anti-Conservative forces, as were the 1987 and 1992 polls. They gave rise to the celebration of 'Thatcherism', a term predictably coined by defensive left-wingers at *Marxism Today*, carrying out Thatcher's work for her, elevating her populist pragmatism to a philosophy which was capable of conquering all that stood in its way.

But it was never really like that. The Conservatives' support hardly moved in her three election wins, hovering throughout at around 42 per cent. This was a reasonable achievement, but considering the economic prosperity enjoyed by most people most of the time in the 1980s, not an especially spectacular one. By fighting each other at least as much as they fought Thatcher, Labour and the Liberal Democrats made her dominance much more spectacular than it really was.

A majority of voters were still seeking an alternative to Thatcher throughout her triumphant years. If Blair and Ashdown had been leaders of their respective parties in 1984 rather than 1994 – and such a scenario implies, of course, that their parties would have been altogether different beasts as well – Thatcher may well have been doomed. Together they would have contrived a credible alternative. Her victories were not inevitable. Indeed, for much of the time she was in government she was behind in the polls. She had a knack of becoming quite popular, but not excessively so, just as she was about to call an election. The rest of the time she had a precarious electoral base. Thatcherism was a myth brought about by a split opposition.

Blair, having more in common with the Alliance than his own party for much of this period, recognised the problem. The least tribal of politicians, he stood back from the fray, identifying the progressive tradition in both parties and their electoral potential if they moved closer together. But Blair is also a politician interested, first and foremost, in achieving and exercising power. Therefore all routes are kept open. The alternative route of destroying the Liberal Democrats always remained open even as he flirted with its leaders.

The key text for Blair's ambiguous assessment of the project is his Fabian lecture delivered in July 1995. In it he identified Liberals such as Lloyd George and Beveridge, as well as Hardie, Attlee and Bevan as being part of the progressive tradition of the twentieth century. No other Labour leader had incorporated political giants from other parties when navigating a radical path. It was time, he declared with a flourish, to forge a 'new coalition' of the radical centre. 'Paddy Ashdown will be in the Shadow Cabinet within a month', one senior Shadow Cabinet member said to me after hearing the speech.

Characteristically, though, Blair left a gaping hole in the speech. The clarity of tone disguised deft evasiveness. What form was the 'new coalition' going to take? He left it perfectly open for New Labour, alone, to be the vehicle for radical change in the new progressive century.

However intense his exchanges with Paddy Ashdown in the run-up to the last election, Blair was keeping his options open. We know this because of what happened next. After the landslide win, Blair did not invite Ashdown or any other Lib Dem to join him in government.

A myth has arisen subsequently that the size of his majority prevented Blair from cementing his relationship with the Lib Dems. Privately Blair has said it would have been 'quixotic' to have formed a coalition in such circumstances.

Journalist Robert Harris, who was with Blair on the night of the election, has reinforced this myth. He has written since that Blair was in a subdued mood as the sensational results were announced around the country. Harris sensed that the reason for this unlikely reaction from a leader who was winning by a landslide was the realisation that his project, in the short term at least, was doomed.

I have always believed the opposite, that a triumphant landslide was exactly the circumstances in which Blair could have implemented his project. More precisely, there were only two scenarios in which Blair could have formed a coalition. Obviously a hung Parliament would have necessitated some kind of formal arrangement. Given Blair's open flirtations with the Lib Dems he would not have forged ahead with a minority Labour government as Harold Wilson did in February 1974. Parliamentary arithmetic would have legitimised the formation of a coalition.

The only other situation in which a coalition would have been possible is one where Blair had been so triumphant, rendered so politically invincible, that he was in a position to take on his fiercely hostile Cabinet colleagues. Brown, Prescott, Straw and co. were all opposed to Blair's relationship with the Lib Dems, as was his Press Secretary, Alastair Campbell. Blair would have been a relatively weak Prime Minister if he had secured an overall majority of 30 or 40. Even so, with a working majority, he would not have been weak enough in terms of seats in the Commons to have a coalition thrust upon him. Nor would he have been strong enough to take on his colleagues:

Tony: 'Gordon, John ... I know I have failed to get the landslide everyone was predicting, but I am still going ahead with the project.'
Gordon; John: 'Over our dead bodies.'

On the other hand, winning with a majority of 180, say, and he could have done what he liked. That is the majority Blair secured. He chose to do nothing.

Ashdown, too, had his own problem. His party was his problem. He would not have been able to stride into the Cabinet without extensive consultations. Delay and hesitation as to who would be in his cabinet would have marked Blair's opening days in government. This would have been a fumbling, uncertain start for someone who wanted to lead with a Thatcherite glint in his eye.

This was part of Blair's curiously schizophrenic approach towards his 'project'. He sought strong, disciplined government from the beginning. Later, his experience of the Balkans War, in 1999, when he could act in virtually any way that he wanted while many of his European colleagues had to consult their coalition partners, turned him against governing with other parties. The experience in Scotland also hardened him. But from the beginning his attitude towards government would have made coalition impossible. Alastair Campbell even wanted to know whom ministers were meeting for lunch. Stray Liberal Democrats, unaccountable to the rigidities of the New Labour machine, would not have been acceptable in such an atmosphere.

The headlines which greeted the publication of Paddy Ashdown's *Diaries* in the autumn of 2000 suggested that the two leaders were even closer than we had all imagined in the run-up to the last election. That is not my reading of the full text. Blair's attitude changed at every meeting described by Ashdown. One moment he is striding willingly towards coalition and proportional representation, the next he is having doubts about the whole damned thing. And this is the view from Ashdown, who wanted to convince himself as much as anyone else, that Blair was a true believer.

Although Blair has a tendency to say what his companion at any given time wants to hear, he was surprisingly candid with Ashdown at times. On his off-days he told Ashdown that there were problems with Gordon over the project and then, most damning of all, he reported back that the focus groups were not impressed. Most of the time Blair seemed to be agonising aloud, openly honest with Ashdown about his dilemmas in forging ahead.

Not all the time, though. At one point Ashdown records his horror at an interview Blair gave to the *New Statesman* in July 1996 in which, for the first time, the great equivocator said he was against proportional representation. In his *Diaries* Ashdown records Blair as saying that his remarks were wrongly reported. I conducted that interview with the editor of the *New Statesman* at the time, Ian Hargreaves. I am sure we are capable of misinterpretation when writing up long interviews, but not on this occasion for the simple reason that there was no interpretation. For the only time when I was at the *New Statesman* we transcribed the interview and published it in its original form. There were no complaints from Blair's office about the accuracy of the transcription. It was there for all to see in front of their eyes. Ashdown saw it in that form too. Somehow he was more desperate to believe Blair's excuses than to believe the original transcript.

So is that it? Has Blair accepted now, a few years down the line, that the coalition of the centre-left will be New Labour alone?

No. In the same way as he kept all options open in his Fabian lecture in 1995, he keeps them open now. He has wooed the Lib Dems enough to keep the dream alive. They have a Joint Cabinet Committee, a share of power in Scotland and Wales, and a form of PR for the European elections. More important, events can change the political context, making Blair thankful for his political flexibility. In the latter half of the first term events have moved back in favour of the 'project'.

In the autumn of 2000, for the first time since he became leader of his party in 1994, Blair began to acquire enemies. Although he always claimed to want them, to need enemies to help provide clearer political definition, he did not really mean it.

People moved of their own accord. The newspapers, the business leaders, the tax haters turned on him. The fuel crisis in the autumn of 2000 was the defining moment. The government's genuine friends came to the fore; the trade unionists, assorted progressives, and some fickle allies walked out of the big tent.

In spite of himself Blair has discovered that a Labour leader, even a New Labour leader, has traditional enemies. The newspapers, which he wooed so assiduously, turned on him. He had never fully realised that they would only like him as long as he said what they wanted to hear. As soon as he moved a few inches away from their terrain on Europe or tax they would pounce, mauling him as they had mauled his predecessors. Some business leaders proved to be unreliable friends. The steely, nearly anonymous oil managers were not exactly helpful in the early days of the fuel dispute. Were they complicit in the tax revolt? A bemused Downing Street so in awe of business, so proud that business had turned to Labour, asked the question too.

Suddenly Blair needed genuine allies, and he will continue to do so as long as he seeks to retain power. Just as obituaries of the 'project' were being written, even by its founders ('That was the past. We must look to the future now', Paddy Ashdown told the *Today* programme in September 2000), the political heat blew life into the embers. The need for a genuine progressive alliance rather than an artificially contrived big tent became more important than ever.

On all the big issues of the day – Europe, race, crime, tax-and-spend – there is broad agreement between the two parties. Some members of both the parties might squirm at such a statement, but it is correct; most obviously on Europe, but on the other issues as well. The differences have been tactical. At times Labour have been pathetically weak on race, playing to the *Daily Mail* gallery. But their instincts are different and sometimes they show it. Blair refused to play to any gallery on asylum, agreeing always with Charles Kennedy in the Commons when the Lid Dem leader bravely – and, as the Romsey by-election showed, politically astutely – attacked Hague's populism. The government is spending more than the Lib Dems advocated at the last election. They present the spending case a little differently, that is all. Both parties agree that the chronic underinvestment in Britain's public services is the essential issue that any government has to address. Given Britain's propensity to indulge in tax-cutting feasts, they will need to be strong about this. Two parties working together are stronger than one.

Charles Kennedy opposes the Conservatives with the same ferocity and for the same reasons as Tony Blair. In the 1980s there was an informal anti-Labour alliance. Now there is an anti-Conservative one.

Hague dreads its formal realisation. In the autumn of 1998, when Blair began to equivocate about holding a referendum on electoral reform, Hague told his Shadow Cabinet, 'I thought he had a strategy for destroying the Conservative Party. Instead he obviously doesn't know what to do.' One of the biggest arguments in favour of electoral reform is that the Conservatives are terrified of it.

The question, then, is not whether the two parties should work much more closely together, but how. What happened after the election in 1997 serves as a guide. If two party leaders at the height of their power could not contrive an effective arrangement, there should be no further attempt at such contrivance in the future. The experiment should evolve naturally from a local level. Proportional representation in local councils is the next logical step, to be followed by a referendum on electoral reform in the Commons.

1997 might well have been the exception and the elections in the 1980s more typical. After all, in a voting system which allows for only two parties to flourish, the one which occupies its own space alone on the right has more room to flourish, especially if it faces a divided opposition. Or, as Neil Kinnock put it: 'June 9th, 1983, never, never again.'

6
Is There a Progressive Electorate?

David Cowling

The twentieth century began and ended with massive parliamentary defeats for the Conservatives – at the hands of the Liberals in 1906 and of Labour in 1997. Yet the greater part of the intervening years saw Conservative governments in Whitehall. Towards the end of Labour's post-1979 wilderness years, a view developed that differences with the Lib Dems were not irreconcilable; and from there it was not difficult to move on to propose that co-operation could create a formidable centre-left majority that would dominate the twenty-first century as much as the Conservatives had dominated the twentieth.

However, as is so often the case, such a theory is more easily expressed than proved. We know that many individuals respond positively when asked whether they favour less gladiatorial and partisan politics. Yet they continue to vote for parties and politicians that sustain the system they insist they despise. The proponents of big tent, centre-left co-operation argue that such ambiguity is under-standable when parties are so relentlessly and publicly addicted to a polarised political system. However (the argument continues), if Labour and the Liberal Democrats challenged the sterile politics of the past by offering a real alternative of constructive engagement then the public would respond positively. What evidence is there that the electorate is willing to subscribe to such a strategy? And do these theorists reflect a real desire for change among electors, or are they simply moving paper armies around a political gameboard?

Our Westminster electoral system is not proportional, but those on the centre-left have been haunted by the fact that massive fractures in the anti-Conservative vote at successive elections in the 1980s delivered Mrs Thatcher enormous parliamentary majorities to push through her policies. Table 6.1 sets out the share of the vote for the three main parties in general elections over the past three decades.

Table 6.1   Three-party voting in General Elections (GB)

	Conservative (%)	Labour (%)	Liberal* (%)
1970	46.2	43.9	7.6
1974 (Feb)	38.8	38.0	19.8
1974 (Oct)	36.7	40.2	18.8
1979	44.9	37.8	14.1
1983	43.5	28.3	26.0
1987	43.3	31.5	23.1
1992	42.8	35.2	18.3
1997	31.5	44.3	17.2

*Lib/SDP in 1983 and 1987.

It is easy to see why such figures tantalise those who advocate closer co-operation between Labour and the Liberal Democrats. If only they could yoke together the separate votes of the two parties, who could withstand them? For many of them, the 1997 general election epitomised what they hope will become the new political hegemony: a spectacular harvest of Labour seats plus the biggest crop of Liberal Democrat MPs in 60 years, combining to reduce the Conservatives to a narrow rump in Westminster. However, the assumption that seems to underpin their thinking, namely that many supporters of the two parties are virtually interchangeable in terms of shared attitudes and beliefs, is not exactly borne out by history.

In January 1949, Gallup asked Liberal supporters how they would vote if there were no Liberal candidate in their constituency at the next election. By a ratio of two to one, they said they would vote Conservative. There is also the example of Labour's narrow 1964 election victory. Almost five years earlier, in the 1959 election, securing 44.6 per cent of the vote, Labour had suffered its third defeat at the hands of the Conservatives and found itself crushed by a 100-

seat majority. In the 1964 general election, Labour's share of the vote was 44.8 per cent – virtually unchanged from 1959 – but this time the outcome was a Labour majority of four seats. A major reason for these very different results is found in the increased Liberal vote – some 1.4 million higher in 1964 than in 1959 – largely due to the fact that the Liberals contested 149 more seats in 1964. The political consequence of this great increase in Liberal candidates was that they siphoned off key voters from the Conservatives and eased Labour's path to victory. But whilst this intervention played a critical role in Labour's success in the election, it hardly portrays a world where Liberal voters were virtually indistinguishable from Labour ones. On the contrary, it suggests that in a whole raft of seats in 1959, where they had no candidate of their own, Liberals preferred to vote Conservative rather than Labour.

Almost 30 years later, at the 1992 general election, the NOP/BBC exit poll asked respondents who had just voted how they would have cast a second preference vote. Among Liberal Democrat voters, 37 per cent chose Labour and 35 per cent chose the Conservatives: statistics that explain why for so long the party's leadership followed a policy of maintaining political equidistance between themselves and the Labour and Conservative parties. The caution of those years, amongst other reasons, reflected the painful experience of the Lib-Lab pact.

The pact (which lasted from March 1977 to August 1978), negotiated between the Labour Prime Minister, James Callaghan, and the Liberal Party leader, David Steel, meant that 'for the first time since 1931, Britain had a government explicitly dependent on an understanding with a party not in government' (Butler 1979). The terms of the pact required that the Liberals be consulted in advance of all major policy initiatives. It also committed the government to bring forward legislation on devolution and direct elections to the European Parliament, as well a free vote in the Commons on proportional representation. Throughout most of the period of the pact Gallup asked a question that very quickly exposed the political complexities involved in sustaining such a venture. Table 6.2 sets out the net figure between those who thought the pact a 'good thing' (+) and those who thought it a 'bad thing' (–).

Overwhelmingly the pact was seen as a good thing for the Labour government. This is not too surprising given that it guaranteed their survival after by-elections had eliminated their small majority in the

Commons. Also, after an initial dose of scepticism, the public came round to the view that the pact was good for the country. However, they were hardly ever persuaded that it was a good thing for the Liberal Party. In the subsequent election of 1979, the Liberals lost 1 million votes and two parliamentary seats.

Table 6.2   Q. *'Do you think the agreement between the Liberal Party and the government is a good thing or a bad thing, (a) for the country, (b) for the government, (c) for the Liberal Party?'*

	(a) Country (%)	*(b) Government* (%)	*(c) Liberal Party* (%)
May 1977	−5	+19	−24
July 1977	+ 6	+33	−1
August 1977	+ 7	+40	+ 2
September 1977	+ 9	+30	−3
October 1977	+25	+37	−4
November 1977	+15	+37	0
December 1977	+13	+40	−1
January 1978	+13	+35	−7
February 1978	+17	+39	−2

This experience does not provide any sort of 'proof' that co-operation between parties is doomed to failure. The 1979 election was fought in a highly charged and polarised atmosphere, following the 'winter of discontent' which makes direct links between Liberal losses and the pact at least questionable. Equally, however, the experience showed that there is no automatic electoral reward for those who practise consensus politics.

Many would doubtless say that the Lib-Lab pact has no relevance to the current debate on co-operation between the two parties. However, if nothing else it reminds us that timing is crucial in politics. The Liberals in 1977/78 found themselves propping up an exhausted and wounded government, besieged by an aggressive and self-confident Conservative Opposition. The obvious lesson from this is that co-operation is likely to survive longest and retain more credit when it results from principled agreement between strong partners rather than when it is perceived as a desperate piece of crisis management.

But if the Lib-Lab pact was followed by a tidal wave of polarised, partisan politics, can future models of co-operation, however cast, survive similar assaults? We have no crystal ball that provides an answer, but we do know that the great historic blocs of party support are diminishing. As Table 6.3 shows, over the past four decades not only has overall voter identification with the three main parties declined, but *strength* of identification has declined even faster.

Table 6.3   Identification with the three main parties

	1964 (%)	1979 (%)	1997 (%)
Conservative identifiers	39	38	30
% identifiers 'very strong'	*48*	*24*	*14*
Labour identifiers	42	36	23
% identifiers 'very strong'	*51*	*29*	*23*
Liberal identifiers	11	11	13
% identifiers 'very strong'	*32*	*14*	*6*

One does not have to subscribe to the fashionable but facile notion that voting today is simply an extension of consumerism, to recognise that the perennial competition for votes is becoming an increasingly complex affair. Not only is the electorate more rootless now compared with the allegiances of previous generations, but from 1997 onwards they have shown themselves significantly less interested in voting for anybody. In the fuel crisis of September 2000 it was quite clear from the party's collapse in the polls that the public wanted to punish Labour, but at the same time they showed no equivalent determination to reward the Conservatives: support (at Labour's expense) rose almost equally for the Conservatives and the Liberal Democrats.

Has the drift to the right in the Conservative Party hindered their recovery and created an opportunity for the advocates of co-operation on the other two main parties? A poll conducted by Harris Research in December 1998 asked respondents to describe their views in political matters on a scale of left and right. The average of the two polls published that month gave the following voting intention: Labour 52 per cent, Conservatives 28 per cent and the Lib Dems 14 per cent (Table 6.4).

One in five respondents in the Harris survey did not identify themselves within the scale offered, but 42 per cent described their political views as of the centre. Of the remainder, 18 per cent defined themselves in terms of the right and 22 per cent in terms of the left. Interestingly, Conservative voters were the most polarised – 49 per cent describing themselves as of the right, compared with 38 per cent of Labour voters who described their political views as left. These figures doubtless reflect the fact that the low level of support for the Conservatives at the end of 1998 included a disproportionate number of core voters, whereas Labour's high ratings encompassed a dispro-portionately large number of people who were not traditional supporters. But for the advocates of centre-left co-operation these figures could be viewed as potential building blocks for their project.

Table 6.4   Q. *'In political matters, people talk of the right and the left. Generally speaking, how would you describe your views in these terms?'*

	All voters (%)	Conservative voters (%)	Labour voters (%)	Lib Dem voters (%)
Right	5	19	2	2
Towards the right	13	30	10	14
Centre	42	36	37	55
Towards the left	16	3	26	16
Left	6	1	12	4
Don't know	15	8	11	8
Refused	4	4	1	1

However, hanging over all this is the essential question: What form does any centre-left co-operation take? For those who are determined that the centre-left should dominate the next hundred years as decisively as the Conservatives dominated the last, then there is only one answer. And this is the subject that dare not speak its name: pro-portional representation.

It is not my intention to rehearse the issue of PR here (not least because I am agnostic on the subject), but if the purpose of those advocating co-operation is to deliver something tangible and lasting then, it seems to me, only a fundamental change in our voting system will do. Our current electoral system has both strengths and weaknesses but few would argue that its outcomes stimulate co-operation: in the 1983 election the Conservatives secured 43.5 per cent of the national vote and won 61 per cent of the seats in

Parliament; and in 1997, Labour's 44.3 per cent of the vote resulted in them winning 63 per cent of the seats. Proportional voting, on the other hand, has resulted in Lib-Lab administrations in the Scottish Parliament and the Welsh Assembly with real power-sharing based on shared objectives.

There seems little evidence that the British public is greatly absorbed by the theoretical advantages of co-operation between Labour and the Liberal Democrats. They support the idea that politics should be less aggressive and divisive but show a propensity to change their minds about this depending how passionately they feel on specific issues. Past history suggests that we cannot automatically assume that the overwhelming majority of Liberal Democrat voters would be comfortable at developing closer relations with Labour as opposed to the Conservatives. But it also seems to me that there has been no better time than now in living memory for the advocates of closer co-operation to advance their cause. New Labour has dismantled large chunks of its ideology that proved such an obstacle to co-operation in the past. The major constitutional reforms that produced devolution in Scotland and Wales and a directly elected Mayor plus Assembly in London do pose a real and profound challenge to the historic Westminster model of politics. With a speed that takes my breath away, if nobody else's, over the past three years the 'first past the post' glacier has melted. That traditional voting system is now reserved for Westminster and local government elections alone (and in the latter case proportional voting is being seriously considered for local elections in Scotland and Wales). The result is that one-party government is under siege across great swathes of the UK. If the advocates of centre-left co-operation cannot advance their cause now, then the project truly has no future.

References

Butler, D. (1979) *The British General Election of 1979*. Basingstoke: Macmillan (now Palgrave)

Part 2

Giving Government Legitimacy: New Structures and Culture for a New Century

7
The Second Wave of Constitutional Reform

Pam Giddy

The concept of a 'progressive century' can only take shape as a new form of politics if it is rooted in a new form of democracy. Is New Labour up to the challenge?

The most tangible result of New Labour's first term in government will be its constitutional reform programme. For those in Scotland, Wales or London, the results of the Government's constitutional reforms are clear: a Parliament with some tax-varying powers; an elected Assembly; an elected Mayor presiding over a pan-city Assembly. It might be slightly harder for the rest of us to taste the fruits of democratic change – a Human Rights Act, *most* hereditary peers have been cast out of the Lords and proportional representation has been introduced to some elections, but not all.

This is beginning to have an impact on where power lies, for most of these measures are designed to move power away from the centre. The details can be argued about, but reform has happened on an amazing scale.

However, there is a striking absence of principled justification for the reform agenda as a whole. No Cabinet Minister has stood up on a major public platform and declared New Labour's reforms to be a success in which we should take pride. In fact, the grudging implementation of the later reforms may cause one to wonder if the government is merely going through the motions with no commitment to the outcomes. It is as if the government's most radical programme is one from which they prefer to hide.

And now there are those who say that this was an agenda that it may have been unwise to embark upon in the first place and argue that it is one that New Labour should leave well alone in its second term.

Labour's conversion to constitutional reform has been slow. The British left has traditionally been ambivalent towards the constitution. In general, Labour governments have been more concerned with social and economic policy than 'constitutional meddling'. Their concern has been to concentrate on what the state does rather than what the state should be.

It is important to bear in mind that the Westminster model of government allows an enormous amount of power to be centralised in the hands of the British executive and Prime Minister. It is a model, therefore, which holds attractions to any incoming government with radical ambitions. Our 'first past the post' electoral system, which tends to deliver substantial majorities, and the legislative dominance of the Commons over the unelected Lords, mean that governments can, with rare exceptions, pass whatever policies they wish. It is not really in their interest to reform a constitution which delivers such advantages.

And yet the winning 1997 Labour government came into power with a raft of constitutional reforms. By implementing them, arguably they have recast the British constitution more in the past three years than any government has in the past 300 years.

So why did the Labour Party turn to reforming the constitution? Historically the answer to this is found in the Conservative Party's reaction to opposition in the 1970s. They realised that it was possible for a Labour government with only the slimmest of popular mandates to use the British state for radical socialist ends. The fear that the conventions which kept government in check would not hold led Lord Hailsham to label the powers of the Prime Minister and his Cabinet an 'elective dictatorship'.[1] Conservatives began to call for a written constitution to act as a check on the government. Most, however, lost such reformist zeal after the 1979 election delivered them power again with an economic and social agenda so radical that it was only deliverable by this same 'elective dictatorship'.

The reality of electoral politics in the 1980s gave Labour the impetus to turn its mind to reforming the British state. A party which looked unelectable started the process to reform itself and began to see the advantages of reforming the rules that determined how politics was played. The political juggernaut of Thatcherite majorities seemed to be without challenge under the existing constitutional settlement. It was a deathbed conversion to help save the party.

However, the final and most powerful push came in the late 1990s when New Labour made a strong electoral link between the sleaze of the previous Conservative governments and the constitution: for the first time, constitutional reform of sorts became a 'tabloid' issue. The Labour Party argued that the Tories could not be trusted; a New Labour government would be cleaner. If elected, the party would reform government to be more open and more accountable and less prone to sleaze; it would be a government in touch with the people.

The question is: did the architects of the New Labour 'project' really believe in the reforms they signed up to? Most of the reforms that Labour put forward in its 1997 manifesto – and has acted on – primarily grew out of commitments that the late John Smith had persuaded the party to take on board.

Smith's passion for constitutional reform was rooted in the belief that the British people believed in government. However, he was worried that government would lose its legitimacy if it could not reform itself to become more accountable to the people it sought to serve. He said: 'the role of government in our society ought to be instrumental and subordinate – subordinate, above all to the democratic will'.[2] Smith's constitutional reform programme had an overriding purpose: to create institutional and legal checks that made it impossible for future governments to impose their will on society as Thatcher had done. He also recognised that without a root and branch reform, the body politic would never recover from the effects of an increasingly cynical electorate.

However, the democratic agenda was never truly part of Blair's mission. One only has to observe the manner in which New Labour has governed. There is much talk of giving power to the people, moving power away from the centre, empowering and consulting the people; but its instinct is to centralise. In sharp contrast to its theoretical constitutional reform programme, in practice it wants to retain rather than disseminate decision making. New Labour in power reeks of a government which believes that only a strong centre can deliver and imposes its will on an unwitting electorate. At the heart of the New Labour machine, democracy is regarded as inefficient and outcomes are considered better served through the iron will of the centre.

And so in implementing its programme of reform, New Labour has taken care not to meddle with anything which preserves its own unique position. The prerogative powers, the secrecy and the executive discretion remain largely untouched. Take freedom of information, a policy to which Labour has long been committed: this reform has been so compromised that the release of advice and factual information is left to the ultimate discretion of Ministers. Ministers will decide which reports from authorities like the Health and Safety Executive can be released. The culture of secrecy, which meant that warnings about BSE were hidden from the public for so long, will remain largely unchanged. And reform of the House of Lords, arguably Labour's most 'popular' constitutional change, has been compromised by the same reluctance to challenge the fundamentals on which the system is built.

The narrative which accompanies New Labour's programme of democratic reform does not concede the need to create a modern state which is responsive and aware of a new time. There is no overarching ambition to create new and varied centres of power and governance. Ultimately, the government has fought to ensure that its own position remains largely untouched. One is left wondering whether, if New Labour had had more time before the 1997 election, whole rafts of the democratic reform programme might not have been quietly cast off.

So now it may be easy for New Labour strategists to sit back and think that they have kept (most) of their promises on the constitution (with reform of the electoral system for Westminster being the most glaring omission). For those who took up the constitution for narrow electoral advantage or because it was an inheritance they could not lose in time, it is not difficult to turn away from these rather dry reforms. Few grab headlines and fewer still (as they see it) will act as 'eye-catching initiatives' to inspire voters to turn out and re-elect New Labour for a historic second term. If they used the constitution in 1997 because it was then politically advantageous, next time round a new set of advantageous ideas might take New Labour somewhere else.

There is a painful logic for those who argue this case. But it is a logic based on a misapprehension of the constitutional reform agenda and the effect of New Labour's reforms. Whether New Labour recognise it or not, they have only just begun on the constitution. It is no longer an issue which can be left behind. The reforms have a dynamic of their own and the genie cannot be put back into the bottle. The question at stake now is, who owns our political system – the politicians or the people? There are three clear reasons why New Labour has no choice but to continue with the reform agenda.

First, it linked constitutional reform to the idea of new politics. The impetus for reforming the constitution may have been the result of inheritance and narrow electoral advantage, but New Labour strategists linked reform to a new project with a new politics. An illustration of how the project was seen as inextricably linked to reform of the constitution was the publication, just two months before the 1997 election, of a joint constitutional report with the Liberal Democrats. To abandon the constitution now is to abandon the concept of a new politics.

Second, Labour's changes are not traditional piecemeal reforms that build on or refine the past and thus preserve the essence; some are too radical for that. The principles which guided the old constitution have been broken, except for centralisation, without replacing them. Most of the pillars of the past have been broken, leaving intact the powers of the Prime Minister and only tinkering with the rule of law and winner-takes-all voting. The absolute sovereignty of Parliament is fatally undermined by the Human Rights Act, the unitary state is no more but we have no mechanisms by which to negotiate new relationships and settle disputes. The independence of the civil service has been further eroded. Cabinet government is weaker. While New Labour has broken or disregarded the old principles, it has not replaced them.

Third, it is a question of trust and legitimacy. The Prime Minister made much of the lack of trust in the run-up to the 1997 election. He promised us a government that would be more open, more accountable and more in touch with the people. Trust, however, is a two-way thing. The government call on us to trust them, yet show pitifully little trust in us. Research shows that people feel alienated from politics: they do not believe what politicians say. Turnout for all elections is falling. Feelings of dislocation are growing. Some dismiss this as apathy. But we are still interested in the outcomes: it is our faith in the process that has declined. This should be a wake-up call for politics itself. We are a different electorate even to that of only 20 years ago. Deference is dying, our communities changing, our loyalties increasingly dissipated. The British system functions to deprive voters of their sense of relevance.

New Labour seems content to continue as if none of this matters. But for how long can it behave like this? The challenge now for the Prime Minister is to establish his own democratic credentials.

It is time to question the remnants of the old constitution which New Labour has shied away from challenging. It cannot any longer talk about empowering the citizen, if it refuses to question its own centralising zeal. Its behaviour in Wales and in London, its desire to impose on the electorate rather than let us choose for ourselves, exposed a distrust in both its own reforms and the people.

New Labour's democratic reform programme has ironically increased rather than sated our feelings of disillusionment with our democracy. New Labour has failed to address those issues of representation and participation which exclude the majority of us from being involved in the decisions which affect our lives. Power remains distant from us. The challenge for Blair and the architects of New Labour must now be to find innovative and creative ways of including the electorate rather than expecting us to bend to their will. Including us means accepting that what we want and need in our different regions, cities and communities may be different from the grand vision held at the centre. Constitutional reform is not an end in itself. We believe in it because updating our institutions and reconfiguring where power lies will lead to better outcomes.

After the 1997 election New Labour rejected the argument that a new constitutional synthesis was required. It decided that it could push through the various commitments inherited from John Smith because they were of little significance – except as promises which had to be enacted to ensure that Labour kept its all-important image as a party that delivers on its commitments.

But it does matter now. The forces that New Labour has unleashed will lead to a new settlement. The question for the party is whether it wants to help define this journey. Without a defence of the ambition that unites its various reforms, New Labour is likely to continue to suffer the accusation of being inconsistent, ad hoc, perhaps unwise and certainly incoherent.

And New Labour must also realise the totality of its ambition for new politics. A major part of this means a new electoral system for Westminster, one which is more representative of society as a whole and which creates a Parliament in which the executive has continually to seek greater consent for its policies. Labour's interest in electoral reform, like much of its constitutional proposals, may have come out of its experience of Thatcherism but it must now place it at the heart of its recasting of both British politics and also the British constitution. New politics cannot be built on an informal behind-the-scenes deal between parties. Electoral reform to ensure that parties can work together is a real and open way – agreeing and working together where they can but maintaining an open ability to disagree when they do not. This should be the first reform in the second wave of constitutional reform, and by instituting it Tony Blair will begin to define his own democratic credentials.

Plural politics was a touchstone during the creation of New Labour. It should be a guiding principle behind the continuing evolution of New Labour and the recasting of the constitution. Pluralism has always been part of the vocabulary of Labour and it is now time to institutionalise it and not see it as just one policy among others.

Notes

1. Lord Hailsham, Dimbleby Lecture, 1976.
2. 1993.

8
The Sociological Foundations of Pluralist Politics[1]

Michael Rustin

We tend to forget in these days of post-Cold War, post-ideological politics, how far political parties and movements of the right and left have usually drawn sustenance from systematic bodies of social thought. Distinct philosophies, conceptions of human nature and social scientific paradigms have given shape and direction to the political programmes of traditional conservatives, economic liberals, collectivistic liberals, social democrats and Marxist revolutionaries alike. We only need think of such figures as Adam Smith, Alfred Marshall, Joseph Schumpeter and Friedrich von Hayek, on the side of capitalism; and Marx, Gramsci, Bernstein, Polanyi, William Morris or Tawney, on the side of the various socialisms, to see the importance of these connections. There is also a third tradition of 'social liberalism' represented by the ideas of Keynes, Beveridge and Hobhouse (and today perhaps by David Marquand and Will Hutton) which has also continued to find expression, for example, in defence of 'Keynesian' and 'stakeholder' approaches to the economy against the economic liberalism of the new right. These various political positions have drawn much of their analytic, programmatic and persuasive force from such theoretical underpinnings.

One can doubt how far the 'Third Way', as it has been constituted thus far, is based on any such coherent theoretical foundations. It originally had all the appearances of a cover story, representing as a fresh compromise what was at first more of a caving-in to capital. Critics have been scathing about this, observing the role of branding and techniques of marketing in the construction of New Labour politics, and noting also the borrowings[2] from the New Democrats in the US, whose principal skills lay in the techniques of political competition. It sometimes seemed that the effort to give intellectual sense to the Third Way came after rather than before it had been politically invented. It could even be described as a brand in search of a product.

The negative aspects of much New Labour campaigning contributed to this impression. Its foundation lay after all in the battles for the 'modernisation' of the party, against Old Labour, long before it was elected to government. Because in its early stages most of New Labour's venom seemed reserved for those to its left, it was possible to see its politics as largely one of adaptation to the demands of a market society, even while it presented itself, though nebulously, as distinct from it. Whilst the Third Way proclaimed itself as neither state socialist nor free market capitalist, its positive commitments were much less clear. In respect of its processes and procedures, it also remained in many ways a majoritarian Old Labour formation, as its difficulties in adapting to the more open political environment of national devolution and mayoral government showed all too clearly. We seem to have lost the benefits of the old kinds of formalised Labour Party democracy, while so far gaining little from the wider enfranchisements promised by constitutional reform. It remains to be seen whether New Labour will proceed further with electoral reform, which remains crucial to the opening up of new democratic spaces.

There can and must be some principled basis for a 'post-socialist' politics. What is essential to this is a commitment to pluralism, to the idea that all sources of social power should be limited and balanced against one another. The power of large-scale private property and of market forces might be made less intolerable if vigorous democratic institutions existed to challenge their excesses, to ensure a fair distribution of resources and to nurture values other than those of materialism. I shall argue that if this pluralist position were more fully articulated, Labour's current project would be much strengthened.

Yet it does seem possible that there are deeper forces in play which are now pressing New Labour to locate a more independent political space of this kind, as a condition of its electoral survival. The second phase of new Labour policy making has been significantly more radical than the first. There does now seem to be a firm intention to achieve some measure of redistribution of income, and to remove at least the worst levels of poverty. There is a conception of economic citizenship and social inclusion inherent in the government's plans to bring about full employment and to link welfare to employment. Recently announced plans to increase expenditure on the National Health Service and on education have indicated that the government expects to be judged on the solidity of at least these two pillars of a modernised public sector. It is not difficult to adduce many examples of the government's inclinations in the opposite direction, in its timidity regarding taxation, its authoritarian approach to many issues of law and order and its undue subservience to the corporate sector on many issues. But nevertheless, it emerges after three years that there is a measure of deliberate balance, one might almost say pluralism, in the government's programme, even though its agenda has hardly yet been articulated in these terms.

Supposing that there is after all an emergent political basis for such a pluralist position, where might we look for a theoretical justification of it?

The social scientist who has been most prominently identified with the project of the Third Way is of course the sociologist Anthony Giddens, the most prolific and well known British sociologist of his generation, and now the Director of the London School of Economics. He has written a succession of books – *Beyond Left and Right* (1996), *The Third Way* (1998) and *The Third Way and its Critics* (2000), for example – developing a case for a new left-of-centre politics, which is opposed both to the right-wing version of the free market and to traditional state socialism of both communist and old social democratic varieties. One of these books, *The Third Way*, appeared at the same time as a Fabian pamphlet by Tony Blair which had the same title, and set out many of the same arguments, making these connections plain. Anthony Giddens is a leading sociologist, and it seems appropriate to look therefore to the academic discipline of sociology for an understanding of what the theoretical underpinnings of the Third Way might be.

It is worth remembering that the academic subject of sociology in the first instance – that is to say in the second half of the nineteenth century – was itself conceived as a 'third way', positioned deliberately in between and as an alternative to the theoretical ancestors of the modern liberal right and Marxist left. Of course, these ideologies provided the theoretical underpinnings for the political positions which the contemporary political Third Way has set itself politically to displace from their hitherto dominant positions. It is also worth noting that social democracy as a political formation was also originally invented as a political 'third way' for an earlier era. It aimed to provide in its programmes an acceptable synthesis of liberalism and Marxism, combining the constitutional democracy of the former with the latter's critique of capitalism and markets as the dominant form of social power. We know how much social democracy was limited in its ambitions to surpass capitalism, both in practice and in conception, but this was one of the aims which defined the classical social democratic parties of the continent, and even the Labour Party under the banner of Clause IV of its constitution. (In Britain, there was a more direct connection between the founding of sociology as an academic discipline and the alternative stream of social liberalism via Leonard Hobhouse.)

In the construction of the new social science of sociology, in the latter years of the nineteenth century, 'founding fathers' like Emile Durkheim in France insisted that the atomistic individual should not be the primitive unit of analysis of social behaviour. Instead, he sought to demonstrate that social structures, norms and social solidarity should be given explanatory priority. Durkheim and his sociological peers argued that individualism and individuality were not primordial facts of human life, but had only emerged as the outcomes – as the precarious achievements – of a complex division of labour and of new forms of legal and moral regulation. There was a risk, thought Durkheim, that such individualist societies would leave their members unduly exposed to isolation and anxiety – and to what we might now call social exclusion.[3] Durkheim accepted too that such societies were inclined to generate systematic injustice and inequality, and that their stability would be endangered by these divisions if governments did not take preventive action. Social solidarity needed to be cultivated to avoid these various dangers; not least, in a curious parallel with New Labour priorities, by means of an expanded system of public education.

Max Weber, Durkheim's great German contemporary, was a more direct adversary of Marx's theory of history and society, which by this time in Germany had achieved a considerable political influence through Germany's Social Democratic Party. Weber set out the seminal sociological arguments against economic reductionism, insisting also on the scope and necessity for choice and moral judgement in political life, against conceptions of historical determinism and inevitability. Weber's thinking was explicitly pluralist, calling for balances to be struck between the place of the market and capitalist enterprise and the role of law, government and administration in society.

Since its modern founding moments in the period when the early capitalism of small entrepreneurs was transmuting into the modern organised capitalism of corporations and imperial states, sociology has continued to elaborate and advocate its models of pluralism and equilibrium, against the competing poles of the revolutionary and statist left, and the unbridled free market.[4] Anthony Giddens, who began his career with a notable exposition of the foundations of the sociological tradition in the work of Marx, Weber and Durkheim,[5] has set out in his work above all to update and modernise these perspectives, in the light of the many new theoretical resources that have become available for thinking about different aspects of societal life. Just as a second phase of development of the field of sociology was induced by the coming of the New Deal and the welfare state and their later vicissitudes, so further developments in the subject are now being provoked by the phenomenon of globalisation, and the breakdown of the 'organised capitalism' of the recent era. Globalisation looms large both in recent sociology, that of Anthony Giddens included, and in the justifications for the need for a political third way, 'beyond left and right'. The main reason given for the need for a radical rethink of traditional social democratic institutions – trade unions, welfare states, public sector bureaucracies – is that these have been rendered obsolete by the tide of globalisation, in much the same way that even the most firmly built sandcastles are liable to be washed away by the sea.

One can and should argue with what is ascribed to globalisation, and in particular with its representation as an unstoppable force, no less inevitabilist and triumphalist than some versions of the Marxism which global capitalism now believes to have been defeated for ever.

There are signs that Giddens himself is now taking a more critical view of these globalisation processes and of the counter-balances that may be called for in response to them, than he did earlier.[6] But what I want to argue here is that it is to sociology, in its historically pluralist, equilibrium-seeking, social-reformist role that one should look if one wants to clarify the theoretical resources that the Blairite Third Way (and a pluralist politics more broadly) has available to it, and has implicitly been calling upon.

For reasons of realism, if nothing else, one might choose to accept that any successful left-of-centre government (perhaps, after Thatcher, any successful right-of-centre government too) will have to be a government of balance and compromise if it is going to succeed. Capitalist corporations and the markets in which they operate are not, in the foreseeable future, likely to be abolished or socialised in large measure. Thus the powers that they represent, and the benefits they bring, are going to have to be recognised in the policy making and ideology of any feasible government. But societies do not only consist of markets, and the well-being of citizens requires that governments legislate, provide and regulate on the citizens' behalf, where necessary setting boundaries to what markets and the economically powerful are allowed to do. Even the market itself requires a substantial legal and moral framework as its precondition of success, as the recent experience of post-Soviet Russia, seeking to introduce a market economy in the absence of an effective and dependable state, has made entirely plain. The question of what is the appropriate scope for the operation of economic competition within markets, and what should be determined by legislated political decisions, remains fundamental to political debate. Indeed this question, unwelcome as this fact has been to New Labour, continues virtually to define the political left and right. Such choices between the appropriate sphere of markets, and that of legislated decision, continues to touch almost every area of political life, whether this be minimum standards of material welfare, the acceptable limits to inequality, standards of health care or education, the quality of the environment or of public culture, such as that represented by broadcasting.

Another dimension of choice, distinct from the balance to be struck between states and markets, lies in the moral order underpinning society. The Thatcher governments set a pattern in their upfront advocacy of a particular social ethic – individualist, self-improving, hostile to dependency, entrepreneurial. New Labour has echoed the idea that a moral agenda of this kind is both legitimate and perhaps ideologically enabling. Unfortunately in practice it has more often pursued its own version of a modernising capitalist ethic, and has followed in the wake of conservative campaigns for a tougher moral order, rather than choosing a distinctive direction of its own. But the idea that the moral order underpinning a society is a central issue for political debate, and underpins many political decisions, can hardly be avoided.

Here too, the perspectives of sociology offer resources which could make it possible to think these alternatives and choices out more clearly. The founding principles of sociology include the ideas that there are different modalities of power and co-ordination – those based on economic advantage and self-interest; those based on coercion and the framework of law, and those based on moral assent and commitment. Clarifying where real powers lie in an actual social formation, and deciding what different balances of power might be desirable, is the essence of what politics is or should be about.

So far, New Labour has shown little capacity to reflect on the complexities of this agenda. Instead, it seems to have merely given its own inflection to Thatcherite individualism and to its authoritarianism in the social and moral sphere. It has, it is true, favoured a more active and constructive role for government than the Conservatives (though in its destructive role the Thatcherite state was hyperactive), but largely in the service of inculcating the ethic of self-help and responsibility among sections of the population whom the Tories had deemed addicted to the dependency culture.[7] New Labour believe in putting active government to the service of the market, in rather the way of the Benthamite reformers of the nineteenth century. Obstacles and resistance to the market having been largely broken, the new government sees its 'modernising' role here in creating a governmental system adapted for the nation's survival in the new globalised marketplace.

In the social and moral sphere, there are continuities with the intolerance of the populist right, in regard for example to asylum-seekers, and to crime. Some of this is an opportunistic response to agendas set by the tabloid advocates of the right. But parts of the New Labour coalition identify with repressive aspects of public opinion, more punitive in outlook than the liberalism of the professional classes. There is a populist idea that those who live in more difficult circumstances are more exposed to problems of delinquency and to competition for scarce resources than the privileged middle classes. Thus the representation of less tolerant attitudes comes to be seen in a populist way as expressing New Labour's commitment to the less privileged. Thus this authoritarian part is played by some government ministers with conviction.

Although one might have little sympathy for the particular approach to moral questions which have so far dominated New Labour in office, there is value in the idea that the moral order underpinning a society is a proper issue for political debate. (This has also been a contention of cultural critics of capitalism, in the tradition described by Raymond Williams, as well as of advocates of a 'learning society', like Marquand.) The problem has been the shallowness and fearfulness of New Labour's approach. The government has decided that it is expected to deal in answers, not questions. The foray into 'ethical foreign policy', which might have been a fruitful basis for reflecting on Britain's role, connecting with a long internationalist tradition, proved a short one, as its contradictions emerged. Educational policy, in which questions of competing values and perspectives are central, has been conducted as if everything could be reduced to simple output measures and a tough-minded approach to failure. Tony Blair's recent remark that comprehensive education should not mean one size fits all, announced, as if it were a new discovery, the original pluralist tenet of comprehensive education, which was that comprehensive schools needed to respect and further a diversity of values, and not merely the stratifying goal of academic achievement. (The fullest manifesto of this position, the Hargreaves Report (1984), was issued by the Inner London Education Authority.)

Some of the intellectual resources needed to develop a reflective moral agenda are also to be located in the sociological tradition. One of the constituting ideas of sociology is that moral norms are as important to social cohesion as either the market or the framework of law. Different societies are based on different balances between the competitive, the coercive and the consensual, as principles of co-ordination. It is surely clear that a more generous and more equal society (equal at least in respect of mutual dignity and respect) will not emerge as an outcome of tougher economic competition. On the contrary, such competition reduces social trust, rather than increases it. Nor can a more generous society be coerced into existence by tougher laws. What such coercion seems most likely to generate are backlashes of public opinion against over-mighty governments. The development of a society which shares common values can only take place if governments take on an educative role. And education, in political matters, depends on tolerance of differences and debate.

Modern governments need to maintain a very broad basis of support, extending well into the 'centre ground' of politics and society. Clarifying the appropriate limits and boundaries of different kinds of power is crucial to the task of winning such support. It is obvious that market forces, and corporate power, have to be constrained, and even confronted from time to time. It is obvious too that government also has its limitations – there are kinds of 'non-market failure', as well as innate kinds of 'market failure'. 'Moral communities' can be strengths in some circumstances, but unduly coercive and restrictive of individual freedoms in others. For example, even though powerful sentiments are aroused in response to crime, victims of crime should not be allowed to determine sentencing policy.

A left-of-centre government in these times should be articulating these central questions of balance, of necessary choices between competing norms, powers and priorities. It should, as a matter of principle, make clear that its task is to articulate new boundaries between market and government, between public and private spheres, between competing ethics and different views of the social good. Government can accept that there will be persuasive arguments on each side of these different divides, but that sometimes choices must be made between them. Confidence in democratic decision making is sustained if those who stand for different interests at least feel their positions are understood, even if their claims are not always accepted. It will be helpful to a government which intends to be inclusive and consensual, and to retain office for a long period, if it displays itself as capable of reflection as well as action, and if it is usually seen to act after, rather than before, it has reflected.

In this chapter I have argued that sociology is a social science discipline which has uncannily tracked, throughout its history, the political 'third way' between capitalism and communism. The New Labour Third Way has not yet provided itself with a sufficient foundation in social theory. Even its leading social scientist, Anthony Giddens, has made few positive connections between his own abundant work of social theory and the political Third Way which he advocates. A politics without a foundation in social scientific analysis is in the long run vulnerable, since it will lack capacity to clarify its own agendas and purposes.

The sociological perspective has always aimed to clarify the different sources of power and value in the development of industrial societies. It has been pluralist, opposing the one-dimensional claims of markets and states. Although committed to social levels of explanation, it has sought to explain the emergence of individuals as agents and subjects in modern society. Here is a theoretical foundation, clearly distinct from both economic liberalism and statist Marxism, on which a new pluralist politics could be based. If these links between social theory and political practice could be developed, there might be a better chance of establishing some countervailing balances to the power of capital in the age of globalisation.

Notes

1. A fuller version of part of this argument will shortly be published as a chapter in P. Arestis and M. Sawyer (eds), *The Economics of the Third Way*, London: Edward Elgar.
2. For example the concept of 'triangulation', or positioning an aspiring government for election-winning purposes mid-way between the main competing parties, including the party from which the aspiring government itself comes. Hence, in the US, 'New' Democrats, and in Britain, 'New' Labour.
3. Durkheim famously set out this concern in his studies of *Suicide* (1897) and *The Division of Labour in Society* (1893).
4. This interpretation of the self-positioning of sociology in a field of ideological conflict was developed by Goran Therborn in *Science, Class and Society. On the formation of sociology and historical materialism* (1976), London: New Left Books.
5. Anthony Giddens, *Capitalism and Modern Social Theory* (1971), Cambridge: Cambridge University Press.
6. See, for example *On the Edge*, London: Jonathan Cape, 2000, a book Giddens has edited with Will Hutton, and his *The Third Way and its Critics*, Cambridge: Polity Press, 2000, which invites constructive dialogue with left-wing critics of New Labour.
7. I have explored these issues more fully in 'The New Labour Ethic and the Spirit of Capitalism', *Soundings* 14, Spring 2000.

9
Politics with a Purpose: Reforming the House of Commons

Greg Power and Peter Riddell

Parliament is increasingly isolated and marginal. The public knows it, those with real power in Whitehall, business and the media know it, and MPs now know it and do not like it. Power has shifted elsewhere – to European institutions, to the courts, to the broadcasting studios, to pressure groups, to regulators and, most recently, to devolved bodies. As the Phillips Inquiry into BSE showed, ministers and civil servants are now more constrained by European regulations and the threat of judicial review, and by the need to have a persuasive line for the media. The *Today* programme is as important a forum for debate as the floor of the House of Commons.

The Commons has played a large part in its own marginalisation. Despite the changes in the scope of government and of society, Westminster has been slow to respond. To the general public, the House of Commons looks more like a museum than a modern law making body. The proceedings of Parliament appear arcane, the content of debates often seems irrelevant and news coverage focuses on the more gladiatorial aspects. The club-like atmosphere and the tribal loyalties of Westminster are out of kilter with public attitudes which are more sceptical and detached and less bound by lifetime loyalties.

The urgent need is to reform the Commons to ensure that government is made more accountable and executive decisions and legislation are scrutinised more fully. Many ideas for reform have been made by both insiders, such as the Liaison Committee (consisting of select committee chairmen) (2000) and the Conservative commission under Lord Norton of Louth (Norton Commission 2000); and outsiders, notably the continuing work of the Hansard Society. But these proposals challenge the traditional view of Parliament dominated by the executive and party loyalties. The government is reluctant to give a greater role to select committees which might embarrass them, while the instinctive oppositionalism of the parties often undermines attempts to scrutinise legislation or to hold the government to account.

This chapter examines the role of party politics at Westminster and argues that it is not adversarialism *per se* that is the problem for Parliament so much as the quality of the party political debate. At its best it should illuminate key political issues for the general public, but at its worst it can simply mean point-scoring between the two main parties, reducing serious issues to the level of a playground argument. Removing the adversarialism of the Commons is attractive to many, but is not realistic. The real challenge for those seeking a more collaborative form of politics is to recognise the value of the political parties and improve the quality of party politics at Westminster so that we get something approximating politics with a purpose.

The function of Parliament was defined by Gladstone in 1855 as 'not to govern but to hold to account those who do'. Parliament's role, in essence, remains the same today. It can be broken down into a legislative function (ensuring that laws are properly examined before they come into force and where necessary amended) and an accountability function (ensuring that ministers are responsible for the activities of their departments and held to account for their actions). MPs pursue these tasks through debates and questions on the floor of the House, through the departmental select committees responsible for investigating the policy, administration and finances of their ministry and the standing committees, which undertake the 'line by line' scrutiny of bills.

However, it is generally acknowledged that Parliament is performing neither task as effectively as it might. Debates do little to improve the scrutiny of government or legislation. It is rare for a six-hour debate to shed any new light on a subject as debates tend to place 'a higher premium on the trading of insults than the analysis of problems' (Adonis 1990, p. 142). The quality of debate and the level of attendance is usually poor.

Questions to ministers tend to be orchestrated affairs with whips on both sides of the House planting questions with pliant backbenchers. For the Opposition this means ensuring that the minister is given a sustained questioning on a particular policy failure. Government whips, on the other hand, will try to arrange favourable questions or give the minister an opportunity to announce a new initiative.

Scrutiny of legislation is also beset with problems. For the most part the government's overriding objective is to get the legislation through with a minimum of fuss and, in particular, give away nothing that would bring credit to the Opposition. The standing committees responsible for the line by line scrutiny of legislation replicate the worst elements of the chamber. Members are rarely chosen for their expertise in a particular policy area, but because of their willingness to toe the party line. It is impressed upon these MPs by the whips that if they are keen for promotion they should simply vote the right way. As a result, it is not unusual to see backbench MPs in committees spending the entire time going through their constituency casework or, depending on the season, writing their Christmas cards.

The adversarial nature of the legislative process means that the lines are drawn early on. The government is almost always unwilling to accept Opposition amendments, because they know that if they do the Opposition will portray it as a U-turn and thus their victory. Tony Blair, in opposition, bemoaned the fact that 'it does not help produce good government when almost every change in every clause of a Bill is interpreted as a defeat for the government' (Blair 1996). Yet little has changed since 1997. Bills are regularly pushed through Parliament with the government accepting few amendments from the Opposition parties. The Lords has become more important in scruti-nising legislation than the Commons – though even here most of the amendments are put forward by the government and in the Lords procedures are often as time consuming as in the Commons. But there have been some experiments – both via the publication of draft bills to allow consultation before the provisions are finalised and, more rarely, to permit scrutiny by select committees. The Freedom of Information Bill was, for example, closely examined and strongly criticised by select committees of both Houses. This led to some changes in the bills, though producing considerable irritation within government and a reluctance to put more bills to select committees.

The problem is that Parliament is built around confrontation. The set-up of the Commons chamber itself, which sees the two front benches facing one another, contributes to suit the adversarial style of the place. Yet, in fact Parliament is built around not one but two separate confrontations. The first is the party political battle between the government and Opposition parties, the second is that between Parliament and the executive.

While the dividing lines for the party battle are clear at the outset, the participants in the second are less clearly defined. The parliamentary task should fall as heavily on the governing party's backbenchers as on MPs across the floor. Their role, as much as that of the Opposition, is to scrutinise and hold government to account.

This presents a problem for many MPs. Individual MPs need to balance three distinct but overlapping roles, reflecting the interests of the party, the constituency and Parliament. It is difficult for MPs, and particularly government backbenchers, to balance their party role with the parliamentary task of scrutinising and holding government to account. Being an effective scrutineer will inevitably mean criticising and undermining the government, but religiously toeing the party line devalues Parliament. It is a dilemma faced by politicians in many legislatures and one which 'is resolved usually – almost invariably – in favour of party' (Norton 1998, p. 194).

Scrutiny is therefore often regarded as synonymous with opposition. Research from the Study of Parliament Group shows that MPs tend to define their role according to their party's position in government or opposition. MPs were asked to rank the constituency role, influencing policy, supporting the party or scrutinising government, in order of importance. In 1994, the most important role for Conservative MPs was representing the constituency, and scrutiny of government the least important. By 1999 the constituency was the second most important role, after the scrutiny of government (Rush 2000).

According to two senior commentators, the dominance of the party conflict means that it is 'revealed and articulated in almost every parliamentary action of every Member of the House' (Griffith and Ryle

1989, p. 13). By contrast there is little in Parliament which promotes the MP's parliamentary role as a counterweight.

Parliament, in short, has no corporate ethos. It is rare for Parliament to do anything collectively. In some senses (and paraphrasing a recent Prime Minister) there is no such thing as Parliament. When the House is said to have expressed its view, this usually translates as the view of the majority party in Parliament. Parliament is a collection of 659 individuals, each one acting as their own public relations officer.

Outside of the select committees, the structure of parliamentary activity reinforces the party conflict. The procedures of the chamber are characterised by adversarialism, premised on the existence of two parties. The motivation for most debates is a party political one, and the content usually reflects this, with the quality of contributions poor and speakers tending to stick to the party line. There are virtually no opportunities for MPs to work with those from other parties to force debates on substantive issues.

A case in point is that of the Passport Agency. The first sign of difficulties arose in February 1999 when the Passport Agency decided to prioritise applications by date of travel. By the end of April it was clear that most MPs were dealing with constituency cases relating to passports. A question to the Leader of the House, Margaret Beckett, revealed the extent of the problem when she replied that, 'I think that the whole House ... will be aware of how great are the difficulties being experienced by the Passport Agency and of their serious effect on the service available to people' (HC Debs, 29 April 1999, Col. 487).

However, Parliament did not discuss the issue properly until the Conservatives held an Opposition Day debate on 29 June 1999, two months after it was originally raised and by which time the situation was reaching crisis point. By the end of June there was clearly a political value in the Conservatives holding such a debate. But the case highlights the difficulties for MPs to force debates on topical and substantive issues. there was no effective way of translating these concerns into a constructive debate.

In addition to these procedural constraints MPs are, quite simply, not taught how to be parliamentarians. The selection and training of prospective parliamentary candidates (PPCs) pays little attention to the sorts of skills needed to scrutinise government. PPCs are trained by Millbank, or Smith Square, or Cowley Street to deal with the media and campaign in their constituency. They are instructed on the intricacies of their party policies, the weaknesses of other parties' arguments and given a 'line to take' on topical issues. But little effort is spent explaining the role of Parliament or what duties MPs, as a breed, are expected to perform.

Such induction as there is remains the province of the House authorities. This tends to explain some of the most important procedures and ways of working, but given the resources and time available they tend to be cursory. The most valued source of advice is the experience of longer-standing MPs. As a result the party role tends to be reinforced.

Given this situation it is not surprising that attempts to reform the Commons have tended to concentrate on enabling scrutiny before the party political battle begins. A much heralded initiative of this government was to publish more bills in draft form and allow for greater consultation before presenting the legislation to Parliament. The process of revising and amending therefore takes place in a more objective manner. Because the bill is in draft, the government, in theory, is more willing to consider amendments, and there is less capital for the Opposition in crowing about a change to the bill.

Similar reforms have been tried. Special Standing Committees were used on several bills in the early 1980s, which effectively allow legislation to be scrutinised in a select committee format rather than the more adversarial standing committee. In November 1999, a new semi-circular chamber was introduced into Westminster Hall to allow MPs more opportunity to debate non-partisan matters and constituency matters.

The thrust of these changes has been to move away from the traditional opposition mode of working and to a more collaborative format. As such the reforms are welcome and have, in varying degrees, been regarded as successful.

However, this analysis misses half the equation. The scrutiny of government is not solely an administrative exercise, it is a political one. Although the technical task of scrutinising legislation would benefit from a greater attention to detail, it also requires an improvement in the quality of political activity. Parliament must provide a political interpretation of events and issues for the electorate. It should illuminate an issue – highlighting the key points and allowing the electorate to distinguish between the political parties on their performance. Reforms which aim solely at removing the politics from the scrutiny of legislation or government ministries are an implicit acceptance that party debate is of poor quality, and that little can be done to improve it.

The style and content of most debates has little to interest the average voter. The spectacle of Prime Minister's Questions makes for watchable TV but, according to most opinion polls, voters think it a turn-off. Most people seem to regard the 'yah boo sucks to you' politics as pointless. And for most of the electorate it is. The principal motivation for MPs to speak in debates is to attract the attention of one's colleagues, not the general public. An MP regarded as an effective debater will be the one who effectively dishes the other party on a regular basis. Such qualities may not have much attraction for the electorate, but they may well improve that MP's chances of promotion.

Making Parliament more effective means improving scrutiny, but an integral feature of this is that reforms must also seek to improve the quality of the party political discourse. At present, it is petty and insular. It serves little other purpose than maintaining the current system, so that minor or artificial differences between the parties, become major issues of contention, or occasionally even 'resigning matters'. Yet, the clash between the two main parties will always be of most interest to the media. Unfortunately, the present quality of that party political debate merely increases the public perception of a Parliament out of touch with the population.

Given that solutions to the current problems lie partly in the culture of the Commons, and partly in its structure, there is no automatic guarantee that reforms will improve the situation. The partisan nature of the Commons is deeply embedded, and is passed on from one generation of MPs to the next. Reforms should, though, seek to foster a more productive form of discussion and debate which recognises the importance of distinct political parties but does not actively amplify those differences for the sake of argument. Improving the quality of the party political contest should focus on changing the culture by providing more opportunities for MPs to work on a cross-party basis, in the committees and in the chamber.

In the first place there should be more emphasis on committee work. The House of Commons is unusual amongst legislatures for the amount of time the chamber sits. In most Parliaments the bulk of the work is done in committees and the Parliament meets in plenary to discuss this work. Westminster should follow this model. It could meet one day less each week – a day that would be devoted to committee work.

The select committees themselves should be extended. They should be given greater responsibilities to monitor the work of government, given greater resources and more backbench MPs should sit on a departmental select committee. In the first instance this would extend MPs' experience of cross-party working and, taken with other recommendations, might have a knock-on effect on the chamber.

A suggestion made by the Liaison Committee in 2000 was for more prime-time debates on select committee reports. This gives a purpose to the select committees' work and would improve the links between the chamber and the committees. It would mean that MPs could tackle substantial issues, on the basis of recommendations from select committees. Given that any select committee report worth its salt is the product of cross-party agreement, this would help to foster a more productive form of political debate.

In addition there should be more opportunities for MPs to call for debates on pressing matters. The Passport Agency problem, highlighted above, could have been identified earlier if there was a more effective mechanism for MPs to filter their concerns into the chamber. In the Scottish Parliament the Petitions Committee performs this function with members of the public allowed to present a petition which could then trigger a debate. At Westminster a 'public interest debate', initiated by a quota of MPs from all parties, in response to the concerns of their constituents, could do a similar job.

The biggest problem facing Parliament at the beginning of the twenty-first century is one of relevance. The growth of single-issue politics and direct action, as a challenge to Parliament, appeared to reach its peak with the fuel crisis in the autumn of 2000. Although the crisis would have played itself out differently had the Commons been sitting, Parliament looked marginal.

If the House of Commons is to improve its relevance it must become more effective in scrutinising and holding government to account on behalf of the electorate. But, equally important for those 'progressives' who want a more collaborative form of politics is to make the party political battle more productive, purposeful and topical. It's the political parties that remain the most important mechanisms for aggregating and articulating public opinion. If the public are not to lose faith in parties' ability to do this, the Commons, as the principal arena for those debates, must be reformed so that the public takes an interest in what is said and done in Parliament.

There is no shortage of ideas for reform. The problem is a lack of will on the part of MPs, and the vested interests of government and Opposition in keeping the system the same. The solution ultimately lies on the back benches. There are numerous changes that MPs could make immediately. Wider reform requires a more co-ordinated approach. Yet it is for MPs to decide how seriously they regard the threat of irrelevance and what they are going to do about it.

References

Adonis, A. (1990) *Parliament Today*. Manchester: Manchester University Press.

Blair, T. (1996) John Smith Memorial Lecture, 7 February.

Griffith, J.A.G. and Ryle, M. (1989) *Parliament: Functions, Procedure and Practice*. London: Sweet & Maxwell.

Liaison Committee, (1999–2000) *First Report, Shifting the Balance: Select Committees and the Executive*, HC 300.

Norton, P. (1998) *Parliaments and Governments in Western Europe*. London: Frank Cass.

Norton Commission (2000) *Strengthening Parliament: The Report of the Commission to Strengthen Parliament*. London: Conservative Party.

Rush, M. (2000) Evidence submitted to the Hansard Society Commission on the Scrutiny Role of Parliament.

10
A Third Sector as Well as a Third Way

Olly Grender and Kate Parminter

The last century saw charities and voluntary organisations play an important role in responding to the social and environmental problems that Britain faced. Their value, however, was not universally acknowledged, with some on the political left believing they provided help 'motivated by pity and laced with condescension' (Leadbeater 1997, p. 24). For them the state was the appropriate means to solve social problems. Those on the right were more attached to charities, but for some it was no more than a convenient way of passing responsibility for society's problems from the state to someone else. What is now clear is that without the active engagement of the third sector there can be no delivery of the progressive politics and policies that those on the centre-left want.

A progressive age cannot be a reality without a healthy, efficient and, yes, even disagreeable third sector. But to achieve that will require changes in attitudes and practice both from the politicians and from the third sector itself. What is needed is a new partnership between the state, the business community and the third sector. Achieving that new partnership is what this chapter is about.

Change must first be provided in the form of a new framework that enables the sector to provide the moral leadership and social entrepreneurship that society needs. Second, the contribution the sector can make to improve people's work–life balance must be nurtured.

Finally, a redefined market is needed in which organisations in the third sector can compete and co-operate with the state, with the private sector and with each other.

The third sector in the UK is a broad church, comprising a wide range of organisations that help, enable and advise millions. The sector covers 'not-for-profit', charities, voluntary organisations, education establishments, church groups, co-operative associations, pressure groups and think tanks. There are over 135 000 charities in the sector with a combined annual income of around £13 billion that employ around 2 per cent of the total UK workforce.

One strand holds all these organisations together – the aim of improving society. Whilst there is a welcome and increasing trend for some commercial organisations to engage in socially responsible activities, they hold the profit motive as the primary purpose; engaging in socially responsible activities is not their *raison d'être* as in the third sector.

A key distinction for a number of organisations in this sector from the private and state sector is their advocacy role. This moral leadership is increasingly important as traditional sources of such (the church, politicians, and so on) fail to command the respect and support they once did. The third sector can and should point to the failures of civic society and seek redress. Witness the potency of recent campaigns such as Greenpeace's Genetically Modified Organisms (GMOs) campaign that pits the belief in the primacy of science against democratic control and the precautionary principle. Challenging the status quo can create an uneasy relationship with some in politics. Indeed, it can make it hard to maintain the relationships with politicians who are vital partners in helping meet the social and environmental goals of the sector.

Given the adversarial nature of the current political system, with easy point-scoring fanned by a critical Opposition and the media, it is a rare politician who is prepared to be criticised about the failure of their policies or lack of action and then work with that criticising organisation to effect change. What we would hope is that, in a more consensual political system that progressive politics implies, such a dual role of chider and partner can be more readily accepted for the sector by the political forces of the day. Indeed, as political parties learn to compete and co-operate, is it too much to ask that politicians understand that of this sector?

The advocacy role that the sector performs is vital in a healthy democracy. It is as valuable as the role of service provider, meeting social needs, which many organisations in the sector provide. Progressive politicians must therefore ensure that the increasing trend to channel state funding (either directly or via sources such as the National Lottery) solely to service providers is stemmed. The advocacy role of the sector is vital to ensure a progressive civil society, and its value needs to be reflected in a commitment to provide funds to those third-sector organisations who undertake that role. In return the sector must be truly accountable to stakeholders, acting with probity in any whistle-blowing and exposé activities.

Finding innovative answers to social problems has been one of the voluntary sector's greatest strengths. The leanness of the typical third-sector organisation, combined with the expertise of staff and experience of volunteers means they are often best placed to find practical solutions to social and environmental problems. It is why this sector is the most fertile source of social entrepreneurs – developing leading-edge ideas to provide effective services that tackle some of our more pressing social and environmental problems.

Let us give you just two examples. First, the RSPCA, which devised and monitors the Freedom Food scheme, an accreditation scheme for food produced in a humane way. In so doing it harnesses the power of the consumer, to achieve animal welfare goals. Second, WWF's timber mark which harnesses the power of the market to achieve environmental goals. These are solutions that move beyond a mind-set that sees legislation as the only way to bring about improvements to society and the environment.

But in order to maintain that fertile ground for new ideas and new services there must be a restored balance in the funding framework for the sector. Money from the National Lottery and a significant number of trusts, both very large funders of the sector, are increasingly only available for third-sector organisations willing to deliver *their* agendas and social objectives.

Progressive politicians must ensure a balance in funding arrangements for policy and research development and service provision for less fashionable issues. If they don't, they'll not only be stamping on the organisations that can provide the social entrepreneurship we need, they'll also be creating a climate for more aggressive marketing to enable the third sector to access money from the public – which has the advantage of having no strings attached.

But it's not just what the sector can offer society – in the form of moral leadership and innovative solutions – that's critical to secure a progressive age. It's what the sector can offer the individual in terms of improving the quality of their own life through participating in the opportunities the sector has to offer.

How often do we hear the phrases, 'I'm stressed out', 'I'm overworked', 'I've no time for myself', 'I've no time for my loved ones', accompanied by questions such as, 'How do I contribute?', 'What am I doing this for?', and 'What do I get out of it?'

If the goal of a progressive age is to deliver a better quality of life for all – both as members of a more civil society and as individuals – then these issues of work–life balance have to be addressed. Looking at the prism of the third sector from a new angle reveals a huge capacity to respond to this pressing issue of the imbalances in individuals' lives, so that whilst the object of the exercise may be the 'giving' process, either through engaging in this sector with time or money, we would argue that there is also the opportunity for people to 'take' out of the process something of value.

Involvement in the third sector – as a volunteer, an employee or a trustee – has the potential to materially add to quality of life as well as adding to the quality of life of the beneficiary. Giving time and sharing talents does a lot to make people feel better about themselves and give value to life.

What are now needed are the conditions that enable more people to participate. This government has taken some important initiatives, such as Millennium Volunteers, to encourage young people to volunteer. However, it will become increasingly important, given demographic trends, to move away from the focus on merely encouraging the younger population to volunteer, important though that is. With an ageing population and an ageist work environment there will be many older, still active, skilled people who have much to contribute as well as the available time to contribute: people who have the time to participate in critical 'knowledge' volunteering; for example, literate older volunteers passing on their skills to those marginalised by low levels of literacy. Schools could benefit massively from such a programme. Research suggests that children who read one to one with an adult once a day will learn at a much faster pace than those who can only read one to one once a week with their hard-pressed teacher. It is these older people's experience and patience that will liberate new practical solutions. For example, the Refugee Council asked volunteers to spend time with asylum-seekers. The result was practical suggestions of how to make the asylum-seekers comfortable, without recourse to the sophisticated form of 'help' provided.

To enable the sector to utilise the time and skills of this increasing pool of older, often highly skilled people means creating an environment which allows them to give those skills creatively, without the straightjacket of centralised control. Whilst the increased professionalism of the voluntary sector should be encouraged (particularly when it comes to efficient use of donors' money), increased professionalism in the sector can be to the detriment of fulfilling volunteering.

The problem will only be made worse as governments search for new ways to provide social welfare – and rightly focus on the quality of provision rather than the ideology of who provides it. There is a real danger of the 'Contract/Best Value' culture alienating the enthusiasm of volunteers. A welcome focus on outcomes by progressive politicians must allow the sector flexibility in deciding how targets should be achieved. A new framework in the progressive society must ensure engagement in drawing up tenders and a continual mature dialogue as services are delivered. There needs to be a balance between a professional organisation and creating the climate to get people involved.

Opportunities for those in employment already must also be opened up to ensure maximum benefit for the 'feelgood' factor of volunteering. Employers must look to new ways of working to enable participation in third-sector volunteering and in return receive better motivated and fulfilled employees. In the same way that people are given time off to study, they could also be given time off to volunteer. At present there are a small number of schemes where senior staff in charities spend time with senior staff in the corporate sector in order to learn from each other. Under a scheme now run by Business In The Community (BITC), KPMG employees spend time as mentors to more than 100 head teachers. Other examples include employees of Marks & Spencer who are encouraged to become governors of schools. Further, a number of the large financial institutions in the City of London provide staff to assist in schools in the East End, particularly when learning about money skills. But whilst BITC has been at the forefront of encouraging its 650 members to do more to promote corporate social responsibility, more can be done. Its recent document 'Winning with Integrity' (BITC 2000) offers a useful route map to improved social corporate responsibility and is part of an agenda that a progressive government must champion.

Business would be receptive. Two recent polls underline this. One of larger business showed that, across Europe, increasing pressure for social responsibility was ranked second only to the recruitment of skilled staff. The other, amongst smaller business, showed that 83 per cent strongly or tended to agree that 'social responsibility will become increasingly important to businesses, such as mine, over the next five years'.

If the private sector could be persuaded to allocate more human resource to this endeavour then the third sector has a responsibility to match that. This means a more flexible approach on the part of the sector to encourage more regular exchanges between the voluntary and private sectors – for example, creating opportunities for 24 hour volunteering and regular but limited time volunteering. It will also require a sophisticated response mechanism to link employees through their employers to volunteering opportunities. As technology advances the internet will become the ideal broker for volunteering opportunities, building on the approach pioneered by TimeBank's National Database of Opportunities.

Increasing access to the opportunities for volunteering is necessary to increase participation but so too is increasing the incentives to give. The welcome new fiscal incentives to encourage people to give money to charities are already beginning to bear fruit, including the removal of the Gift Aid limit, allowing virtually any gift now to be used in the Gift Aid scheme.

What is clear is that progressive governments need to pioneer fiscal incentives to encourage volunteering as well as building on the policies to give money tax efficiently. For charities, a person's time is often as valuable a commodity as money. More fiscal incentives to encourage volunteering would make a reality of Tony Blair's 'giving age'.

A progressive government must recognise time as a commodity – allowing people to participate in creating a better society with the resources at their disposal. Time exchange systems already work successfully in the US and Japan. Innovative schemes using time as a kind of money include one New York State college allowing students to pay off student loans in time hours, by doing volunteer work in the local community. It should be possible to give a tax break to people who volunteer their time and effort for recognised third-sector organisations. In the same way that you fill out a form to the Inland Revenue, you'd tick a box on the tax return form to get a tax reduction or tax credit, if time has been given up to volunteer. As more people do their tax returns online it should be possible to provide internet links to volunteering activities as a means to encourage further participation. Clearly, third-sector organisations would have to verify the amount of hours and there would need to be checks and balances to ensure that people weren't 'clocking up' hours without adding value. But increasing professionalism in third-sector organisations and the monitoring they are already having to undertake means this process would not be as alien or impractical as it may have seemed in the past.

Providing incentives would help persuade employers to encourage staff to volunteer. If companies were required to produce annual social reports it would force companies to review their activities, and the third sector, through volunteering opportunities, could become a partner in meeting the corporate social responsibilities of business. An osmosis of human resource and skills between the corporate and voluntary sector would make corporate social responsibility more than just a public relations exercise, merely an adjunct to business.

What is also needed is a new market in which the third sector can compete and innovate. A common call from commentators and the general public is that charities should work together more, as though there is something almost distasteful about competition in the sector. It is time that competition in the sector is recognised as the healthy force that it is, allowing innovative ideas and services to develop and challenging complacency in some of the more institutional third-sector organisations. Competition for resources and contracts ensure the innovation and competitiveness in service provision is maintained.

A process of rationalisation is starting to happen in the market, but much more can and should be achieved. In 1964 there were 47 000 charities in England and Wales, today there are 185 000. Charitable trusts and other funders are starting to question adverse duplication of expertise and services and refusing to fund activities of 'duplicate' charities. Clearly freedom to establish a new charity, where appropriate, is an important part of the voluntary sector's independence from the state, but more mergers or take-overs would create greater efficiencies in the sector. This reality is already affecting the plethora of HIV charities in London and the over 700 cancer charities in the UK, to give two examples. What is clear, though, is that there is room for greater rationalisation that would mean fewer but stronger national charities, alongside a wide range of local volunteer groups.

Britain has a strong and vibrant voluntary sector. The challenge for those on the centre-left is to forge a strong partnership with the sector that builds on its success and encourages it to further develop. Government will have to realise that the partnership won't always be comfortable, but that it is vital to encouraging self-reliant individuals and strong communities. At the heart of this are the three challenges for the voluntary sector, for government and for business that we have tried to address. The voluntary sector has to continue on the path of professionalism and rationalisation if it is to be a viable partner. The government has to ensure that the funding it provides via the National Lottery and other programmes isn't making too much of the third sector over-reliant on and over-directed by the state. Government also needs to create incentives to volunteer to rival those being put in place for giving. Business needs to encourage its people to volunteer as part of the drive towards effective corporate social responsibility. These are the challenges which, if met, and met in partnership, will help lay the foundations of a progressive century.

Reference

Leadbeater, C. (1997) *The Rise of the Social Entrepreneur*. London: Demos.
BITC (2000) 'Winning With Integrity' in *A Guide to Social Responsibility*, London: Business Import Task Force.

11
Scotland: An Experiment in New Politics

Kirsty Milne

Journalists were jumpy, commentators confused. The aftermath of the first Scottish parliamentary elections was a time of cheerful chaos and tense improvisation.

Instead of the easy handover of power that follows most UK general elections, there was an unaccustomed hiatus. For one week in May 1999, as Labour and the Liberal Democrats thrashed out a coalition deal, nobody knew what was happening. Political correspondents, used to formulaic briefings and photo opportunities, were reduced to old-fashioned doorstepping. They haunted bars on Edinburgh's Royal Mile, hoping for titbits from exhausted negotiators.

Until then, attention had focused on the birth of devolution, on the drama of voting for the first Scottish Parliament since the Act of Union in 1707. Suddenly the implications of the new electoral system hit home. Labour had won 56 seats, too few to govern with an overall majority in a parliament of 129. The party's Scottish leader, Donald Dewar, needed the 17 Liberal Democrats for another constitutional experiment: to form the first coalition government in mainland Britain since the Second World War.

Tony Blair's 1997 landslide denied Paddy Ashdown a place at the Cabinet table. But where Mr Ashdown was locked out of Number 10, the leader of the Scottish Liberal Democrats, Jim Wallace, was welcomed into St Andrew's House as Deputy First Minister. His partner in government was not some blurry young Blairite but Donald Dewar, last of the Gaitskellites, whose Labour loyalties went back more than 40 years.

It happened with the minimum of fanfare. The nearest approach to theatre was when Dewar and Wallace signed their Partnership Agreement in the new National Museum of Scotland. But the implications were bigger than most people realised. This was 'realignment' in action. Not as a subject for pamphlets or fringe meetings, but as a constitutional fact, challenging civil servants and journalists as much as politicians. Dewar, who was to die suddenly of a brain haemorrhage 18 months later, is regarded as the father of the Scottish Parliament. He is also the father of post-devolutionary 'new politics'.

For those who support co-operation between Labour and the Liberal Democrats, Scotland is seen as a trailblazer. What has been remarkable is the lack of comment from those who oppose it – even for the three months in the summer of 2000 when Dewar was convalescing from heart surgery and Jim Wallace was formally in charge. To see Scotland being run by a Liberal Democrat cannot have enchanted John Prescott or Gordon Brown. But after the initial shock, it caused astonishingly little fuss among Labour MSPs (Members of the Scottish Parliament).

Coalition was not inevitable. In the National Assembly for Wales, Labour governed for 18 months as a minority administration, negotiating with other parties for every vote. Not until October 2000 did the First Secretary, Rhodri Morgan, form his own coalition with the Liberal Democrats, taking advice from Scotland's First Minister the week before his death.

For Donald Dewar, the Assembly's first turbulent year vindicated his decision to do a deal which could deliver stable government and an agreed legislative programme. He characterised the arrangement with Jim Wallace as 'a Partnership for Scotland, founded, as every honest coalition must be, on a common approach'.

There was plenty of overlap between the two manifestos (although, on paper, the Liberal Democrats' ideal partners would have been the Scottish National Party (SNP), so closely were their policies aligned). The big divide was over student tuition fees, which the Liberal Democrats opposed, and which featured heavily in the Scottish parliamentary election campaign.

Tuition fees were the Liberal Democrats' strongest card because the SNP and the Scottish Conservatives were also committed to abolition. Without the support of Jim Wallace's party, Labour could have faced an early defeat on the floor of the Parliament.

The solution was, in thoroughly Blairite fashion, to shelve the problem for six months by setting up an independent inquiry on student finance, and to find a compromise that allowed the Liberal Democrats to claim they had fulfilled their election pledge of scrapping tuition fees. At his party's annual conference in September 2000, Jim Wallace was able to brandish the letter sent to the Student Awards Agency, proclaiming, 'Liberal Democrats – making the difference in government!'

The reform of student finance signalled the biggest devolutionary divergence between Scotland and England since the Parliament started work. Yet the change went through more easily than might have been expected, since few Labour MSPs felt much allegiance to tuition fees. Most of the resistance came from London, where Gordon Brown and David Blunkett resented the idea of Scotland opting out of a policy they had defended in the teeth of a backbench Commons rebellion.

Tuition fees were the Liberal Democrats' talisman. But in other respects, they are much the weaker partners in the coalition. Jim Wallace can claim just two members of an eleven-strong Cabinet – himself and Ross Finnie – with two junior ministers in the wider executive. Experts on coalitions overseas suggest that the Liberal Democrats could have demanded at least one other Cabinet member, in line with their parliamentary numbers.

Jim Wallace insists he is content with the outcome. 'I don't think we'd have got more ministers, and I'm not sure that we necessarily wanted more ministers.' With a small parliamentary group, he wanted to see 'a good strength in numbers' on the back benches, not least for committee work. (Quoted from a personal communication.)

A problem for the Liberal Democrats, in dealing with Labour and maintaining their profile as a separate party, has been the inexperience of their MSPs. Old hands like Menzies Campbell, Malcolm Bruce and Robert MacLennan chose to stay at Westminster. With David Steel lost to the post of Presiding Officer (equivalent to the Speaker of the House of Commons), the parliamentary group is short of talent, and of politicians who understand the ways and wiles of Labour.

Yet Ross Finnie, an accountant from Greenock who was virtually unknown before he was catapulted into the new rural affairs portfolio, has proved an unexpected success. The party looks to him to advance the interests of its predominantly rural voters. Jim Wallace, at justice and home affairs, is responsible for Freedom of Information, where he plans a slightly more liberal Act than Jack Straw's UK equivalent, and a Judicial Appointments Board, which Derry Irvine has scorned for England and Wales.

The Cabinet appears to operate surprisingly well. More than one minister reports that it can be hard to tell the parties apart. During the controversy over repeal of Section 28, the law which forbids councils from 'promoting' homosexuality, some Labour ministers found themselves disagreeing with colleagues and forming tactical alliances with the Liberal Democrats. Much of the tension in the months before Donald Dewar's death came from Labour politicians competing to succeed him.

The executive has been criticised, by the press and even by its own MSPs, for being timid and conservative. But this cannot automatically be blamed on coalition government. Dewar was an instinctively cautious politician – a trait he shared with Jim Wallace – and sought to move carefully in devolution's early days. His successor, Henry McLeish, looks unlikely to pursue a more radical agenda or one that is more distinctively Scottish.

Labour ministers eschew tribalism, at least in public. When Wendy Alexander – who describes herself as 'a great fan of the coalition' – upset the Liberal Democrats by failing to mention them in a speech about social justice, she made amends in subsequent speeches with inclusive language and pointed references to Beveridge.

'Sometimes you wish you could do things in the old, less transparent way, because that's easier', says Jack McConnell, Finance Minister under Dewar, who challenged McLeish for the succession. 'But there are other times when it is just so exciting to be involved in something that is different and more open and ultimately more successful for Scotland. That's a very powerful day-to-day motivation' (personal communication).

Civil servants had to make adjustments of their own, not the least of which was to drop the habit of writing in official documents, 'This government has, since 1997 ...', as Liberal Democrat ministers understandably refused to buy into anything predating the coalition.

Wallace and his fellow ministers have fallen over backwards to behave honourably and shoulder the burden of collective responsibility, sometimes to their own detriment. Even at moments when Wallace has looked exposed, as when facing parliamentary defeat over a private member's bill to abolish warrant sales (Scotland's equivalent of sending in the bailiffs), his advisers did not move to protect his personal position but stuck to the agreed executive line.

Nor did the Scottish Liberal Democrat leader make political capital from his first spell as acting First Minister, apart from slipping out a consultation document on a Scottish Human Rights Commission, an idea Jack Straw has rejected for England and Wales, and one which did not figure in the Partnership Agreement.

Labour ministers have been astonished by this apparent meekness. In private, some view Jim Wallace as an apolitical figure who leans towards the establishment. They wonder why he does not seek to carve out a more distinctive Liberal Democrat agenda based on civil liberties. MSPs in the Scottish National Party are openly contemptuous, referring to the Liberal Democrats as 'Labour's lapdogs'.

Coalition carries the risk of being swallowed by the Labour whale, with damaging electoral consequences. So far, the evidence is mixed. A year and a half into the first Holyrood term, the party's poll ratings were holding up. In the Hamilton by-election (for Westminster) and the Ayr by-election (for the Scottish Parliament), Liberal Democrat candidates suffered the humiliation of losing their deposits. But neither were seats in which the party had a hope of doing well.

Jim Wallace concedes that his party must learn to take credit for its achievements and to campaign independently of the executive. 'I would be the first to admit that I don't think we've cracked it yet.' He has dismissed a proposal by the chair of his parliamentary group, George Lyon, to follow the continental model where the party leader, or another senior figure, stays outside a coalition government.

The issue will become urgent as the general election approaches, when Labour and Liberal Democrat Cabinet ministers could find themselves on opposite sides of a campaign platform. The next Holyrood poll, due in 2003, is a subject rarely addressed. Though Wallace insists the two parties will fight 'separately', he hopes that debate will be more civilised. 'I would find it very difficult to slag off a person I had been sitting around the cabinet table with' (personal communication).

It helps that the two parties represent, in the main, different parts of Scotland, with Labour's support concentrated in urban areas and the Liberal Democrats' in rural seats. Scotland lacks the crusading anti-Labour activist base that the Liberal Democrats have built up in English cities like Liverpool and Sheffield – a role usually occupied by the SNP.

Donald Dewar's death in October 2000 was a shock to the coalition, which depended heavily on the trust between the First Minister and his deputy. Just as Charles Kennedy does not have the rapport with Tony Blair that Paddy Ashdown enjoyed, so the dynamic between Wallace and Dewar's successor, Henry McLeish, will be different. Equally, a more combustible Liberal Democrat chief than Wallace would mean a more combustible coalition.

But links between the two parties in Scotland go deep. Ministers such as McConnell and McLeish knew Wallace from the Scottish Constitutional Convention, which worked from 1989 to 1995 to devise a cross-party devolution blueprint. 'If the Convention hadn't happened, this would have been a very challenging period for us all', thinks McConnell, a former general secretary of the Scottish Labour Party (personal communication).

In Wales, the two parties discussed power sharing in the Assembly's first year but did not come up with their own version of the Partnership Agreement until October 2000. Rhodri Morgan, on a visit to Edinburgh in August, pointed to the lack of a shared project like the Convention: 'We have not yet learned to trust the Liberals and they have not learned to trust us' (personal communication). One function of the Joint Cabinet Committee set up by Tony Blair after the 1997 election may be to forge those links in case they are needed in future.

Liberal Democrat ministers in Scotland have another relationship with Labour: at the UK government level. Jim Wallace and Jack Straw, a Liberal Democrat bogeyman, have co-operated smoothly on home affairs, even at moments of stress such as the Home Secretary's decision to allow Mike Tyson into the UK for a fight in Glasgow, which the SNP attacked in the Parliament.

By contrast, Ross Finnie's dealings with his opposite number at agriculture, Nick Brown, have been fraught. Finnie asked for, and received, a public apology after it emerged that Brown's department had delayed passing on information about crops contaminated with genetically modified seed. But Labour ministers have also had difficulties with Whitehall departments. Dismissive attitudes to devolution are probably more to blame than party antagonism.

If the coalition in Scotland offers one lesson for any arrangement between Labour and the Liberal Democrats at Westminster, it is the need to keep the infantry informed and involved. This was apparent from the start, when the two leaders took the Partnership Agreement to their MSPs. While the Labour group supported Dewar 54 to 2, three of Wallace's 17 Liberal Democrats declined to back the coalition deal.

Jim Wallace's need to consult his parliamentary colleagues slows down decision taking. But Labour ministers have also realised they must communicate better, after lack of consultation surfaced as an issue in the contest to succeed Donald Dewar. Within the Parliament, a backbench liaison committee allows MSPs from the two governing parties to swap information. Labour ministers attend meetings of the Liberal Democrat group – and, very occasionally, vice versa – to discuss policy.

What neither side has devised, however, is a way of securing the endorsement of MSPs and party activists for the coalition's evolving programme, ensuring that both parties are signed up to new measures that were not in the Partnership Agreement.

The coalition's path is less stony than it would be at Westminster, with devolution shielding the Liberal Democrats from what they would regard as the more offensive aspects of Blairism. Benefit changes, vouchers for asylum-seekers, and Jack Straw's Terrorism Act are all reserved matters. The Prime Minister's plan for elected mayors has been rejected by the executive. The use of private firms to run local education authorities has not penetrated north of the Border.

There have been tensions, especially over local government spending and the accountability of quangos. The handling by the Labour education minister, Sam Galbraith, of a crisis over late and incorrect exam results caused strains in the Liberal Democrat group.

But the issue that will put the coalition under strain for the rest of the Parliament's first term is voting reform for council elections. The Partnership Agreement promised no more than 'progress' in this direction, to the surprise of some Labour politicians who assumed the Liberal Democrats would demand a more concrete pledge. A committee chaired by a former Labour councillor, Richard Kerley, came out in favour of the Liberal Democrats' preferred system, the Single Transferable Vote (STV).

Labour councillors are deeply opposed – with good reason. Under STV, the party could expect to lose half the 15 local authorities it currently controls, including Edinburgh. The leader of Glasgow City Council, Charles Gordon, has been a prominent and powerful critic.

A cabinet subcommittee began examining the Kerley proposals in September 2000. Wallace would probably accept a delay in implementing reform until after the next local elections in 2002, as long as legislation was passed by the end of the parliamentary term in 2003.

That could be a step too far for the Scottish Labour Party. Such is the hostility among councillors that by the time Kerley's report was published in June 2000, even Labour ministers sympathetic to proportional representation were showing signs of retreat. Yet according to one Liberal Democrat MSP, Donald Gorrie: 'If we don't get it, I believe most of my colleagues and the party in general would decide that the coalition should stop' (*Scotsman*, 9 September 2000).

With the fate of Lord Jenkins' recommendations on voting reform for Westminster still uncertain, what happens in Scotland has UK-wide implications. It would be a tremendous boost for the Liberal Democrats to secure STV for councils north of the border, strengthening the case for further co-operation with Labour. Shelving the Kerley Report would not only threaten the coalition in Scotland but breed mistrust between the parties at Westminster.

Some Blairites see co-operation as a way of marginalising the left and neutralising the traditional attitudes of 'Old' Labour. Within the executive, Liberal Democrats have been useful in overcoming resistance to Freedom of Information and in holding the line on Section 28.

But the issue of PR for council elections shows that coalition does not magically change the culture of either party. Outside government, political battles still need to be fought and won. The danger is that too much energy is devoted to sustaining the coalition, leaving little for campaigning and persuasion.

Of course, the coalition might break down – an event that would be, as Jack McConnell observes, 'Titanic in terms of its impact on Scottish media and politics, but in reality not such an unusual occurrence in countries that are more used to that style of politics.' Scotland, he adds, must prepare for a future in which coalitions will come together and fall apart – 'and that's not a bad thing' (personal communication).

But an equal risk is that this first attempt at partnership government will remain a lonely passion for a small group of ministers, advisers and civil servants, who conscientiously believe they are practising 'new politics', but fail to share their passion with the world outside.

Acknowledgements

With thanks to my former colleagues Alan Ruddock, Tim Luckhurst, Peter MacMahon and Richard Neville, who made the *Scotsman* the best possible place to write about devolution.

12
The Progressive Council: The Case for Collaborative Local Politics

Dave Sullivan and Andrew Stevens

In *They Only Look Dead*, American political commentator E.J. Dionne Jr (1996) claimed that progressives would dominate the twenty-first century. This side of the pond, any such claim is based as much on optimism as reality. If the last century was a sentence then Labour merely provided the punctuation and arranged the syntax. On base facts alone, there is much to provide a sanguine analysis of the current political situation. The Labour Party has held together a coherent coalition of Middle England and its heartlands. Despite the pessimism of some who would seek to exploit any kind of electoral meltdown, the government looks on course to achieve a second, if not a third, term. It remains committed to modernisation, both within the Labour Party and the country at large. The prospect of a Hague–Widdecombe administration, with all its attendant extremism, is enough to scare off any floating voters from returning to the Tory fold. Even in the event of a hung Parliament in the next 10 or 15 years there remains the prospect of a Lib-Lab coalition administration, the relationship between the two progressive parties of the centre-left being more constructive and healthier than ever before. There are many reasons to be cheerful.

This is the perspective from the ground. However, we are not national policy practitioners and this chapter will seek to explore the possibilities and means of achieving a progressive pluralism in the other sphere of national politics – local government. This, we are often told, is the territory of political anoraks and those whom Governor George Wallace used to refer to as 'pointy-headed intellectuals'. Local government is where most Labour members experience contact with the Liberal Democrats, the 'pavement politics' of *Focus* being much to the chagrin of many a Labour councillor or activist. However, it must be accepted that the Liberal Democrats are here to stay as a local government party. In councils and wards where Labour has been inept or out of touch, the Liberal Democrats' opportunism knows no bounds. Erstwhile Labour strongholds in Liverpool, Sheffield, Hartlepool and Islington have handed over the keys to town halls to Liberal Democrat Groups following crushing defeats at the hands of the electorate. Even in more solid Labour areas, councillors can cite wards in which 'the Lib Dems are chasing us' or wards which the Liberal Democrats have taken from Labour where 'once they're in, they're buggers to get out'.

Natural partners or old enemies?

It cannot be taken as given that Labour will achieve a third term with an overall majority. In that case, the best scenario we can hope for is for a hung Parliament and a Labour-Liberal Democrat coalition. Other factors may have come into play by then; the electorate may use the mid-term referendum on changing the voting system as a plebiscite on the government's overall performance and vote in favour of electoral reform for Westminster, and this would alter the face of national politics forever. Even more likely is the introduction of electoral reform at the local level, perhaps as a means to placate the Liberal Democrats under a reduced majority in the second term. Both of these scenarios mean that Labour has to learn to live with the Liberals.

Not since the division of Labourism and Liberalism in the early twentieth century has any kind of partnership between Labour and the Liberal Democrats (who contain many former Labour members) been mooted in the way that it has recently. Phillip Gould stated in *The Unfinished Revolution* that either Labour and the Liberal Democrats should merge or Labour must modernise itself to the point that the Liberals are 'driven to the margins and New Labour alone becomes the broad progressive church of British politics' (1998, p. 398).

Providing that Labour continues on the path of modernisation and the rivalry between the two parties remains at the local level then Gould's second option appears more likely to transpire. This is, of course, based on politics at the national level and the Lib Dems are highly unlikely to be willing to relinquish their position in local government. In addition to this, much of the talk surrounding a merger or pact with the Liberal Democrats remains national and was largely confined to the post-Blair ascendancy to the Labour leadership era when it was not certain how large Labour's majority in Parliament would be. Indeed, in *The Blair Revolution*, Peter Mandelson and Roger Liddle, both former Labour councillors, argued, 'There is no barrier to cooperation in terms of principle or policy' (1996, p. 207). The departure of Paddy Ashdown has seen such talk reduced to begrudged co-operation on Labour's constitutional agenda. And whilst George Dangerfield's 1935 authoritative work *The Strange Death of Liberal England* may be the Prime Minister's preferred holiday reading, most Labour members on the ground attribute the Lib Dems as being the party of those who sought to divide the Labour Party in 1981 or, at best, their natural opponents to the left of the Tories.

Not an apologia for the Liberals

It has been established that the Liberal Democrats have supplanted majority Labour councils in key northern cities and towns (not to mention 'New Labour' Islington), and even in unshakeable Labour strongholds they hold key wards in unlikely territory. The London Borough of Lewisham is a different story, however. In the 1998 local government elections, Labour won 61 out of 68 seats on Lewisham Council. Even after a poor by-election result (Socialist Party win) and one defection (to Independent), Labour remains the pre-eminent party in the Borough with 59 seats on the council, three Labour MPs in the Borough and a Labour GLA member. When the Labour Group was re-elected in 1998 with its large majority, the Group leadership tried to play the co-operative politics card with the tiny four-member Liberal Democrat Group. The Liberal Democrat leader simply didn't want to know. The Liberal Democrats in Lewisham draw their support from two wards in the South of the Borough, and even then they share one ward with Labour where that councillor (a former unselected Labour councillor) was elected on a majority of four over

Labour's vote in 1998. The Liberal Democrats are fortunate to be the largest Opposition party in the Borough – the Tories obtained more votes across the Borough but less seats on the council (2 out of 67). When we modernised our political structures in 1999, our new Executive Mayor and Cabinet system accorded the two opposition parties two non-portfolio seats within the Cabinet. Whilst the Tories gratefully accepted theirs and remain in a constructive and co-operative relationship with the Labour Group to this day, the Liberals have always refused to take up their seat in the Cabinet.

On the strength of this, an observer could be forgiven for thinking that there is no future for co-operative politics in Lewisham. However, playing a long game affords a different view. There are a number of factors that make an increase in the number of Liberal Democrats on the council on the cards. First, it is accepted that despite the low turnouts in local government elections, voters often use them to send a signal of discontent to the government of the day. Rather than this being in favour of the Tories, recent evidence has shown that Labour voters choose Liberal Democrat as a protest vote. In their current extremist guise, the Tories may lose protest votes to the Liberal Democrats from both their own voters and discontented Labour voters. The net result of this is an increase in the fortunes of the Liberal Democrats (Fishman 1998, p. 105, in Coddington and Perryman 1998). Second, the 'first past the post' system is well known for providing results that are wild in the extreme; namely the minor exaggeration of Liberal Democrat support in Lewisham. In the long term this may become more acute and despite their purist preference for the single transferable vote (STV), the Liberals may actually benefit from the inherent inequalities of first past the post. Particularly in former Tory strongholds such as the City of Canterbury, it has been seen that the Liberal Democrats have proved adept at overturning majorities in both Tory and Labour wards, resulting in coalition rule between Labour and the Liberal Democrats after a period of Tory dominance.

From pavement politics to better services

The London Borough of Lewisham's Select Committee on Political Management which reported in 1999 recommended many changes to the political structures in the Borough. It also made a firm recommendation that a system of proportional representation be used for future council elections. To this end, we enlisted the services of political scientists Helen Margetts, Patrick Dunleavy and Simon Bastow to undertake a study on the effects of electoral reform in relation to the political composition of Lewisham Council. Their report gave a bottom-line analysis of what it would take for Labour to lose political control of Lewisham Council under a directly elected mayor system. The prospect of political behaviour altering under directly elected mayors is something we will cover later. However, Margetts, Dunleavy and Bastow (2000) argue that Labour support in the Borough would have to dip below 35 per cent for the Conservatives to win the Mayorship and 30 per cent for the Liberal Democrats to win the post. They conclude that, 'Both the Additional Member System and the STV would work well in making elections in Lewisham much more democratically proportional, in both cases leaving Labour with a sizeable majority but giving much fairer representation to all the other parties' (p. 30).

Following the research undertaken by Margetts, Dunleavy and Bastow, Steve Leach and Chris Game undertook a similar analysis of the effects of electoral reform on local government in wider national context (2000). Their report for the Joseph Rowntree Foundation, *Hung Authorities, Elected Mayors and Cabinet Government*, argued that hung authorities had proved to be a learning experience for those involved, parties 'modifying approaches' (p. 23) as they progressed under hung council relationships. They allude to the fact that hung councils can 'operate as effectively in terms of speed and consistency of decision-making as do majority-controlled authorities, and often with the bonus of greater transparency and openness of public debate' (p. 23). However, they also draw upon the fact that 'hung authorities can be chaotic, slow-moving and full of rancorous political conflict, producing fragmented and inconsistent decisions, and proving extremely difficult to manage' (p. 23). Whilst no one would argue that hung authorities are desirable to the interests of local political management, it remains the case that they constitute over one-third of local authorities in Britain and this trend is on the up (Leach and Game 2000, p. v). Even under first past the post, there is no guarantee of one-party rule of local councils and often when this has happened it has led to disenchantment amongst the local electorate and ultimately a change in overall control. Leach and Game conclude thus:

Labour/Liberal Democrat co-operation is less likely where there is a history of electoral rivalry between the two parties in a local Parliamentary constituency. However, the general trend is clear. Programmatic co-operation between Labour and Liberal Democrats – which may take the administrative form of a *de facto* coalition, shared Chairs, a minority administration, or even rotating *ad hoc* Chairs (depending on the political arithmetic and local preferences) – is now a dominant feature in hung authorities, to which it lends a new degree of stability and integration. (2000, pp. 24–5)

Therefore, it remains to be seen whether local government will become the new scene of co-operation between the two parties. Whether or not it transpires will depend not on political will but forced circumstances arising under the new Local Government Act.

New Labour, New Alliances: Mayoral perspectives

The prevailing culture in most local authorities, as personified by the committee system originating from 1835, generally promotes one-party rule except in the case of one-third of councils. The challenges and opportunities afforded by the new Local Government Act are many in number. Former preconceptions of what local government is about and how it acts will be thrown to the baying dogs of modernity. Professor Ian Loveland of Brunel University argues that:

One can count on the fingers of one hand the 20th century politicians whose prominence on the national stage was the direct result of their eminence in local government – Joseph Chamberlain and Herbert Morrison are the only real political heavyweights whose careers have followed that path since 1900. British councils are at most a training ground, an apprenticeship, a sparring ring for the people who will much later in life become our nation's senior politicians. For many, they are not even that. (Loveland, in Blackburn and Plant 1999, pp. 311–12)

This will come to an end shortly. The seriousness with which people, politicians and electorate alike, treat local government figures will alter under the new mayoral systems that will breathe new life into local democracy and challenge previous assumptions on political behaviour. The idea that Parliament is the only route to a national political career came to an end the day that Ken Livingstone was elected as Mayor of London, thus ushering in a new era of pluralistic politics in the capital (Simpson and Stevens, in Bechler 2000). A future Nye Bevan would not have to leap from tier to tier of government to locate real power.

More importantly, political behaviour inside town halls will alter irrevocably. Rather than 'government by seminar', new forms of executive power will accentuate the executive/scrutiny split that already exists in many town halls. Those councillors not in the Mayor's cabinet will have to adjust to a role whereby they are expected to scrutinise the cabinet's decisions *and* provide a frontline community representation function. One would expect that this community slant on local politics would receive the nod of approval from the Liberal Democrats. Unfortunately, with the brave exception of Liberal Democrat leader Charles Kennedy, Liberal Democrats nationally and locally remain opposed to directly elected mayors for one reason or another. However, like the Labour councillors who may have to adjust to sharing power with their doorstep opponents, the Liberal Democrats will have to accept that directly elected mayors will become the norm in local government, and the sooner they become accustomed to them the better.

Labour's attitude towards the Liberal Democrats needs to be fashioned on the basis that, as Martin Summers writes, 'local community politics [has] made them significant power brokers in most council chambers' (Summers, in Perryman 1996, p. 222). However, this is merely a starting point that accepts their *current* position in local government – as significant powerbrokers rather than serious contenders for majority control (save Liverpool and other notable examples). The challenges of mayoral politics and electoral reform alter that basis altogether.

By far the most detailed analysis of political relationships between Labour and the Liberal Democrats under cabinet systems in local government is contained in Leach and Game's recent study. This is brought into context by the likelihood of Labour mayors having to work alongside a hung assembly or even a Liberal Democrat majority-controlled one, which, as has been witnessed of late, can happen under first past the post. Whilst electoral reform is not a panacea for all local government's ills, it is part of a package of modernisation designed to overcome the crisis of legitimacy facing local government and to instil greater accountability and transparency than is currently afforded to local democracy. Electoral reform is necessary to bring about assemblies worth their salt as scrutineers of mayors. Therefore we cannot discount the possibility of more hung councils. For Leach and Game, the most salient issue is that of the relationships between cabinet members of differing parties and their selection:

> The reality is that ... choices would be the subject of intensive, inter-party discussion and negotiation – as they are now. The knowledge that cabinet posts would have to be filled at the first meeting of the council would act as a strong stimulus for at least two groups to agree an acceptable outcome in advance. (2000, p. 35)

In reality, the relationships between the Mayor and his/her cabinet would be determined in the way that committee chairs were distributed amongst the parties on hung councils and how they interacted with the leader of the council under the old system. It would have brought a degree of formalism and transparency to the proceedings, with positions being settled on the basis of agreed manifestos rather than behind-the-scenes horse-trading as party managers would be relegated to supervising rather than driving the process.

Also, it may simply be the case that better services are equally as likely to be provided by a Labour Mayor and Labour-Liberal Democrat cabinet as with a Labour Mayor and cabinet.

This brings us to the role of the progressive council in the progressive century. If Labour and the Liberal Democrats are different sides of the same progressive coin (forget the refrain about 'Scratch the surface of a Liberal and you'll find a Tory underneath') then some thinking should be devoted to where Labour stands in relation to the Tories. Whilst we should not fall into the facile and dogmatic trap of dismissing the Tories as our natural enemies, we should carve out a position whereby we, as progressives, consider them to be a regressive force in local government. There are, of course, examples, Lewisham for instance, where relations between the Tories and Labour are con-structive and worthwhile. This is of course merely when the Tories are so small in number that their needs necessitate this. Once in a pivotal position within an authority they revert back to type. As such,

Labour may need all the friends it can find in local government. A study of intraparty rather than interparty relations can only determine whether this is possible or if the will exists to do business.

References

Bechler, R. (ed.) (2000) *Beyond Good Governance*. London: New Politics Network.

Blackburn, R. and Plant, R. (eds) (1999) *Constitutional Reform*. London: Longman Higher Education.

Coddington, A. and Perryman, M. (eds) (1998) *The Moderniser's Dilemma*. London: Lawrence & Wishart.

Dionne, E.J., Jr (1996) *They Only Look Dead*. New York: Touchstone.

Gould, P. (1998) *The Unfinished Revolution*. London: Little Brown.

Leach, S. and Game, C. (2000) *Hung Authorities, Elected Mayors and Cabinet Government*. York: York Publishing Services, Joseph Rowntree Foundation.

Mandelson, P. and Liddle, R. (1996) *The Blair Revolution*. London: Faber & Faber.

Margetts, H., Dunleavy, P. and Bastow, S. (2000) *Applying Alternative Electoral Systems in Lewisham*. London: LSE/UCC Public Policy Group.

Perryman, M. (ed.) (1996) *The Blair Agenda*. London: Lawrence & Wishart.

Part 3

The Issues for the New Century

13
Progressive Economics: Trust the People

Christopher Huhne

This chapter comes in macro-economic and micro-economic parts. The macro-economic issue that will dominate the progressive agenda is Britain's adoption of the euro. In the first part, I set out some of the key reasons why Britain's euro membership is an essential element of the progressive consensus. In the second part, I turn to some of the micro-economic measures – particularly changes in education and in the structure and powers of local government – that we need to adopt to make the UK economy more responsive to a globalised, competitive world economy.

Britain and the euro

A key objective of the creation of the euro was to regain some of the economic stability that was a feature of the golden years of post-war growth. One of the reasons why the euro creates that stability is precisely because it insulates its members from the vagaries of the foreign exchange markets (Huhne and Forder 1999). The overshooting of currency values upwards and downwards has been the most consistent feature of floating exchange rates (such as sterling's rate) since the breakdown of the Bretton Woods system of fixed rates in 1971. Such overshooting on the upside causes output, investment and job cuts in trading industries as we discovered in 1980–81, and have discovered again in 1998–2000. Yet upwards overshooting is usually succeeded by an equal and opposite undershooting with potentially inflationary consequences as import prices rise. These episodes of overshooting appear to be an inherent part of the foreign exchange market, as they are of other financial markets. They cannot be avoided merely by means of better domestic policies. Yet they create instability, raise risks, undermine investment and reduce prosperity.

The European countries have always been too small economically – and hence too interdependent – to ignore these realities (in contrast to the continent-sized and largely self-sufficient US). In most of Europe's modern economic history, with the brief and disastrous exception of the 1930s, European countries have been linked by some fixed exchange rate system (for example, Bretton Woods, European Monetary System) or by a quasi-monetary union (for example, the Gold Standard, particularly from 1880 to 1914). In a world of increasing capital flows, we can expect floating exchange rates to become even more volatile. Equally, the half-way house of fixed but adjustable exchange rates is no longer sustainable. The euro is a modern response to an age-old policy problem, enabling monetary stability in a world of massive speculative capital flows. It is a way of regaining control over our economic environment, and of exercising some real monetary sovereignty.

The macro-economics of the euro are clear. But the issue of British euro membership is also increasingly urgent for micro-economic reasons. The longer we are out, the greater the risk that our big businesses will essentially just become Euro-based, regarding their UK operations as a side-show. And our medium-sized and small businesses will not participate in the new wave of competition that is flowing from the creation of the euro.

Price differences are gradually being eliminated by many multinationals in anticipation of the changeover to physical euro notes and coins in the first half of 2002. This is creating a much more competitive environment. In turn, businesses are investing and consolidating to create the economies of scale that will allow them to survive in the new pan-European market. The scope for consolidation is vast: Europe's segmented markets still have seven car makers against three in the United States, ten makers of turbines against two in the US, and so on. As the euro creates a genuine single market, the value of mergers and acquisitions in Europe is running at a level six times as great as the peak of the last European merger boom in 1992. In short, the euro is a key part of creating the pan-European businesses of the same scope and efficiency as those in the US. While Britain is outside the euro-area, we are inevitably less subject to these incentives for change and efficiency.

Then there is also the political imperative. It may be possible for a small country like Denmark, with far fewer industrial, commercial and financial interests than a country ten times its size like Britain, to be a member of the European Union but not of the euro-area. Denmark's influence would be marginal whether in or out. But Britain's political position – our ability to influence the EU debate on industrial standards, consumer, workplace and environmental protection measures – is clearly weakened by being outside a key project of the Union. Britain's representatives have less status in negotiations, and are regarded as less committed to the whole. Moreover, the creation of the euro inevitably creates real differences of economic interest between euro-area members and non-members. Gradually, our economies will be shaped by different forces, and we will have different interests.

For example, cross-border financial services, spurred by the internet, are likely to grow even faster in the euro-area than outside. And that in turn will require an increasing emphasis on cross-border supervision and regulation of financial institutions. When the euro-area countries want to establish a common markets regulator, or banking supervisor, as in time they will, will Britain want the same if we are outside the euro? Yet such a proposal could currently be made by the EU Commission, and would be adopted by co-decision (that is, by getting a simple majority in the European Parliament plus a qualified majority of 71 per cent of the votes in the Council of Ministers). And that qualified majority in the Council exists in the Eurogroup on its own. Britain could not veto such legislation.

What would the Conservatives say then? Such a development would be a natural consequence of their view that we can comfortably stay within the EU but outside the euro, but somehow I doubt that they will see it that way when it happens. Instead, they will scream that the EU is treating us unfairly, and will gradually move to a position wholly against our membership. In reality, the Conservative policy of being in the European Union but not in the euro is only sustainable for Britain in the short term. We have a window, but the clock is ticking. In due course, if we fail to join, we will be on the way out of the European Union altogether. The consequences for our economy would be grave, but the consequences for our politics of the rampant little Englandism that would surely follow would be even more dire.

If we win the battle within Britain over the euro – as I believe we can and must – we can then throw ourselves behind those who want to see improvements in the operation of the system. The euro is far from perfect. The council of the European Central Bank should be much more open in the way it makes decisions, publishing votes and minutes of its meetings as the Bank of England Monetary Policy Committee has done for the last three years. We also need to ensure that the stability and growth pact – the essential commitments to fiscal responsibility that all euro-area members sign up to – is properly interpreted to allow public investment, defining the 3 per cent deficit limit as applying to current spending. But these changes cannot effectively be pushed from outside the euro-area. That is like arguing for a change in the club rules before joining. We need to be inside as soon as possible to help shape the developing and changing institutions of the Eurogroup.

Micro-economic reforms

Turning to micro-economic measures, let me start with a negative point. Governments need to do what governments do well, which is mainly rule setting and framework building. Ask politicians to make micro decisions – about, for example, the future of the Nissan plant in Sunderland – and more often than not they will get the decision wrong. Their incentives are all bound up with their own interest in marginal seats, rather than with the public interest in long-term sustainability. That is why progressive economics must continue to avoid case-by-case discretionary subsidies. Fortunately, Britain spends less on such subsidies per head than any other member of the EU, and presses the Commission to cut back our partners' unfair state aids. This is the right policy: we are so far short of some of their spending that we could not hope to match them within our own budget constraints even if it were desirable (which it is not). The best strategy is to reduce theirs, thereby benefiting British jobs.

Instead of specific subsidies that try to direct rainfall on to particular hills, we must concentrate instead on the sort of legal and other changes that can alter the climate for prosperity. The big item of unfinished business continues to be education and skills. It is hard to overestimate the importance of education both in broadening people's life-chances and in improving our success in a global, knowledge-based economy. Yet we are still far from getting the framework right, since we have still not given parents the tools to enable them to assess whether schools are doing well or badly for their children. The key has to be much more information about the effectiveness of your particular school – compared with others in the area, a regional and a national average – in improving standards between different benchmark tests.

League tables that merely measure final exam results are virtually meaningless. They play on the widespread lack of understanding of the concept of probability. Let me give an example. A selective-entry school that successfully selects 20 Einsteins in a class ought to get them all into university. If it gets 19 out of 20 into university, it is probably topping the league tables, although it has failed the twentieth Einstein. The neighbouring school that admits one Einstein and 19 Jo Slows, but gets Einstein and another of the 20 into university has actually performed better than the first. Any Einstein stands a better chance of university entry in the second school (100 per cent versus 90 per cent) even though its league table results are far worse. Without an accessible, specific measure of value-added – of looking at how schools improve the life-chances of their pupils between assessment at one age and the next – the consumer-parent will compare apples and oranges. Sensible information for parents would provide a real incentive for schools, and would also help to break down the barriers between the state and independent sector by demythologising the more selective schools' results.

Much economic research stresses the importance of a good education precisely because it empowers people to go on learning, which is another area in which progressive government should play a key role. In a dynamic economy, the only constant is change. Over the last year, nearly 3 million people signed on to the unemployment register (out of a workforce of 28 million) but the creation of new jobs meant that overall unemployment continued to fall. So new jobs are the key. The Government rightly subsidises training for information technology and many other areas where there are skill shortages that can act as a brake on growth. There is abundant evidence that the social returns to education and training are even higher than the returns to the individual in higher pay. But the subsidies themselves are often just adding icing on to the cake, and people have not noticed the cake because of a lack of information. A three-month Information Technology course may cost £8000 plus £5000 in three months' loss of earnings: a total of £13 000. If it usually raises someone's pay from £20 000 to £25 000, the course will pay for itself within three years. This is the sort of investment that many businesses would die for, but many people do not see the advantage.

People also face uncertainty in assessing the usefulness of the course: once again, there is an important role for public authorities in providing information about the likely increase in earnings and its certainty (based on past results). There is also a role in facilitating funding. This need not be a simple subsidy, but could be linked to the risk that someone would not see an increase in earnings. People could also be allowed to mobilise their own savings, which are often locked away. The Canadian Liberal government, for example, has allowed people to take money from their pension fund savings for lifelong education and training. If the likely increase in earnings is high, this is a thoroughly sensible decision. The government may also have a role in persuading mortgage lenders to roll up interest during a course when the student is not earning. We need to find practical ways of removing the obstacles to self-improvement, because that way lies a successful economy.

I have stressed the role of information in making these markets and quasi-markets work better. Information is power. Information is increasingly the means by which central government can have some indirect influence over what are necessarily and properly devolved decisions. It makes no more sense for Whitehall to decree what is going on at 11 a.m. in every secondary school classroom in the land – with all respect to our French friends – than it did for Gosplan in Moscow to specify left shoe production in Nizhny Novgorod. In a more complex society, central government has increasingly to be the persuader and ringmaster, devolving decision making to those who understand all the considerations that need to be brought to bear. This applies to the public sector as much as to the private sector.

So government itself must change. Britain remains, with France, one of the most centralised industrial countries in the world. Our local government has been neutered by the extension of central powers wholly inappropriate for the complexity of our world, and which fly in the face of trends in decentralising big businesses. Moreover, economic history tells us that the systems that have built-in policy competition are more innovative and successful than monoliths. The primary reason why Europe overtook China was policy competition between European states: if Florence introduced anti-business policies, the merchant could up-sticks to Venice. But Shanghai and Beijing both suffered the same emperor, with the same centralising and often suffocating policies (Landes 1998).

Within Britain, the great Victorian cities were economically successful in part because their systems of local governance were responsive to the needs of the local community whether for education, transport or water and sewerage (Briggs 1990). Prosperity has always been a question of public–private partnership. We have 30 cities in Britain with a population of more than 100 000. Each of them has the potential to be a thriving centre of innovation and renewal, competing with each other to attract the best brains, build the fastest-growing businesses and provide the most attractive environment in which to live. By encouraging local elites to take responsibility for local decisions, we would also help to regrow entrepreneurial capacity throughout the country. The skill to innovate crosses the public–private sector frontier.

So my last plea is for a rethinking of the structure of government, with a radical devolution of financial and economic decision making. W.E. Gladstone once said that the principle of conservatism was mistrust of the people qualified by fear, whereas the principle of liberalism was trust in the people qualified by prudence. There is certainly room for prudence, but there must be more space for trust. Given the low quality of many of our local authorities, particularly those that have been controlled for many years by a single party without any real prospect or threat of change, the devolution of serious powers is a leap of faith. A necessary condition is electoral reform to ensure that there can be change and responsiveness to the electorate. Directly elected mayors may also help. But it is a leap of faith that we must make if government is to become more sensitive to the communities it serves.

It matters less whether the devolution of power is to regions or cities, or to both, than that the devolution should be far-reaching and financial. If authorities are to be responsible, they must be able to raise or lower a series of taxes, and should ideally raise as much tax as they spend. Spending without taxing is the way to irresponsibility and waste, and Britain's tax system is highly centralised: we spend 78 per cent of total government tax revenues centrally compared with just 27 per cent in Switzerland, 30 per cent in Germany or 43 per cent in the US (Bromley et al. 1999). This means devolving a serious part of central government revenues – including perhaps a large slice of the income tax base – to regions or cities. In some parts of Spain – the autonomous communities in the Basque country, for example – the local authority raises all the tax revenue, and passes a part to the federal government in Madrid. Devolution means allowing local authorities to experiment with their own taxes, as happens in the US. Thus some cities, for example, might want to zero-rate any developments or improvements as an incentive to regeneration (as have several cities in Pennsylvania) (Plassmann and Tideman 1998).

This independence of the tax base should go hand in hand with the power to borrow money directly as a local authority for the purposes of investment, again as occurs in the US. In the cases of large investments, approval might need to be gained through a local referendum with a notice that clearly sets out the consequences in debt-servicing costs for the local rate, variable excise duty or income tax. Each local authority would be subject to a clear 'no bail out' rule by Westminster: if it failed, it could not expect other authorities to pick up the pieces (although there might be New York City-style safeguards such as a commissioner with special powers to run any authority at risk of bankruptcy). Each authority that borrowed would be assessed by the marketplace. The terms of its own borrowing would depend on its creditworthiness, track record and administrative competence: authorities with poor records would pay higher interest rates.

This does not rule out an equalisation subsidy from the centre designed to help poorer areas, so long as that grant is clearly based on objective criteria and is set for several years so that it can be the basis of planning. The key point is that local authorities should be able to succeed or fail in their own way. The role of rewarding and punishing local authorities should not fall on Westminster – rate-capping and other Whitehall-imposed penalties belong in the old Gosplan world – but on their own local electorates. Ultimately, it is the people who live in an area who are best placed to judge whether they are getting what they want, and who will certainly be told by the opposition if there is any failing on the part of the ruling party.

There will, of course, be failures in any system that seriously devolves power. But those failures will be a lesson to others, and part of the learning process of policy competition. Such failures would not entrap the country as a whole – unlike, say, the poll tax. And the successes would prove a model that other authorities would quickly emulate, particularly if Westminster were to take its role as ringmaster and information-provider seriously. Competition works in government as effectively as in the private sector. Diversity and experimentation are the sources of success. It is not an accident that one of the most successful and acclaimed changes introduced by the 1997 Labour government – very much supported by the Liberal Democrats – was the delegation of power over monetary policy to the Bank of England. Delegation, decentralisation, devolution are the keys to responsive government in the twenty-first century. The progressive agenda for the new century needs to put an old Liberal message back at the heart of reform: trust the people.

References

Briggs, A. (1990) *Victorian Cities*. London: Penguin.

Bromley, N. et al. (1999) *Funding Federalism: A report on systems of government finance*. London: Centre for Reform.

Huhne, C. and Forder, J. (1999) *Both Sides of the Coin: The case for (and against) the euro and European monetary union*. London: Profile.

Landes, D. (1998) *The Wealth and Poverty of Nations*. London: Abacus.

Plassmann, F. and Tideman, T.N. (1998) 'A Markov Chain Monte Carlo Analysis of the Effect of Two-Rate Property Taxes on Construction, Virginia', Virginia Technical University Working Paper E98–01, <http://www.econ.vt.edu/research/papers/wps98.html>

14
The Globalisation of Power

Paddy Ashdown

On the wall of my study in my home in Somerset, there is a photograph of my grandfather. The year is 1897 and he has just returned from the Paris exhibition with what he always claimed to be the first car in Ireland – certainly the first car in Northern Ireland. And there he is, proudly sitting in it, in front of the stable door of his house in Rathfriland-on-the-hill.

I also have his diaries. They say that these things – motor cars – will change the world. His friends say they will only ever be rich men's toys. But he predicts that most people will have one. And they will change everything: our relationships with each other; the look and shape of our countryside; the structure of our society.

He was right. The twentieth century was the motor car century.

I believe that we are now embarked on a new revolution which will be just as big. That we, too, are at the very beginning of it. That this revolution, too, when it has run its course, will change everything – perhaps even more in the twenty-first century than the motor car did in the twentieth.

This revolution, however, is not about a machine, although there are machines – computers – at the heart of it. It is about a process – a fundamental shift in the accessibility of knowledge, in the patterns of commerce and in the distribution of power. If there is a similarity with the past, it is not with the motor car but with the invention of printing.

This silent revolution has many facets, but one principal result – the globalisation of power. And it is, in my view, the biggest event of our time – even if most national politicians would prefer to pretend it wasn't happening because it challenges their role and poses questions they would much prefer not to confront.

The essence of this change is that power, which used to be centred on the nation-state, is now being sucked upwards at an ever-increasing rate into the hands of the global players, and downwards into the hands of ordinary citizens.

Try this little test. First, list all those institutions which are growing in power, size and influence; and note how nearly all of them operate in ways which pay no attention to the borders and frontiers which are so important to nation-states – the currency speculators, the commodity traders, the satellite broadcasters, the transnational corporations, the internet operators, the international criminals, the drug-traffickers (not all of these are benign).

Now list those institutions which are under threat or challenge – monarchies, police forces, political classes, the establishments of power. Note how all of these depend for their existence on the notion and borders of the nation-state.

This does not mean that the nation-state is going to vanish, or even that it is going to cease to be important. To the contrary. When it comes to governance, the management of the common wealth or the expression of individual identity, the nation-state will remain of greater importance than any of the other institutions, either above or below it. But it will no longer be the *only* framework for the exercise of power, the expression of identity, or the securing of our safety and well-being.

Perhaps the greatest function of the nation-state in the last two centuries was to tell us, as ordinary citizens, who we were. We were British. And we had a flag and a national anthem and a lot of dead on foreign battlefields to prove it. With the unitary nation-state came the notion of unitary identity. So our national currency has come to be judged, not by whether it is stable or advantageous to trade, or helpful for investment, or better for jobs – it is none of these – but by whether it has our Queen's head on it.

In the meantime our identities could be simply judged by Norman Tebbit's cricket test.

But nowadays the unitary notion of identity will no longer do. Indeed, where we try to make it do, it nearly always ends in bloodshed, as Ulster, Bosnia and Kosovo bear witness.

Speaking personally, if you had asked me who I was 30 years ago, when I was a British soldier, I would have said that I was British and that would have been enough. Nowadays, I have to give you a rather more complex answer. I am Irish by blood – and proud of it. I am West Country by choice and love – that is where my constituency is. I am British, of course. And I am proud of that, too. But I am also a European. And unless I can describe myself in all these ways, I cannot tell you who I am, or describe the space in which I want to live – or, more importantly, the space in which I want my children to live. The unitary identity is no longer sufficient. It is no longer safe. We do not have to choose between being British and European. We can be both. Just as we can be British and Asian, or Belfast and Chinese, or Muslim and Yugoslavian, or Bermondsey and Bangladeshi, or Protestant *and* Irish *and* British *and* European all at the same time. Now that can be confusing to some, and even threatening to others; but it has its advantages, in helping to resolve our ancient quarrels and cope with new ones.

This has huge implications for the way we relate to our government. We politicians ask for votes on the promise that we can solve all at Westminster. But globalisation is making frauds of us.

We offer security for the nation. Yet we discovered 50 years ago that security even for a medium-sized nation like Britain, can only be obtained if we pool our defence (surely one of the key sovereignties of the nation-state) in collective security agreements such as NATO. We offer a clean environment, yet pollution is no respecter of borders – a nuclear power station running amok 3000 miles away in Chernobyl contaminates the grasslands of Cumbria. You cannot have a clean Britain unless you have a clean Europe – indeed, increasingly, unless you have a cleaner world.

The House of Commons, that greatest of all British job preserva-tion conspiracies, detests the idea that its majesty, power and scope for action is now far less than it was 100 or even 50 years ago. But the voters recognise it – and they show their recognition in increasing apathy and abstention at the ballot box. The fact is that the old contract between the politician and the voter is breaking down. Westminster claims it can, alone, deliver all that Britain wants: from peace to jobs; from a strong economy to a clean environment. But in fact, almost all of these things are no longer within our power to ensure and almost all require us to sacrifice (I prefer 'pool') some of our sovereignty with others if they are to be delivered to our citizens.

Meanwhile, below the level of the nation-state traditional politics isn't working, either.

Since the Second World War, Westminster has quite deliberately gone about destroying or emasculating all the proud intermediary democratic institutions which stood between it and the citizen. Local government has become little more than the land agent for Whitehall.

Of course, some alternative intermediary structures have been set up as the independence of local government was, piece by piece, torn down. Local management of schools, primary care groups for health, and so-called 'arm's-length agencies' for the delivery of welfare are examples. But the democratic connection between these institutions and the citizen has been almost non-existent, and their accountability, at best highly tenuous. The quango is *not* an intermediary institution. The fact is that, for the average citizen – used to being treated as a discriminating customer, and capable of handling choice in every other part of the marketplace – finds that in politics, he or she is offered a choice of two and a half at election time and take it or leave it in between.

This applies just as much above the nation-state as below, even if sometimes only by accident. What we are actually creating in Europe is the world's first working experimental test bed for a supra-national structure. Of course, this was not one of the motivations of the founders of the European Union. But we have, as it were in a fit of absent-mindedness, nevertheless come up with an accidental but intelligent response to the challenge of globalised power – if only we would realise it. One of the responses to globalisation will, increasingly, be regionalisation.

Yet, as every politician knows, all is not well in Europe. The concept of Europe may be in tune with the drift of history, but it seems increasingly out of tune with the sentiments of its people. The pro-European argument is failing to convince both at the level of the citizen and at the level of strategic vision. This is a deadly combination of failures. Writing in the *Independent* newspaper, Anne McElvoy drew the comparison between the grand (and convincing) vision of Europe's founders and its current obsession with the petty and pettyfogging. She said: 'The secret shame of the European Union, is not that it seeks to steamroller national sovereignty in pursuit of some great advance for mankind, but that it no longer believes in very much at all' (16 February 2000).

Crucial amongst these failures is the fact that Europe still fails to answer the most important questions in the European debate: What are the limits of the power of the centre? And what are the inalienable powers which will always be left with the members? If we cannot answer either of these questions we cannot either calm the justified suspicions of our voters about creeping European interference in our lives, or create a capacity for effective and unified action in Europe. This is true on both the political level and on the level of security. And it is true especially on the economic level too.

The euro is now the world's second most powerful currency and, some argue, capable of challenging the dollar for first position. The euro and the dollar combined now enjoy between them an economic ascendancy in world markets which is incomparable today and has only occasionally, if ever, been equalled in history. In addition, the position of monetary strength is matched by a political alliance across the Atlantic which, for more than half a century, has represented the fundamental axis of global power in our times. We have been able to act through this alliance to suppress conflict, assert the rule of inter- national law and preserve peace from Korea through to Iraq, Bosnia and Kosovo.

Should we not similarly be prepared to act to create a stable climate for world trade and the currency system which supports it? The setting up of a new form of Bretton Woods-type structure through the establishment of a currency stability pact between the dollar and the euro would be a major step towards economic global governance and a bulwark against currency instability which can nowadays damage even medium-size economies – as we saw on Black Wednesday.

Of course, in a world of freely floating currencies and freely flowing capital it may be that this would achieve little more than a broad underpinning of stability. However, the fact of active co-operation between the US and Europe and expectations of greater stability which policy co-ordination would itself bring benefits and helps to boost real trade flows.

It would also, incidentally, take much of the foolish proto-nationalism out of the single currency debate in Britain. And, on a less altruistic plane, it would also be strongly in the interests of both the US and Europe, greatly strengthening the Atlantic Alliance, which I believe will remain the only effective basis for developing our emerging framework for international law in the crucial decades ahead.

But maintaining a strong Atlantic relationship is not a substitute for creating a greater capacity for Europe to act more cohesively and, if necessary, independently where it must. If, as Europeans, we do not develop the ability to project power in order to prosecute our interests and, where necessary, defend them, we may well find them being marginalised. Europe may not wish to become a superstate, but it cannot avoid being a superpower.

Europe is not alone in facing these challenges. Every region will find it has new economic, security and political imperatives. We have already seen new challenges to International Law, bought about by increasing globalisation. And we have discovered that the old rules of International Law, based as they are on the notion of the inviola-bility of the nation-state, will no longer do.

If you believe, as I do, that the campaign to reverse President Milosevic's policy of ethnic cleansing in Kosovo was just and right, even if there were flaws in its execution, then logically you have to question whether the assertion of domestic sovereignty in Article 2, paragraph 7 of the UN Charter can be seen anymore to hold.

What we need is a new approach which, though still based on the presumption of non-intervention, sets out clearly those circumstances in which that presumption can be challenged. In essence, we need to define the circumstances in which the international community has a right, if not a moral obligation, to defend people from oppression, even when the oppressor is their own government. I suggest four criteria for international intervention. The first three are matters of principle, the fourth is a judgement of practicality:

- First, is the State in question acting in gross violation of International Law or the Universal Declaration on Human Rights?
- Second, have all available diplomatic avenues for resolution been exhausted?

- Third, does this action threaten the wider stability of the region; for instance, by creating floods of refugees?
- Fourth, is it militarily and politically practicable?

If the answer to any of these questions is no, then intervention is not justified. If the answer to all of them is yes, then intervention can proceed, provided it is conducted in accordance with the wider body of International Law. In this way the UN acts as the author and guardian of International Law, even if it subcontracts the enforcement to others, such as NATO in the Balkans. But the UN's role is not finished once the military intervention is over. It also has a role as a validator and protector of the peace that it has sponsored. This diminishes fear of colonisation; provides a better context for reconciliation; and stronger, multilateral guarantees of lasting peace than any other organisation could.

But for the UN to do this effectively we need to tackle its own internal problems. Britain, with its leading role in each of the four key circles of power in the world (the Security Council, NATO, the Commonwealth and the EU); with its assets of military effectiveness and diplomatic experience and with its residual capacity to take a world view, has a unique position to lead the process of reforming and strengthening the UN, particularly in relation to its ability to maintain and, where necessary, make peace.

We will also need to create new institutions capable of tackling other global problems which now confront us: global pollution, scarcity of natural resources, proliferation of weapons of mass destruction, the internationalisation of drug-trafficking and crime, and many others.

If power is becoming increasingly global, government must start to become global, too. If this frightens you, take comfort from this fact: power sometimes does migrate outside the institutions we have created to control it, and, when this happens, change becomes inevitable – so it was at Magna Carta, in the time of Cromwell, at the glorious revolution of 1688 and in the Great Reform Acts of the nineteenth century, and so it is today. The globalisation of power is the big challenge of our time. How we respond to this by globalising at least some of our institutions and our thinking is going to be one of the big debates of our future.

15
Socialising Markets

Philip Collins

The hardest thing in philosophy, said Descartes, is to know where to begin. For most of the last century, social democratic thought has begun with the conflict between capital and labour. It is not clear that the left any longer has a viable critique of capitalism. It is not clear that the left any longer has any critique of capitalism at all beyond the insight that markets sometimes fail, which all but the most extraordinary of neo-liberals would also accept.

There are a number of candidates as the primary value of the left: social justice, fairness, the two senses of equality. In a sense the search for a single defining idea is itself thoroughly misconceived. Politics has always been far too complex to submit to singular ideas. The legacy of applied utopian blueprints is egregious and not to be emulated. Amongst the enduring lessons that Isaiah Berlin has for the contemporary centre-left, one of the more pressing is that not all good things can be had at once. The really difficult conflicts in politics are not those between good and bad but between good and good.[1]

The intellectual position that the left has inherited includes a rather romantic hope that equality, fairness and social justice can all be had at once. Indeed, in many recent works these terms are used interchangeably, as if they were all exactly the same thing.[2]

There is one central value not yet mentioned. The idea of liberty has been a conspicuous absentee from the public rhetoric of New Labour, as Ralf Dahrendorf has pointed out.[3]

It would be strange, and damaging, if British politics became a race to see who could run away from the term 'liberal' the quickest. The current Conservative Party leader, William Hague, seems determined to make 'liberal' a term of abuse, as it has become in the US. The current government acts at its worst when it follows him on to this barren ground.

This is all very strange when one considers the deep and abiding inheritance of liberal political philosophy on British politics. John Gray has written eloquently of the enduring bequest of liberalism which we can note every day in the best political practices of liberal democracy.[4] Freedom of association, freedom of the press, freedom of speech, and so on, are forever contested. These basic liberties need constant and vigorous defence. But there is no great ideological division on this between political traditions and this is evidence of the rightful triumph of liberal ideas in British politics.[5]

It is precisely because liberal political institutions have become so taken for granted that politicians can blithely declare that they owe no debt to liberalism. In fact the idea of liberty is one which the social democratic and the soi-disant liberals have in common. The idea of extended freedom for all is a value around which all the progressive forces could be expected to coalesce. It differs from purely negative versions of liberty in that it does not accept that the upshot of market encounters is *ipso facto* fair and just. The point from which a person begins makes an obvious difference to where they tend to finish.[6] Material circumstances clearly affect the extent that anyone is capable of exercising the freedom to act. Freedom for the left does not mean simply the absence of external coercion. Raymond Plant has pointed out that all conceptions of liberty include the verb 'to be able' and thereby imply the importance of the capacity to act. Freedom is not just about willed coercion.

The economic counterpart of political liberty is a market. At the moment the conversion to market economics on the left is still superficial. The manifest advantages of markets in allocating most sets of resources has been recognised, grudgingly, reluctantly; in some quarters, not at all. For most goods it simply does not make sense for governments to attempt to gather all the information that is contained in the signal of a price. To that extent, the old argument is now a lost historical relic. However, freedom for a reunited left means a recognition that a market must be social.[7]

The social market is a case which liberals and social democrats alike could take to their hearts. The democratic case for markets is not heard often enough. A market is the most radical tool for decentralising power ever devised by the wit of man. It is far quicker and far more extensive than government in dispersing power. Indeed, global markets, through the development of immediate technology, are becoming quicker, more virally extensive than ever before. A fairly regulated market is a democratic institution which has allowed a more extensive exercise of individual freedom than any regime which has relied on the state to promote liberty.

However, this does not mean the left needs to take on the zealotry of converts. The democratic promise of a market is not real for everyone. There are four related ways in which this endorsement of the market needs to be qualified. They are all ways, in other words, of describing a social market.

First, although the term 'public good' is used in a very slippery fashion, some things are unquestionably better provided publicly.[8] Not everything should be private and in this limited and uncontroversial sense there is a role for government.

Second, a market is very much a communal institution. Functioning markets depend on a range of often unspoken shared understandings. The more a society exhibits high levels of trust or of due observance of contractual regularity, for example, the healthier that market order will be. We have seen from plenty of negative examples that economic stability is umbilically linked to political stability and a graceful transition from one political administration to another is a vital component of a working social market order. The link between economic and political liberty is more intimate than I have space here to elucidate.

Third, it is also perfectly obvious that markets sometimes fail. The intellectual victory of the left over the past decade has been largely won on pointing this out. Markets can have undesirable results.[9] For instance, it now seems decisively clear that the benefits of market economies will not trickle down to the very poorest. The claim that trickle-down will work in the long run is the right-wing equivalent of the leftist claim that real socialism has never actually been tried.

Recognition of this fact is absolutely critical to the concept of the social market. If markets produce drastic inequalities in income, and if one of the consequences is that significant minorities of the rich and the poor do not come into contact with common institutions, then the market order as a whole is thrown into disrepute. Opting out is, on this reading, not an exercise of liberty so much as a threat to the communal stability on which the social market rests.

Similarly, and lastly, a social market order requires a theory of justice. Transactions in a social market need to be seen to be fair. They need to be experienced by participants as fair. If the outcome allows for unwarranted rewards then the market order itself is impugned. It is not good enough simply to reply that the transaction was entered into voluntarily. Not all the outcomes that occur in markets are predictable and wildly divergent rewards can lead to a questioning of the market system itself.

All of this is a way of saying that the market system does not spring out of the air. It is consciously and deliberately made by public policy. The tone and the bias of competition policy, of consumer policy, of regulation can make a market in one good very different from a market in another. There is no straight road from the desire to barter to a developed and sophisticated market economy. The role of government is critical from the very beginning, conceptually and practically. The most substantive thesis that re-emerged from the Third Way debates is that this separation between state and market is thoroughly artificial. The Third Way is really the social market with a less arresting name. The New Liberal thinker Hobhouse put this very well in *Liberalism*, where he writes that economic liberalism 'seeks to do justice to the social and individual factors in industry alike, as opposed to an abstract socialism which emphasizes the one side and an abstract individualism which leans its whole weight on the other'.[10]

There is a very great deal of scope for disagreement over the nature of the theory of justice that the social market order can accommodate, and I shall return to this question below. However, its distance from the neo-liberal position is obvious. On the social market view, social justice is not, in Hayek's infamous denunciation, a 'mirage' but a vital part of a functioning market economy. There is no intellectual argument here between progressive liberals and social democrats and any continued dispute between them is damaging to both parties.

The split is especially senseless when we consider the radical liberal roots of the British left. Eric Hobsbawm has pointed out the 'broad and generic sense in which all Englishmen of the left are the offspring of the radical liberal tradition'.[11] This tradition demonstrates that the association of the left with the state as the first instrument of public policy is not obvious or necessary. G.D.H. Cole has written that the central distinction in Labour intellectual history is that between the centralisers and the federalists. The centralisers have certainly had the better of the argument. The Labour tradition has, to its detriment, been dominated by Fabian *noblesse oblige*. As Hobhouse wrote: 'Mechanical Socialism makes insufficient provision for liberty, movement and growth.'[12] The Labour left has undeniably placed too great a faith in the efficacy of state planning.

But this is not at all insurmountable. The arguments for reconciliation already exist in the writings of the New Liberals of the closing years of the nineteenth century.[13] Hobson and Hobhouse aimed to protect the value of individuality, to reconcile it with social betterment. To put this aim in the more recent terminology of Thomas Nagel, they aimed to satisfy both the personal and the impersonal impulses.[14] Hence Hobhouse looked forward to a day when 'whatever inequality of actual treatment, of income, rank, office, consideration there be in a good social system, it would rest, not on the interest of the favoured individual but on the common good'.[15] I return to this conception of the good below.

The New Liberals did not hold to an unrestrained conception of liberty. Hobhouse defended social legislation on the grounds that it protected the freedom of the individual against the power of the association. In Tawney's famous formulation he stood up for the minnow against the freedom of the pike. He went on to argue unapologetically for a liberal market economy and a strong defence of the power of choice vested in vigorous anti-monopolistic competition policy. In *The Crisis of Liberalism* Hobson joined the attack on vested interests and monopoly power. He calls 'endeavours to recover, for the people and the State, liberties or properties or privileges which had within recent generations been lost or encroached upon by one class, trade or other vested interest'.[16] It is a rallying cry that is still relevant.

I suggested above that a functioning social market order requires a public theory of justice which commands at least silent consent. We urgently need to find such a theory which satisfies the social democrats, the liberals and works for a market economy competing in sophisticated global capitalism. This is not the place to press the following claim too strongly, but I do not think that the old conception of equality can meet all these requirements. Too much current thinking on the left is extremely woolly on this question. Again, Hobson is admirably clear: 'Liberalism will retain its distinction from socialism in taking for its chief test of policy the freedom of the individual citizen rather than the strength of the state.'[17]

An agreement could, though, be struck on a modified version of meritocracy. Inequalities matter greatly at the extremes. There are huge consequences for public policy when whole 'classes of people become detached from the common weal. Inequalities of this kind cannot be tolerated by a social market order for the good reason that they bring it into disrepute. There is a compelling case for corrective intervention especially where minimum standards of decency are not being observed. It is simply intolerable, for example, that anyone in a rich society should be forced to endure inadequate housing. The levels of child poverty are shameful and too many people are living without basic necessities.[18] The case for a minimum income is a good one as a means of upholding the social market order.[19]

However, it does not follow that other inequalities are intolerable if they have been freely arrived at by procedures which everyone involved would agree are fair. As long as we are prepared to allow rewards to accrue to talent (an admittedly huge assumption) then we will have to be prepared for relatively large inequalities of outcome.

The meritocratic case is a very good one but it is important to recognise that it is not the same as the case for equality. It allows the talented child from a poor family to prosper and she only becomes a problem for social policy if she uses her new resources to buy her way completely out of the common order on which the social market depends. As long as nobody ducks under a minimum threshold then the resultant inequalities, fairly arrived at, can be tolerated. And neither should a minimum threshold be limited to basic necessities. There is a good deal more to living in a society than remaining alive. The redistributive implications of a minimum threshold could be extremely radical but they do not derive primarily from the desire to produce a society that is more equal.

Lurking behind these thoughts is a moral instinct on which liberals and social democrats can agree. It is a profound prejudice against unearned, unmerited advance. It is an instinctive animus against privilege which unites the social democratic and the progressive liberal left. It is a battle they should conduct together.

Notes

1. This point is made most forcefully in Berlin's famous essays, 'The Pursuit of the Ideal', in *The Crooked Timber of Humanity*, London: John Murray, 1990; and 'The Two Concepts of Liberty', in *The Proper Study of Mankind*, London: Pimlico, 1998.

2. Two recent examples, though by no means the only ones, are Linton, Raymond and Whitehead (eds), *Beyond 2002; Long Term Policies for Labour*, London: Profile, 1999; and Margaret Hodge, 'Equality and New Labour', *Renewal*, vol. 8, no. 3.

3. Ralf Dahrendorf, 'Whatever happened to liberty?', *New Statesman*, 6 September 1999.

4. John Gray, *Liberalism*, Buckingham: Open University Press, 1986.

5. It is instructive that the great tension in conservative political thought derives from an attempt to reconcile itself to liberalism. David Willetts has tried manfully to rescue his tradition in *Modern Conservatism*, Harmondsworth: Penguin, 1992, and he joined the same debate with John Gray in *Is Conservatism Dead?*, London: Profile, 1997.

6. In *A Class Act: The Myth of Britain's Classless Society*, Hamish Hamilton, 1997, Andrew Adonis and Stephen Pollard demonstrated conclusively once again that life-chances in the UK are very much a function of class origin.

7. This is a very different endeavour from David Miller's attempts to mount a case for market socialism in *Market, State, Community*, Oxford: Clarendon, 1989. The word order is no accident.

8. The best recent guide is Evan Davis, *Public Spending*, Harmondsworth: Penguin, 1998.

9. This tension is again especially acute for political conservatives.

10. L.T. Hobhouse, *Liberalism*, London: Williams and Norgate Ltd, 1911.

11. Eric Hobsbawm, *Labouring Men*, London: Weidenfeld and Nicolson, 1964.

12. Hobhouse, *Liberalism*.

13. The best book on the New Liberals is Stefan Collini's *Liberalism and Sociology: L.T. Hobhouse and political argument in England 1880–1914*, Cambridge: Cambridge University Press, 1979.

14. These terms are taken from Thomas Nagel, *Equality and Partiality*, Oxford: Oxford University Press, 1991.

15. Hobhouse, *Liberalism*.

16. J.A. Hobson, *The Crisis of Liberalism*, London: P.S. King and Son, 1909.

17. Ibid.

18. David Gordon, Laura Adelman et al., 'Poverty and social exclusion in Britain', York: Joseph Rowntree Foundation, 2000.

19. The Social Market Foundation has pressed this case before. See Meghnad Desai's 'A Basic Income Proposal', in Robert Skidelsky (ed.) *The State of the Future*, Social Market Foundation, 1998.

16
Making Society Just

Don Foster

A more just society must be the chief aim of a centre-left government. It is for us to secure the fair treatment *of* all our citizens, *by* all our citizens. By contrast, right-wing parties are obsessed with hierarchies; with authority, deference, pecking orders. Their few winners stand on the shoulders of a mass of losers.

It is natural for the social authoritarians of the right to champion the monarchy, hereditary privilege, the Established Church, Oxbridge, the Inns of Court, the public schools, the 11-plus; all mechanisms that tend to make Britain *un*fair and exclusive. The right want the rich and powerful to be taxed and regulated as little as possible. If disadvantage is to be tackled at all, they want the task left to the voluntary sector. Where taxes are unavoidable they want them to be indirect (like VAT) so they bear on the poor as much as they do on the rich.

Any threats to these totems from their critics at home, or more particularly, from supra-national institutions like the EU are resisted as intolerably corrosive of tradition and national identity.

A centre-left government, however, should move quickly to challenge unfairness and inequality. Government can intervene directly through changing the taxation regime and by directing funds to provide routes out of poverty. It has an even more crucial role as enabler, giving a 'hand up' instead of a hand down. Such a government must certainly tackle discrimination head on through a

Single Equality Act. Governance must be reformed, and a Social Justice Audit introduced to cover all legislation and government initiatives.

In the twenty-first century the centre-left can talk openly about the redistribution of wealth. We can be honest with the electorate in saying frankly that taxation should be progressive. We can campaign on a platform that says that high-quality public services need to be paid for; are, indeed, *worth* paying for.

We have to tackle the problem that among those living in poverty in the UK, we have millions of pensioners, one in three children, and eight in ten people of Pakistani or Bangladesh origin. It is apparent to many in Middle England that to permit the growth of a restive and anti-social 'underclass' is not only unjust but also causes unaccept-able damage to their own personal quality of life.

The logical conclusion of the ultra-right-wing agenda can be seen with grim clarity in some of the cities of South America, where the hilltop mansions of the rich and powerful have to be surrounded with top security and razor-wire, and their owners can only go out by car accompanied by bodyguards. The slums of the poor cluster on the foothills, the beggars are at the gates. Human rights organisations claim that the police sometimes 'cleanse' the streets of beggar children simply by murdering them. You could almost pity the rich, for they live in jail with their quality of life curtailed just as certainly (if a good deal more comfortably) than their victims. Huge disparities of wealth give no one a good quality of life. The reckless greed that underpins the widening gap between rich and poor also threatens the future of the planet.

Elimination of poverty is therefore in the interests of the whole of society. In part this does rely on the redistribution of wealth. The most obvious route is through a small increase in income tax on those on high salaries, which is then used to take those on the lowest incomes out of tax. There are many other things we could do.

We could ensure that the 700 000 pensioners who fail to claim Income Support receive the benefits to which they are entitled, a problem now proved to arise not through pride, but through lack of information. We could entitle to Income Support even those pensioners who have saved a little for their old age. We could include 16- and 17-year-olds in the benefit system, rather than facing some of them with the choice of enduring physical or sexual abuse at home, or going on the street to survive by begging or prostitution.

We could choose to end the cruel irony through which it is very *expensive* to be poor. Higher unit costs are charged by gas, electricity, telephone and water companies to low-income families who have to use pre-payment meters. Expensive and infrequent bus services make it costly to look for work. The disappearance of banks and post offices from run-down neighbourhoods forces poor people to rely on loan sharks charging exorbitant rates of interest.

Credit unions have proved very helpful in enabling such communities to take ownership of their own banking arrangements. The local authority in Eastleigh, for example, has provided the backing for a successful credit union managed by community leaders and local business people. Government should enable and encourage more local authorities to follow suit.

We must certainly alter the ludicrous Social Fund rules under which people in acute need who can't demonstrate evidence of an ability to repay loans are unable to get help. The Social Fund was introduced to give grants for such vital needs as buying a cooker to a help a homeless person begin life in their first flat, or to buy a child shoes for school. Since 1988 the grant was changed to a loan, and now you can only get one if you can demonstrate the ability to repay it. This needs to change.

Beyond direct intervention, both central and local government need to move towards acting as 'enabler'. Ways need to be found of engaging those in the UK who have no worthwhile purpose or means of earning to act together on behalf of their own communities. This can be done only by empowering them to plan their own routes out of poverty, and assisting them to organise their own community initiatives. Professionals and planners should be on tap, not on top.

People, especially in degraded environments, need power and funding so they can have a pivotal role in planning and implementing improvement schemes. This must mean much more than just consulting them about a variety of options dictated from Westminster or the Town Hall. Perhaps it's no wonder that the Dome, through lack of consultation with the local community, although it is now claimed by government to be a regeneration project for Greenwich, finished up by cutting the trade of some local shop-owners by up to 40 per cent.

At all levels government must take care to avoid programmes that merely provide endless opportunities for professionals and administrators. Calderdale Council identified 101 so-called 'partnerships' in its area alone. One had to question whether these were programmes to benefit people in need or to provide job opportunities for professionals.

There are already working models where councils have pioneered an 'area committee' system. All urban areas need local community councils; in rural areas there could be a much bigger role for parish councils (though perhaps it's time they were renamed).

Involving people from the start in environmentally friendly projects works well too. In Sutton, in south London, local people are developing the Peabody/BioRegional Beddington Zero Energy Development, probably Europe's biggest eco-village. Householders on this zero-energy housing project will generate their own power from waste and other sustainable resources. Additionally, there is to be a community car pool, avoiding the need for each household to buy their own car. Sutton Council acts as facilitator, but those who live in the community are in charge.

People should not be campaigning for better services; they should be running them. It would lower the running costs of many thousands of poor households if their roofspaces were well insulated, if damp could be eliminated and double or triple glazing were to be installed. Some of these householders could be trained in the skills to do this work, and perhaps with appropriate grants and workshops restored from derelict buildings might even be involved in manufacturing glazing units or insulation material.

This would have the important benefit that 'regeneration' activity would keep the money generated *in the area* and *among the people* it is intended to benefit. The Social Exclusion Unit (SEU) has looked at the problem in some detail.

The SEU found that if a major company figured as part of a regeneration bid (for example, a supermarket chain building a new superstore), much of the money pumped into the local economy was siphoned out again by the big company. If, on the other hand, an enterprise is managed by and employs local people (like my example of insulation and double glazing), both those with new jobs and those with lower heating bills will have more spending power. This may in turn stimulate the reopening of local shops, creating further employment, and so forth.

'Top-down' initiatives like subsidising huge new factories simply impose a 'cuckoo' in the nest of a deprived area, with the employees (often skilled workers driving in from outside the area) earning and spending their money so that the profits go to already well-off share-holders in wealthy parts of the country. It's essential that the new wealth is created *by* the 'socially excluded' *for* their own benefit and is reinvested so it continues to benefit them.

In the same way, these people should be empowered to take decisions about their own transport and how journeys are made. Communal decision making can make a great difference. A few years ago I saw infant schools in the Canton of Zurich in Switzerland, where young children could walk home safely and unattended by adults because the local community had agreed that no one would drive cars in the streets around the school at 'home time', and because adults watched out for the children, both on the pavements and from the windows of their homes.

It should not be impossibly difficult for local people to lease minibuses and to train and employ drivers to provide a 'Dial-a-Ride' service tailor-made to the real needs of the community (even if this ate into the profits of the giant bus companies). Young people unmotivated by formal education might be given skills to maintain and service such vehicles (and perhaps gain vocational qualifications). Just possibly, *'our'* bus might be rather less likely to be a target for vandalism.

Where major investment goes into a public transport system, it should be 'commissioned' by those who could most benefit from it. Some cities are pondering spending huge sums on light rail systems, which will benefit affluent commuters from the outer suburbs. It may well be that if the residents of the poorest inner-city communities are asked, they might choose to spend some of the money on more small-scale projects, such as their own community buses, cycle tracks, traffic calming, and so on.

Skills are vital in empowering people to take charge of their own lives. The 'enabling strategy' has to start with *people*, not with places or geographical areas. People who are 'socially excluded' usually have multiple problems, and these need to be addressed 'in the round' with a multi-agency approach.

Our schools are ideally placed to provide this support. 'Family centres' have been pioneered in some deprived areas so that parents with very young children can come into school and get help with parenting skills and advice on home management and budgeting. On a visit to a scheme in a Cambridgeshire nursery school, I saw some of these parents preparing to gain vocational qualifications in child care and nursery nursing.

Many more of our schools could be turned into true 'community schools', but the power to manage them needs putting into the hands of all those in the community who could benefit from the facilities (whether in the evenings, at the weekends, or in the school holidays). The local education authority, as the democratically elected body, should oversee the strategic plan and be the 'enabler'.

Library, drama, music and sports hall facilities could all become a community resource. We could guard against private finance initiatives in schools that allow private contractors to exploit out-of-hours use of the premises by ensuring that their local communities are involved in negotiating the terms of such initiatives.

Recently I have been much involved in the politics of the environment. If this has taught me nothing else, it has taught me that we are all equal in the face of the destruction of the planet. Whatever agenda a centre-left government embraces in promoting social justice, it has to convince all our citizens that social justice involves challenging greed, waste and short-term thinking, and that *sustainability* has to become a shared goal.

Young people need to be directly involved in developing school sites into flagships for 'green' projects. How many schools have solar heating panels or high-grade insulation? Why can't they have on-site processing of waste and composting? Unused land could be used to train people to grow organic food. Courses for adult learners could give them the skills to develop and run such sustainable projects. Community enterprises creating jobs *and profits* could work out of school sites.

Other community facilities have this potential too. There are possible multiple uses for libraries, community halls, youth clubs, day centres and post offices. We have to stop just talking about 'joined-up thinking' and have some joined-up action.

For a centre-left government this model of citizens acting on their own behalf at community level should be the inspiration for a radical change in the governance of Britain. For a Britain of four nations, and an England of nine regions, we have far too much government by elites and hierarchies in London.

I believe Westminster should become a very much smaller operation. The nine English regions already supervised by the Regional Development Agencies should elect regional governments functioning much like the Scottish Parliament, with powers passed down from Westminster and from the innumerable regional quangos. And in turn, local government should be passing down power to parish councils, neighbourhoods and housing estates – even perhaps to individual high-rise tower blocks.

However, equality in Britain has another dimension beside that of tackling poverty, enabling our communities to revitalise themselves and underpinning this by radical constitutional change. A centre-left government must also assume a leadership role in changing public opinion on racism, sexism, homophobic attitudes, ageism and other forms of social injustice.

Women are not treated equally in our society. Even those black or Asian people who are wealthy are not treated equally by all our citizens. Nor are gay men or lesbians, transgender or disabled people. The elderly are too often victims of discrimination.

Discrimination against children in our society is in some ways the most distressing form of injustice. We don't even have a minister for children, whose rights and concerns are too often overlooked. Yet we live in a country where a baby is killed every fortnight, the mental health of children is deteriorating at an alarming rate, almost two-thirds of 12- to 15-year-olds claim to suffer some form of victimisation, and 75 per cent of children in care leave school with no formal qualifications.

A centre-left government has therefore to look at civil rights, and to ensure that we are at least all equal before the law.

We should begin by putting a Single Equality Act on the statute book. This would protect citizens against discrimination in a whole range of situations. It would make it illegal to discriminate on the grounds of gender, age, race, religion and sexual orientation.

To support the legislation we need a Single Equality Commission drawing together the work of bodies like the Commission for Racial Equality, the Equal Opportunities Commission and the Disability Rights Commission.

This has already been done successfully in Northern Ireland. The new Single Equality Commission would be a one-stop shop for employers seeking advice on how to become equal opportunity employers, and for citizens seeking redress after discrimination.

Public policy from a centre-left government needs to include a 'Social Justice Audit'. Just as Sir Donald Acheson's Independent Inquiry into Inequalities in Health has recommended that 'all policies likely to have a direct or indirect effect on health *should be evaluated in terms of their effect on health inequalities*', we could do with a requirement that all public policy should be checked to see whether it is likely to reduce inequalities and social exclusion. If not, the policy should be changed.

As part of the Social Justice Audit, the new Single Equality Act would impose on public authorities a positive duty to promote equality. They would have to monitor their performance on equality issues.

This would advance the cause of social justice by giving some 'socially excluded' citizens much better employment prospects and access to services. The economy could only benefit by releasing the potential of all these people.

Government sends signals to the public and to the press through its Ministers and the way they react to events. Punitive rules for asylum-seekers send out a racist message even if one is not intended. The absence of people in top positions who are women, or who belong to ethnic minorities, who are disabled, or gay or lesbian, or who are of the 'wrong' religion, send out the message – no doubt unintentional, but damaging nonetheless – that discrimination is backed by government.

A centre-left government needs to lead public opinion by making its commitment to social inclusion very explicit and by making it clear how much we all lose by excluding people from taking a full part in our society. Each person's exclusion diminishes the rest of us: we are (or should be) involved in humanity.

All in all, a centre-left government would have a lot on its hands. We are talking not about incremental, but radical change to transform Britain from a nation of subjects governed by elites and hierarchies into a society of citizens actively involved in developing their communities. We seek 'another country' where poverty is at an end and where difference is understood and respected.

A government which tackled poverty through taxation and funding, but which acted to enable citizens to bring about their own changes, developing decentralised forms of governance and introducing strong anti-discrimination legislation, would go a long way to secure these aims.

Such a centre-left government could create a climate in which privilege will become less and less acceptable as its citizens construct a socially just society.

17
Sustaining Development

Roger Levett

Mainstream politics has never quite known what to do with 'the environment'. To the average MP or councillor the term seems to encompass a huge jumble of disparate issues from the trivially parochial (dog mess, speed humps) to the ungraspably nebulous and abstract (biodiversity, ozone layer, climate change), united only by their intractability, lack of alignment to party positions, tendency for any action to infuriate some vociferous minority or other, and potential for electoral bad news. 'Sustainable development', with its talk of environmental limits to consumption, public goods and the difference between economic growth and quality of life, looks like a rival and alien political philosophy that breaks cherished taboos with an explicitly ideological and ethical challenge to the private choice and consumerism which the main parties have agreed to compete over delivering.

Sustainable development threatens to release socialism from Blair's closet, paternalism from Hague's, and collectivism from both. It makes the downwards Dutch auction of tax pledges look like a competition to score own goals, and turns both parties' European debates on their heads by making *political* solidarity the goal and *economic* integration the regrettably necessary price. Anyway, there are always more pressing issues like jobs, health, education and poverty. Wisest for sensible politicians to utter platitudes about the beauty of nature when asked, and otherwise leave 'the environment' well alone.

Michael Jacobs, who has incisively analysed this failure of 'the environment' to punch its weight, has argued that environmentalists should respond by dropping the sustainable development language and promoting 'environmental modernisation' instead. This portrays New Labour as some shy creature, a gazelle perhaps, which environmentalists have to entice and beguile into sampling its greens without frightening it off. To do this, we should select the sweetest morsels from the sustainability basket (especially the ones with aromas the creature is partial to, such as 'competitiveness' and 'technological innovation'), chop them up very small lest it gag on the lumps, souse them in a sweet sauce of 'modernisation' rhetoric, and then sit very quietly and patiently, avoiding any noise or sudden movement, hoping to tempt the elusive creature to sidle up and nibble at them.

This presents itself as the 'get real' approach for environmentalists who want to make a difference and not just feel pure. It may well have helped Jacobs and others get a hearing at Number 10 and secure substantial gains, notably the steady introduction of green taxes such as the climate change levy, tougher building regulations and the commitments on fuel poverty (although Britain's greatest environmental achievement ever, decisive leadership in international climate change negotiations, seems due more to the personal moral commitment of that refreshingly unmodernised politician John Prescott).

But 'environmental modernisation' will only remain a good tactic so long as environmental concerns remain marginal, sustainability perspectives obstruct more familiar policy goals, and the ruthless pursuit of inoffensiveness remains a requirement for political success. This chapter argues that none of these three assumptions will remain true far into the new century; and that therefore 'environmental modernisation' is a tactic whose time is already passing, and that it is now time for a new progressive environmental politics which puts sustainable development centre-stage.

First, the consequences of human environmental impacts are becoming hard to ignore. As Sarah Parkin balefully points out, the environment is doing its own canvassing. TV reports a positively biblical litany of storms and fires, floods and droughts, mudslides, desertifications, plagues and famines around the world. The over-cropping, unwise building, forest clearance and other human interferences that precipitate many of them are increasingly reported. The way 'once in a hundred years' freak events now seem to come round much more often must surely make the most complacent TV viewer start to suspect that there's something up.

Britain's middling latitude, equable climate, mixed-up weather and diverse terrain may well make climate change milder and more manageable here than, for example, in small island states that will vanish into the Pacific, in Bangladesh where tens of millions of people face being flooded off their land, or in the Ukrainian and North American grain belts which may become dust belts. And we will be able to buy ourselves to the front of the queue in any global food shortages: poor Africans and Asians will starve, not us. Britain may carry on complacently for some time unruffled by environmental disasters in faraway countries of which we know little.

But what if hundreds of thousands of British home-owners in low-lying and coastal areas received letters from their insurers saying regretfully they could no longer offer cover because of increasing flood or storm risks? The market value of uninsurable houses would plummet, dispossessing a swathe of Middle England, severely jolting the property-owning settlement and creating a furious new protest class overnight.

Or suppose the thousand-year surge that the Thames Barrier was calculated on arrives early? Even if evacuation plans worked flawlessly and nobody drowned, the shock of all the City's and Docklands' commerce paralysed and most of the Tube closed for months to be pumped out, would transform the political salience of global environmental questions. Moreover, climate scientists can't rule out the possibility of more drastic climate change here, if the Gulf Stream ceases to warm Britain's west coast, plunging us into Newfoundland winters without the buildings or infrastructure to cope.

These are speculations. But unless the overwhelming consensus of global climate science is wrong, it is only a matter of time until *something* of this gravity will hit ordinary British people so hard they will make the connections between policies, lifestyles and consequences that the environmental movement has hitherto failed to communicate beyond the broadsheet leader pages. Any politician, any party, that wants to be credible when this happens would be wise to start staking out a serious position on the global environment now. (After this chapter was first written, the October 2000 floods came close. However, their longer-term significance was largely successfully ignored amid the plucky bustle of sandbags and rubber dinghies, and only picked up by a few particularly thoughtful politicians such as Michael Meacher.)

So much for the first assumption that underpins 'environmental modernisation'. The second is that a sustainable development perspective thanklessly complicates and obstructs policy. But consider how evasive, Micawberish, *politically* unsustainable some current policies are.

For example, Labour has taken over John Gummer's 'flagship' planning policy of building at least 60 per cent of new houses on previously developed land. This already fails to provide any framework for managing the 'other' 40 per cent in an orderly or optimal way, makes land most available in regions where there is least housing demand, and flies in the face of most people's aspiration for low-density suburban lifestyles. And it defers bigger problems. Only so much land is left over from old industries, and only some of it is where people will buy houses. Once this is used up, further 'brownfield' housing will entail displacing live industry and commerce (already happening in high-value places like Clerkenwell) or replacing existing housing (often desirable but rarely adding to net capacity).

Rural land is also finite; as Mark Twain pointed out, 'they ain't making it any more'. Developers go for easy sites first, so rural house-building will have to be on increasingly contentious and problematic sites. For as long as government bases policy on finessing which bits of land get designated for market-led house-building in which order, the struggles we already see at all levels from regional planning guidance to individual developments can only get worse.

A sustainable development perspective would help first by acknowledging as banal common sense what is currently an unmentionable taboo: that in a small crowded island, housing can't keep expanding indefinitely without undermining other goals such as functioning, liveable settlements and uncluttered tranquil countryside, so sooner or later we will have to learn to deliver better living conditions without taking any more land.

This turns the policy spotlight on two areas. The first is improving the quality of urban life so that people who want clean air, safe streets, pleasant outlook and good local schools and services (and who does not?) do not feel they have to move to a low-density outer suburb to get them. There is no mystery about the changes required to achieve this, such as much less traffic, shops and employers back in town, lots of park keepers, street sweepers, bus conductors and such like keeping the public realm safe. They are currently blocked by other taboos about intervention and taxation.

The second, less familiar, spotlit topic is the amount of built space people feel they need for a good quality of life, and methods for reducing it. Policies to reduce the number of households who feel the need to devote one of their biggest and best rooms to storing at least one car would be an obvious priority: reclaiming garages for human use could free up as much built space as building a million new homes. Other measures might include encouraging letting surplus space to lodgers, reducing the transaction costs and barriers of trading up and down the housing ladder (for example by replacing stamp duty, a tax on moving, with capital gains tax on house sales, a tax on speculation), and encouraging a return to the shared (and space-efficient) provision of services such as laundry, bulk food storage, guest accommodation and play space and equipment that were the norm until recently.

Building housing at higher density (measured in *rooms* or *internal area* per hectare) achieves nothing if the housing is then sparsely occupied. Many big Islington terraced houses, textbook icons of desirable high-density property, are actually occupied by only one or two people. Families move out because of (among other things) high house prices, poor schools, and conservation policies that thwart efficient and convenient use of space. Thus changes in areas as diverse as letting law, property taxes, redistributive taxation more generally, city car clubs, parental choice in education (which actually means good schools' freedom to perpetuate their advantage by choosing pupils), retail monopoly and buildings conservation are as important for squaring the housing circle as housing and planning policies themselves. None are panaceas; many raise difficulties of their own; but together they could make tractable an area of policy which currently seems so refractory that the government can do little more than procrastinate, and where all the Conservatives can offer is abdication to local Nimbyism. And sustainable development's emphasis on promoting quality of life itself, and not misleading economic proxies for it such as GDP growth, makes them all thinkable.

Transport provides a second example. We have, as it were, a Millennium Dome of a transport policy: designed above all to be inoffensive to the greatest number of people, and hyped as 'better for everyone', a claim which (like the Dome's inflated visitor predictions) sets it up to disappoint. In aiming only to *slow* the rate of *increase* in traffic, it condemns the government just to interfere annoyingly, but ineffectually, with all the trends that will continue to lead to more traffic and all its problems, leaving both the motoring lobbies and the majority who support traffic reduction in opinion polls feeling sold short – just the style of footling, futile intervention that gets the nanny state a bad name.

Paradoxically a radical approach – as it were, a Tate Modern transport policy, not afraid to go all-out for excellence, and damn the critics – might prove more popular. Explicit, unapologetic, vigorous action to reduce car use could flip the current vicious circle into a virtuous circle where less traffic makes people happier to live and work in towns; reducing their need to drive; increasing public transport use; supporting better public transport services; allowing road space to be reallocated to cycling and walking, which more people would choose to do; putting shops to serve them back on to local streets, and so on. Developers would want to build in urban areas and near public transport anyway, so planning could work with the market rather than attempting to thwart it. The pieces of the integrated transport jigsaw would support and amplify each other, instead of fighting a losing battle of attrition and delay against pressures the government bottled out of confronting.

Again, the sustainable development perspective holds the key. The concept of quality of life enables us to argue that people will be *better off* if they have fewer cars, drive them less but can get to the things they need and want in life more quickly, easily, safely and healthily than before. This ought to be an *easier* vision for politicians to sell than the rather dreary one current policy implies which, unspun, is that the extra frustrations for motorists won't be too noticeable, the buses won't be too bad to use sometimes, we'll lose countryside to suburban development more slowly than we might have, and we'll try to reduce the number of villages that lose their post offices and banks by nudging them into doubling up with each other, and for that matter with the pubs, playgroups, sweetshops, churches, library vans and anything else that comes to hand. Er, that's it, as *Private Eye* would say.

Quality of life could get government off further hooks. Employment policy framed in terms of decent livelihoods and fulfilling occupations, instead of the false proxy of possession of a P60, could obviate government blackmailing people into taking demeaning call-centre jobs, bribing inward investors to create them (until somewhere else offers bigger bribes), and throwing huge 1970s throwback subsidies at rust-bucket industries such as volume car manufacturing doomed to eventual closure anyway by the logic of the government's own beloved globalisation. If we measured and aimed to improve *health* instead of *sickness treatment* we could achieve dramatic improvements at much less cost through, for example, diet and exercise changes.

Moreover, we would find policies in different areas 'joining up' of their own accord instead of having to struggle to stop them undermining each other. The approach to housing just sketched both depends on more sustainable transport behaviour and makes it possible. More walking and cycling and less noise and pollution would be good for health. A less competition-obsessed employment policy could concentrate on meeting local needs (reducing the travel intensity of the economy), provide more fulfilling and less stressful occupations (good for health), and encourage employment of the park keepers, bus conductors, station porters, and so on, which make sustainable travel (and the public realm more generally) safe and attractive. And so on.

But what of the third assumption? Didn't the overwhelming public support for the September 2000 fuel price protests prove the political folly, indeed impossibility, of messing with Middle England's private, consumerist interests? Didn't the absence (outside the *Guardian*'s comment pages) of even mention of the environmental case for higher fuel prices show that the only way sustainable development can possibly advance is by stealth, euphemism and indirection – proving the 'environmental modernisation' case?

Certainly the protests were depressing for anyone concerned for sustainable development. However the Three Day Week, Poll Tax and British ERM entry all show that dramatic political lurches can rebound in the opposite direction. The protests showed vividly that less car use could make life much nicer in lots of ways. The problems were all because the reduction in car use was forced, unprepared and chaotic, and could be avoided in a planned, managed transition. The crisis also showed how pathetically dependent our supposedly sophisticated civilisation is on one finite and insecure resource. The way panic-buying of petrol and food turned a blip into a crisis provided a glaring demonstration of how individually rational choices can add up to collective stupidity. These are all sustainability insights.

But the most significant lesson is political. The Conservatives made individual freedom to consume the cardinal goal of government. Blair added admirable social and public service goals but promised they could be delivered without cost or compromise to consumer freedom. The New Labour spin machine neurotically, obsessively, suppressed any criticism of the Thatcherite freedoms or even hinted that they might need to be constrained. No wonder that, when they realised the public goods were actually being financed by backdoor taxes on consumption, people felt the government had cheated on the deal it had offered them, and reacted with fury at being treated as idiots. If politicians encourage infantile political expectations – that we can have good public services *and* low taxes, rampant consumerism *and* environmental sustainability, parental choice *and* all local schools equally good – they must expect an infantile response when these expectations are disappointed.

It is time to rediscover and assert what was the obvious, accepted basis of politics until very recently: that many public goods carry private costs, and that consciously and explicitly negotiating the balance between the two is what politics is all about. If politicians candidly acknowledge this, we can rebuild the contract whereby we all consent to live with decisions irksome to our private interests (at least until the next election) in return for being governed by fair democratic process.

The fuel protests showed the alternative. The government really had no choice but to stand firm against them. However, it must now make some sort of response. Sustainable development offers a 'third way' between surrender and intransigence. No fuel tax cuts as such, but a substantial diversion of windfall revenues into measures to help people – particularly those genuinely worst hit by high fuel prices –

to increase their energy efficiency in general and reduce their dependence on petroleum in particular.

In sum, the case for sustainable development to be at the heart of progressive politics therefore runs thus. The shift in political attitude and rhetoric that sustainable development depends on – in particular, the recognition that private consumerism is only one goal among many – is needed anyway to restore grown-up politics as a respectworthy grown-up endeavour and save us from government by selfish interest group blackmail. Once this is accepted, sustainable development can offer promising approaches to a wide range of 'mainstream' political problems that otherwise look hopelessly intractable, starting with fuel prices themselves. And the environment is going to start to demand these approaches soon anyway.

This argument has centred on the doings of recent governments, and has therefore not yet mentioned the Liberal Democrats. They now have a crucial role in showing Labour how a progressive party can come to terms with sustainable development, and in helping them do so. Alone of the major parties, the Liberal Democrats have never gone infantile. In the 1997 election they acknowledged that better public services mean more tax, accordingly pledged 1p on income tax for education, and still doubled their MPs – a point Labour should remember in the next general election. Liberal Democrat councils like Sutton and Newbury have shown that consistent, explicit green programmes can be election winners. The worldview we now call sustainable development (and many of the specific policies mentioned in this chapter), equally alien and uncomfortable for Old Labour collectivism/producerism and New Labour individualism/consumerism, has been a familiar and thoroughly assimilated strand of Liberal Democrat thinking and policy since the mid-1970s.

The Liberal Democrats can thus supply three kinds of confidence which Labour lacks: *intellectual* ease with the new agenda, gained from long experience of dealing with sustainable development ideas and options as part of the normal policy debate within the party; *political* confidence borne of having fought and won elections with sustainable development policies, and *public* credibility from having long advocated (and, where able, implemented) policies which events are now beginning to vindicate – a record of principled staying power to contrast with New Labour's febrile opinion poll chasing.

These Liberal Democrat strengths will only help Labour come to terms with sustainable development if the 'project' of a progressive realignment of the two parties advances more generally. Sustainable development initiatives can help this happen, starting at the local level. Local Agenda 21 visioning processes all over the UK are arriving with remarkable consistency at the same sustainable development policy agenda. Community Planning – essentially the same thing with different terminology and statutory backing – is likely to reveal the same picture. In many local authorities, behind the party posturing, Labour and Liberal Democrat councillors have worked closely and loyally together to advance initiatives such as Local Agenda 21 and energy, cycling or recycling projects.

Outside the rituals of committee meetings there is often no detectable difference between what councillors from the two parties believe and want. Running sustainable development training sessions for groups of councillors, I have often been unable to tell who is from which party – except that a certain fidgety unease during discussions of the limitations of market individualism tends to betray the Tories. As councillors become MPs and party officials, they will bring not only first-hand experience of how a sustainable development perspective can help achieve what they want for their communities, but also of how much the two parties can have in common.

At national level, cross-party backbench alliances have already achieved excellent green legislation on, for example, household energy conservation and road traffic reduction. Cross-party select committees have produced a stream of cogent critiques that have forced the pace on environmental policy through the Major and Blair periods. Perhaps the question should not be whether the two parties can ever get together, but rather how much longer the fusty and discredited old habits of adversarial bickering will be allowed to obstruct it.

Perhaps, ironically, the fuel price protests will be the catalyst that accelerates the rapprochement. The threat of blackmail is forcing Labour off the fence on the side of democratic process, the social contract, and proud and explicit defence of indirect taxation (especially fuel taxation) for both the public services it buys and the behavioural incentives it gives. This is where the Liberal Democrats already stand. If the two parties can be mature enough to stand shoulder to shoulder rather than tread on each other's toes, the fuel protesters may achieve the exact opposite of their intention: a broad political movement for better quality of life, built explicitly on high fuel taxation, backed by the combined capabilities and credibility of both parties. Against this, the reversion to Thatcherite fatalism, abdication, neglect and atomisation currently offered by William Hague should have limited appeal.

In politics if not in paints, perhaps the best way to make green will be to mix red and orange.

18
Feminism Finds a Foothold in the Centre-Left

Harriet Harman

Feminist politics resides comfortably in centre-left politics. It is certainly more at home with us than it is on the right of politics. But its relationship with New Labour and the Liberal Democrats has evolved differently and it still poses a number of challenges to left-of-centre political traditions. A 'progressive century' worthy of the name must place at its core policies, practices and culture which enables equality across the sexes and which permits the centre-left to take and keep from the right the mantle of the political movement of the family.

In the recent past much has already changed to allow this to happen. The 'Old Labour' tradition was rooted in male organisation in the workplace, determined to improve the lot of men and their families, to challenge class inequality in the name of social justice and to tackle the inequality of the distribution of power and wealth. In the traditional manufacturing industries where the trade unions drew their strength, men were the breadwinners – or at least the principal breadwinners. It is, of course, the case that there is also a strong tradition of working-class women working outside the home. But for the most part, a woman only worked after she had children if the man could not earn the 'family wage'. So the family wage was a centrepiece of trade union bargaining. But it was a justification for inequality between men and women in pay and conditions. If men had to earn the family wage, then it stood to reason that women should receive less from collective bargaining. The family wage concept came under challenge from feminists in the 1970s as women began to identify themselves through their role at work as well as at home and women's wages had become an important and sometimes the sole income for their household.

An example of this challenge to the trade union view that women's work was less important came with a legal case brought by the Women's Rights Unit of the National Council for Civil Liberties in 1981 by Brenda Clarke. Brenda Clarke worked part-time in a West Midlands ammunition factory, Ely Kinnoch, which was making employees redundant. The Transport and General Workers' Union (TGWU) was negotiating the traditional terms of the redundancy – 'last in, first out'. But as was also traditional, the agreement was that before the 'last in first out' rule began to apply, the part-time workers all had to go first. Employment in Ely Kinnoch reflected the usual pattern of employment in that all the part-timers were women – trying to balance their home and work responsibilities. The trade union approach was that all the women had to lose their jobs before any men faced redundancy. Brenda Clarke, a member of the TGWU, challenged this, arguing, with her colleagues in the workplace and with the union, that the income of the women was very far from being 'pin money'. Worse than that, her union attacked her for allegedly harming the trade union movement. Undaunted, and with the support of all the part-timers in the factory, she took a case against the employer. Her union were joined as defendants in the Industrial Tribunal case as they were a party to the negotiated agreement that she argued was discriminatory and in breach of the Sex Discrimination Act provisions against indirect discrimination. She won, and thereafter it became accepted that discrimination against part-timers is unlawful. Later in the 1980s, the conventional wisdom in the trade union movement that women's work outside the home was not important, began to change.

Some 20 years on, the TGWU, on the wrong side in the Brenda Clarke case, have now become leading champions of women's rights at work. But then, women at work were seen by the trade union movement to be not only not as important as men at work, but also a potential threat to the movement. They were not so likely to be members of a trade union. If women were union members, they were less likely to be active and to attend evening meetings. So they were a potential 'weak link' in workplace solidarity.

This view was reflected in the Labour Party and in the Parliamentary Labour Party (PLP). Announcements in Parliament by the Tories of any new jobs created were met by Labour jeers that these were probably 'only part-time jobs'. When I entered Parliament in 1982 I was one of only 22 women MPs. When I raised concerns about lack of child care as an obstacle to women working, there were sneers; not only from the Tories but also from my own side. Women's issues were, as far as the PLP at the time were concerned, not politics.

Yet at the same time, the Labour Party, whose identity was rooted in and remained closely allied to the trade union movement, expressed itself as in favour of equality for all – including equality between men and women. Just as a tension emerged in the trade union movement between the claims of men and women at work, tensions emerged in the Labour Party with women's demands to participate on equal terms with men.

Though women arguing for equality had, I would argue, all the points of principle on their side, we were not powerful. Men dominated the party. And I believe it would have remained so, despite the gap between rhetorical principle and reality, had not women voters intruded into the argument. For even those in the Labour Party who could not be convinced on grounds of principle that women should be able to participate in the party on equal terms, became concerned by the evidence that Labour's loss of successive general elections was in large part due to women refusing to vote for what they saw as a male-dominated party. A Fabian pamphlet by Deborah Mattinson and Patricia Hewitt (1987) exposing women voters' dissatisfaction with the male face and priorities of Labour was the single most influential argument in persuading the party that it had to change, and feminise itself. Patricia and Deborah called for a target of 40 per cent women MPs and reserved places in the Shadow Cabinet for women, backing it up with research evidence that this is what women voters wanted. First Neil Kinnock and then John Smith introduced a programme which included requiring PLP members to vote for at least three women for the Shadow Cabinet and excluded men from competing for selection in half the seats that we hoped to win in the 1997 general election. Though the men in the leadership of the Labour Party in opposition readily acknowledged these arguments and determined to lead the necessary change in the party, for those men aspiring to become an MP or get elected to the Shadow Cabinet, yet not quite there, it was a greater challenge.

The 1993 Labour Conference voted for all-women shortlists. But it could not be said that this was as a result of our comprehensively winning the argument in the party for positive action for women. All-women shortlists became conference policy by being part of an omnibus modernising resolution whose chief aim was to introduce 'one member one vote' for selection of Labour parliamentary candidates. This resolution was passed by a conference which would not, I believe, have passed a stand-alone all-women shortlist resolution. But with strong support for one member one vote, and with John Smith insisting that this was a 'back me or sack me' resolution, Labour adopted all-women shortlists.

The result of the measures to increase the number of women at all levels of the party and to seek to communicate with women in the electorate closed the gap between our commitment to equality and our putting it into action. And it delivered a dramatic closure of the gender gap, which had kept Labour out of office for most of the last century.

The Liberal Democrats' commitment to equality between men and women is expressed in the same terms as Labour's. It is hard to distinguish Labour and Liberal Democrat policy documents from each other. But the key difference is that so far, Liberal Democrats have failed to put it into practice. Despite their strong 'in principle' commitment to equality, out of 71 Liberal, SDP and Liberal Democrat MPs over the last 20 years, only 7 have been women. The Liberal Democrats offer a number of reasons for their inability to make the quantum leap that New Labour women have made. They say that the Liberal Democrat tradition is more committed to its 'grassroots' nature than is New Labour. Whilst Labour does not always find it easy to impose an objective from the top (the choice of our candidate for Mayor of London being a case in point) it was possible to introduce all-women shortlists in half the seats that Labour hoped to win in 1997. Like Neil Kinnock and John Smith, both Paddy Ashdown and Charles Kennedy have backed resolutions which came to their party conference proposing positive action to increase women's selection. But despite the efforts of Liberal Democrat women such as Jackie

Ballard MP, all resolutions beyond the requirement of at least one woman on each parliamentary shortlist have been defeated. Liberal Democrats say that their conferences are more jealous of grassroots freedom of choice even if, as it does here, it frustrates a strategic Liberal Democrat objective. Liberal Democrats also cite a further problem of their having no 'safe seats'. Liberal Democrats argue that they cannot, as Labour do, identify a particular constituency for a woman as there are no Liberal Democrat seats as such. Liberal Democrat seats appear to belong to the individual who wins it for the Liberal Democrats rather than to the Party. They argue that traditionally, Liberal Democrats become MPs after decades of personal work at local level. Jenny Tonge MP, who is now the House of Commons' foremost champion of women's reproductive rights, is typical. She won Richmond after spending more than a decade on the local council, having fought and lost the parliamentary seat in 1992 before she won it in 1997 and never having sought selection elsewhere. Though this is not an unusual pattern for Labour MPs; it is typical for Liberal Democrats. So even if they could overcome the objections of their grassroots the Liberal Democrats claim it is harder to identify seats at national level and set some aside for women.

However, Mary-Ann Stephenson, director of influential feminist think tank the Fawcett Society has challenged the idea that the Liberal Democrats do not have target seats. 'The success of the Liberal Democrats at the last election was based at least in part on a strategy of targeting key seats as a focus for campaigning. And while some Liberal Democrat MPs have been elected following a relatively long period of nurturing a seat over several elections, others have been selected from outside their constituency.' She goes on to say that, 'All the parties give different reasons and different excuses for their relative lack of women, but in truth it comes down to the same thing, a lack of political will to take the action needed' (personal communication).

The price the Liberal Democrats have paid for this is that their commitment to women's equality and their policies to improve women's lives have remained invisible. Though they have had prominent women in the House of Lords championing feminist causes, notably Shirley Williams and Sally Hamwee, they have not had women in the House of Commons in sufficient numbers or for sufficient time to identify their party with feminism in the way they have made the connection between Liberal Democrats and Green politics. And one of their most prominent women, Liz Lynne, who was MP for Rochdale between 1992 and 1997, used her national profile to distance the party from feminism. Though, for the most part, Liberal Democrat commitment to equality for women appears to be very similar to Labour's, it has not been acted on and Labour has had the floor to itself, both facing the challenges and reaping the benefits of being the political home of feminism. Labour have therefore had the equality field to themselves.

Feminism should be a good fit with any party that believes in equality and in the redistribution of power or wealth – women are unequal, and have less power and wealth than men. But it posed a challenge to Labour, which has its roots in male workplace organisation, and it poses a challenge to some aspects of New Labour too.

Anna Coote (2000) identifies a number of broad areas where New Labour has yet to resolve differences with feminism. The first concerns the implications for women of New Labour's particular brand of 'big tent' politics – that the way to include all within it was to espouse a levelling-up approach where there are only winners and no losers. But, Coote argues, equality for women cannot be achieved by levelling up. If women are to have more political power, men will have less. If women are to achieve equality at work, men must take on more of the work at home. It is sometimes argued that equality for women does not take away from men, but helps them too. And it is also argued that more progress will be made towards women's equality if we emphasise the benefits for men so that they accept rather than resist change, seeing it as in their interests too. It is certainly in men's long-term interests that we are more equal. As progressives we believe that we are all better off in a more equal society, in more equal relationships. But in the shorter term women having more power means men having less. And though better child care and good domiciliary support for the elderly can substantially reduce the time needed for care of the elderly and children, there is, certainly within our culture, an irreducible minimum of family care and parenting that people feel must be done by parents themselves – which simply cannot be delegated.

Second, Anna argues that the New Labour leaning towards the traditional family potentially brings it into conflict with feminism. The New Labour model of the family is characterised as a stable marriage where parents supervise homework, prevent truancy, build social capital in the neighbourhood and convey appropriate values to the next generation. This model, without a strong assertion to the contrary, can reinforce the notion that it is women who are expected to makes the time for all these tasks.

A third area of friction between feminism and New Labour is the vanguardist nature of feminism. Feminism has always been ahead of popular opinion; calling for the vote, for equal pay and for the right to choose when to have children long before they were, as they are now, popular demands among women generally. There is friction if New Labour shying away from New Labour vanguardism, wants to go no further than what is understood to be the demands of 'Worcester Woman'. New Labour cannot pray in aid of Worcester Woman when resisting the demands of feminists. Though Worcester Woman may not have demanded all-women shortlists, she was reluctant to vote for male-dominated Old Labour and wants to see more, rather than fewer, women MPs. And she, too, is juggling her work and family responsibilities and needs government help to make that easier.

Whilst the relationship between feminism and New Labour and the Liberal Democrats is not always smooth, the right have what are at present insuperable problems accommodating the challenge of the change in women's roles and aspirations. For some time now, they have been torn between the belief that a woman's place is in the home and their desire to appeal to upwardly mobile, successful, working women. The logic of their free market position leads them to saying that business must recruit the best talent – women as well as men. And right-wing individualism applies to women as well as men – that is, the right to make the most of yourself. So the position of women provides another crunch point between, on the one hand, neo-liberalism, with its extreme free market position; and, on the other hand, traditional conservatism, with its concerns for the family.

Though they have sought, like their Republican counterparts in the US, identification with women's traditional role in the home as carers of children and the elderly, when in government they offered no financial help to make a reality for women of the 'choice' to stay at home. And they offered nothing (except private guilt) to the growing majority of women who are now going out to work. Even those in the Tory Party who want to reach out to working women fall foul of their inability to support new employment rights to time off work and the public investment in child care that working women need. So although there is, from some Tory women, a challenge to their party's 'hankering for the days of the subservient family woman' (Centre for Policy Studies 1999) those women do not offer policies which would support the working women through childcare and better rights at work.

Some Tory women have voiced concern about the lack of female representation in the Conservative Party in Parliament. 'The Conservative Party has been left behind by changes in society. A party ... whose public face is almost exclusively male, is not going to attract votes' (Centre for Policy Studies 1999). But the deep division amongst Tory women is blamed by the party for the failure of women themselves to select women in safe or winnable seats. Tory women seeking parliamentary seats blame other women grassroot members for asking them why they want to be an MP when they should be cooking their husband's dinner, and the Tory men say, 'it's not our fault, it's Tory women who don't want women MPs'.

So with their woman leader many years in the past and Tory women themselves fundamentally split, the centre and left have a headstart. So where should we go as we continue to respond to women's changing role, their increasing educational attainment, their rising aspirations and their continuing responsibilities at home?

We should continue with positive action to redress the lack of women in Parliament and in the leadership of the Labour Party. That remains right in principle, and if we slip back on our commitment to women's equality voters won't like it and will punish us. Evidence that this is already happening is beginning to emerge (Mattinson and Harman 2000). The lack of all-women shortlists for the next general election means that once again we are selecting an overwhelming majority of men. Out of some 30 seats where a candidate has been chosen to replace a sitting Labour MP, only two are women. And though we started out in 1997 with four women in 'frontline' Cabinet posts (Mo Mowlam, Margaret Beckett, Clare Short and myself), Clare Short is the only one left.

We should use the opportunity offered by 'late retirements' to ensure women standing in safe seats. When we are returned, as expected, to government after the next election we need to legislate to make it lawful for parties to choose to have all-women's shortlists. That will be a challenge to the Liberal Democrats both to support government action to change the law and to take advantage of the legality of positive action to improve their representation of women in Parliament. And Labour need to continue to build on the increase in the number of women Ministers and women Ministers in the Cabinet. 'Worcester Woman' might not have called for all-women shortlists but she likes the result and wants to see more, not fewer, women MPs and Ministers.

We should continue to support women in going out to work with better child care and more rights at work. Most mothers now go out to work. But child care remains inaccessible or unaffordable or both. The National Childcare Strategy has made a welcome start in tackling this but we need a quantum leap to deliver the range of choice and quality of child care that parents want. Child care is a missing part of the modern welfare state and needs to be seen as such. The nursery worker will, in the future, be seen to be as important to the economy as the train driver. And to support women in balancing their home and work responsibilities we need to improve the employment rights of new mothers with higher maternity pay, longer maternity leave and more flexibility at work.

We should introduce policies to give women the choice of staying at home as well as going out to work when children are young, and extend that role to fathers. When the state provided neither child care nor financial support to mothers staying at home with young infants, it could genuinely be argued that we were neutral in the debate about whether women should work or stay home when their children are young and that we are in favour of choice. Supporting child care makes the choice of working available to women who previously couldn't afford, or didn't trust the quality of, child care. But we now have to tackle the problem of the lack of choice for women of staying at home when their children are very young. And that means financial support for women in staying at home in the first three years. This is not a 'right-wing' agenda. It is women in low-income families who are forced back to work the earliest because of inadequate maternity pay. It is the poorest women who cannot afford to stay off work until their youngest child starts school, even if they want to. Mothers in well-off families can afford this choice. In Scandinavian countries it is not 'left wing' to help women go out to work and 'right wing' to give them a choice to stay at home. Centre-left governments there have ensured real choice by generous state support for both staying at home and child care. We should not shy away from the staying at home agenda. If we genuinely support parental choice in how women care for their infants, we should pay for it. We should extend the choice of staying at home to fathers too. Paid time off when children are young would enable fathers to be involved with their children from an earlier age, and there is growing evidence that men want a better work–home balance. And it would help mitigate the temptation for employers to discriminate against women employees because they have rights to time off that men don't.

We should offer robust and practical, secular family policy. Women want to see the political agenda take up their concerns about the family. But family policy should focus on practical support for families with children, irrespective of the marital status of the parents. I argue this for five reasons. First, to favour marriage as the best form of family inevitably stigmatises children who are in other sorts of families, such as lone-parent families and step-families, for instance. You cannot argue that one is best without judging as second best those who do not conform to the favoured model of family.

Second, there is no evidence from anywhere in the world that government support for marriage makes any difference to the divorce rate – so supporting marriage makes governments look ineffective. Third, supporting marriage opens government to charges of hypocrisy when politicians and Cabinet Ministers don't conform to the family pattern they recommend to their citizens. Fourth, though women would accept male politicians giving practical help with managing their family responsibilities, they are suspicious of them telling them how to lead their lives. And finally, it distracts from a practical, 'secular' family policy which supports families with children irrespective of the marital status of their parents.

We should change the way we approach policy development so that gender analysis can contribute at every level. The entry of women into the labour market, together with the globalisation of economic activity and the new technologies, demands a new approach to policy making. The traditional distinction between social and economic policy is unhelpful in a knowledge-driven economy, where wider educational opportunity is an economic imperative as well as a desirable social objective. When the success of an economy depends on its 'human capital', the nurturing and developing of that human capital is an economic imperative as well as a social objective. When the labour market comprises women as well as men, the neat separation between economic policy – work outside the home – and social policy for issues inside the home is not possible. What goes on in the home – previously seen as a social policy issue, or not even a legitimate public policy issue at all – becomes important for what has been traditionally regarded as the economic as well as the social agenda. As Patricia Hewitt MP, Minister for Small Business, so neatly puts it, 'Home is where the human capital is' (Hewitt 2000). Thus child care, long understood by many to be important for child development, becomes essential as part of the economic infrastructure, as necessary to enable women to get to work as the roads and railways on which they travel.

This is an agenda which is very hard for the right to adopt. But it should be obvious for the centre and left. A progressive century should deliver economic efficiency and social justice. Women's equality is key to both.

References

Centre for Policy Studies (1999) 'Conservative Women'. London: Centre for Policy Studies.

Coote, A. (ed.) (2000) *New Gender Agenda*. London: IPPR.

Hewitt, P. (2000) 'Social Justice in the Knowledge Economy'. [Speech], St Antony's College Oxford, 28 January.

Mattinson, D. and Harman, H. (2000) 'Winning for Women', Fabian pamphlet. London: Fabian Society.

Mattinson, D. and Hewitt, P. (1987) 'Women's Votes the Key to Winning', Fabian pamphlet. London: Fabian Society.

19
Family Policy: Opening Up Choice

Ruth Kelly

Family policy has signally failed to keep up with the times. It is one of the casualties of our adversarial political system, one of the issues which has become part of a too-often simplistic party political knockabout. In no other European democracy is family policy seen as a matter for partisan advantage as it is in Britain. In the more consensual political systems of continental Europe, with Parliaments and governments elected by proportional representation, family policy is set for the longer term. It is in that context that a progressive family policy could emerge; one that opens up choice for men, women and children. In the last ten years, family life has changed beyond all recognition, with a dramatic increase in the number of mothers of pre-school children taking part in the workforce and a widening divide between families in which both parents work more than they wish, and those in which nobody works at all.

Few parents feel able to choose the work–home relationship appropriate for them and their children. The current system does not support women's choices for combining work and family responsibilities in the way that suits them, and offers hardly any choice at all to men. The result is that children are suffering from inadequate and insecure care; and society is suffering the consequences of the stresses on relationships, family breakdown and juvenile delinquency. Family policy must now be reframed to support families and their choices, as well as to take into consideration the welfare of children.

The impact on children

The choices made by parents about the balance between paid work and care have a direct impact on the well-being of children. The research on the need for 'secure attachments' for children in the early years is well known in the field of child psychology. A recent US report which provides the most extensive survey and synthesis of recent research on children's developmental needs concludes that 'how children function from the pre-school years all the way through adolescence and adulthood hinges in large part on their experiences before the age of three',[1] with the research pointing to the fact that secure attachments are particularly important for babies. It is now virtually indisputable that young children need individual attention from a parent or carer who is reliable and responsive to their individual needs.

For some parents, the answer is to use formal child care. But for very young children, there are many problems to be addressed. First, it is perhaps not surprising that evidence from the Thomas Coran Institute suggests that care in external centres or by childminders is not in general as good as care provided by parents or relatives (although it can be) – partly because children who attend day care have much less one-to-one interaction with adults, and partly because their care is less continuous and the commitment of the carer is often less.

Second, the choice of formal day care is extremely limited. Table 19.1 shows how few public child care places there are in the UK compared with other industrialised countries.

Denmark, Sweden and Finland currently have the highest proportion of very young children in publicly funded child care, while the UK has just 2 per cent of 0–2s in publicly funded child care. The Day Care Trust has estimated that there is a significant 'child care gap' with as few as one place for every eight children – and the gap is much wider for younger age groups.

Third, most formal day care arrangements remain prohibitively expensive for the majority of families, with costs much higher the younger the child, forcing parents to rely on informal care from relatives for their children while they are at work. Many parents – particularly mothers – returning to work feeling extremely guilty about leaving their children.

Table 19.1   Public child care provision

Country	Guaranteed child care coverage (0–2 years)	Guaranteed child care coverage (3–5 years)	% children (0–2) in publicly funded child care	% children (3 to school age) in publicly funded child care	% children in publicly funded after-school care
Australia	None	None	2	26	n/a
Belgium	0–2	None	20	95	n/a
Canada	None	None	5	35	n/a
Denmark	0–2	3–5	48	85	29
Finland	0–2	3–5	32	59	n/a
France	2	3–5	20	95	n/a
Germany	None	None	2	78	4
Italy	None	3–5	5	88	n/a
Luxembourg	None	None	2	58	2
Netherlands	None	None	2	53	n/a
Norway	None	None	12	40	n/a
Sweden	>18 months	3–5	32	79	34
UK	None	None	2	38	<1
US	None	None	1	14	<1

Source: Gornick et al., *Journal of European Social Policy* (1997).

Fourth, whatever the merits of various child care arrangements, the majority of mothers say they wish to remain at home when their children are young. Indeed, according to the DfEE, 87 per cent of mothers of pre-school age children said they preferred to look after their own children; and, if money were not a problem, two-thirds of employed mothers with small children would prefer to stay at home[2] (although these figures switch around sharply once the youngest child starts school).

Perhaps the best way of ensuring appropriate care for children is to trust parents' instincts about what is best for them and their families.

Valuing care

Although many mothers say they would like to stay at home with their young children, many feel that this option is not sufficiently valued by the government or, indeed, by society at large. Recent focus groups run by Deborah Mattinson[3] for Mori and the national

Listening to Women consultation exercises run by the Women's Unit also suggest that women want to be valued at what they consider to be their most important role (Mums matter), and that they think the Government has emphasised work at the expense of valuing caring. As the National Family and Parenting Institute have found, 'in all the debate, parents' voices are faint'.[4]

In addition, many parents feel under intense *financial* pressure to return to work as quickly as possible, often working longer hours than they wish and coming home stressed and tired. The facts are striking:

- one in eight employees works more than 48 hours a week and a third of employees works over 40 hours a week (plus four hours' travelling time)
- over half of all mothers of children under five work, including one in ten women who return to work before the end of 14 weeks' maternity leave (for financial reasons)
- fathers, particularly new fathers, spend very little time at home with their children
- 48.3 per cent of men and 48.5 per cent of women employees experience conflict between work and family
- half of all British workers arrive home exhausted.

For a long time, women have realised the difficulty of combining work and family life, with two in five of women in the Listening to Women exercises saying they thought that all employers should be required to offer flexible working hours and part-time work to mothers in paid work with a pre-school child. Above all, what women say they want is for their choices about how to care for their children to be respected and supported.

What should the government do?

The government has started to recognise the acute pressures faced by many families, concentrating so far on providing practical financial support for parents and investing in the first National Childcare Strategy.

Parents in low-income jobs have been helped to boost their earnings with the introduction of the national minimum wage, the Working Families Tax Credit (WFTC), the new Integrated Child Credit and the Childcare Tax Credit. In addition, child benefit has been significantly raised, providing additional financial support to all families with children. The government has also pledged to introduce free nursery places for all three- and four-year-olds, and is committed to creating child care places for a million children within four years. These steps will undoubtedly make a significant difference to the lives of millions of people.

However, many of the government's current policies implicitly value labour market participation for all families more highly than looking after one's own children, even when children are very young. For example, the Childcare Tax Credit is a substantial subsidy to low-income parents at work who use registered child care, but provides no support to families in which the mother or father opts out of the labour force for a period to look after their children. Other disincentives for parents to care for young children include:

- individual taxation, which, while popular among many working women, means that the tax system is biased against one-earner couples
- the Children's Tax Credit, which is available to Family A in which both parents earn £30 000 a year, but not to Family B in which one parent earns £35 000 and the other stays at home to look after young children/an elderly or sick relative, shares this bias
- by placing a premium on one parent working over 30 hours a week, the WFTC penalises two parents who each choose to work part-time and share child care.

Nor is the work environment conducive to responsible parenting. Despite recent modest improvements (the lengthening of maternity pay from 14 to 18 weeks) maternity provision in the UK is inadequate, lagging up to 20 years behind provision in many European states. At one of the most demanding times in women's lives, they are entitled to only six weeks leave at 90 per cent of their salary, followed by statutory maternity pay of £60.20 a week for twelve weeks. Many women are forced back to work before the end of their official maternity entitlement for financial reasons, and often forced to give up breastfeeding at the same time.

Once back at work, both parents struggle to cope with the competing demands of family and workplace. Britain is one of just six EU countries not to provide financial support for parents of young children who wish to take up their new right of parental leave, for example, and there are comparatively few incentives for firms who wish to offer flexible working to their employees.

Table 19.2 shows Britain's position on maternity pay and parental leave in the international context.

Table 19.2   Maternity leave and parental leave

	Maternity leave (weeks)	Wage replacement rate (% wage)	Paid parental leave (weeks)
Austria (1994)	16	100	104
Australia	12	60	52
Belgium (1993)	15	75–82	260
Canada	15	60	0
Denmark (1994)	18	90	26–52
Finland (1994)	17.5	45–66	Up to 156
France (1993)	16–26	84	156
Germany (1990)	14	100	104
Greece (1993)	16	100	0
Ireland (1993)	14	70	0
Italy (1991)	22	80	26
Luxembourg (1989)	16	100	0
Netherlands (1993)	16	100	208 (part-time)
Norway	18	100	26
Portugal (1993)	18	100	0
Spain (1993)	16	75	0
Sweden (1994)	12–24	90	78
United Kingdom (1993)	14	46	0
United States	6	60	0

Source: Gornick et al., *Journal of European Social Policy* (1997).

We now need a package of policies which enhance families' choices about the appropriate care for children and the balance between work and home life.

Opening up choice: a way forward

For those parents who both wish to pursue careers, the government's main priority ought to be making the work–life balance easier, enabling men and women to fulfil their responsibilities in the home. Many commentators have made the case for:

- better maternity leave and pay
- paid parental leave[5]
- flexibility at work for dual-earner couples
- a massive expansion in good quality, affordable child care
- the right to return to work part-time after maternity leave.

These options are currently being considered by the government in its open-ended review of maternity provision and parental leave. But there is a strong case for completely rethinking financial support for parents in the early years of a child's life. There are four main forms of financial support for children at the moment: maternity pay, child benefit, the Working Families Tax Credit and the Childcare Tax Credit.[6] Child benefit supports all parents – in or out of work; while maternity pay and the Childcare Tax Credit provide significant financial support to families in which the mother was in employment before childbirth and returns to work within 29 weeks of a birth. The WFTC provides some support for families in which one parent stays at home to look after children – but to enable one parent to exercise a real choice to stay at home in the early years, the choice between one parent working or staying at home needs to be broadly financially neutral.

One way of achieving this aim would be to scrap the Childcare Tax Credit in the early years, and replace it with a much higher value child benefit; this flat-rate payment would support parents who choose to stay at home with their pre-school children and allow others who wish to buy in child care to do so and take part in the labour market.

A higher rate of child benefit for children aged up to three, for example, would have the following additional advantages:

- by allowing parents to exercise choice, it would put children first (as the best people to look after children in the early years are those that *want to*)
- it would help the government to achieve its child poverty targets
- it does not discriminate between family type, supporting lone parents as well as couples

- it is gender neutral and does not discriminate between mothers and fathers, either of whom could choose to take responsibility for child care
- by enabling more parents to stay at home with young children, it would, at a stroke, address the lack of child care places for the under threes
- it helps make work pay – that is, it does not deepen any poverty trap
- a universal benefit, it would appeal across income groups
- it would address the gender gap opening up between women's and men's support for the government.

Of course, a much higher rate of child benefit for the under threes of, say, £50 or £100, would be expensive, but it would send a strong practical signal that the government is committed to the family, to parental choice and to children.

Notes

1. *Starting Points: Meetings the Needs of our Youngest Children*, New York: Carnegie Corporation, 1994.
2. Department for Education and Employment, 1994/95 Family and Working Lives Survey, DfEE, 1996.
3. Deborah Mattinson, 'Worcester woman's unfinished revolution; what is needed to woo women voters?', in Anna Coote (ed.) *New Gender Agenda*, London: IPPR, 2000.
4. National Family and Parenting Institute, 'Is Britain Family-Friendly? The parents' eye view', National Family and Parenting Institute, 2000.
5. See 'Plugging the Parenting Gap', London, Fabian Society, 2000, in which I argue for a flat-rate payment to parents of £150 a week when on parental leave.
6. The Integrated Child Credit will be introduced in 2003, bringing together the different strands of support for children including the Working Families Tax Credit, Income Support and the Children's Tax Credit (which will replace Married Couples Allowance from April 2001).

20
More Health, Less Service

Anna Coote

Imagine a National Health Service at ease with itself and the nation. Staff are highly motivated, well trained and adequately rewarded. Buildings are gleaming and efficient. Technologies are harnessed to optimal effect. Hospitals are seamlessly linked with intermediate and long-term care. Waiting times are minimal. Standards are universal. Winter pressures, staff shortages and 'postcode prescribing' are a distant memory. Patients everywhere are satisfied.

This is the vision that seems to have inspired the Prime Minister's announcement of an extra investment of £19.4 billion over four years to create a 'health service fit for the 21st century'. The hurriedly crafted NHS Plan, published in July 2000, set out a programme of 'modernisation' aimed at spending the new money in accordance with ten 'core principles'. Among much else, the principles commit the NHS to providing 'a universal service for all based on clinical need, not ability to pay' and 'a comprehensive range of services' shaped around 'the needs and preferences of individual patients, their families and their carers'. The Plan restates the government's commitment to funding the NHS out of taxes. 'Investment and reform', it says, 'are the twin solutions to the problems the NHS faces'.[1]

There is every chance that, once set on the trajectory mapped out in the Plan, the NHS will improve. After years of relative neglect, it badly needs an injection of resources. But the reforms are essentially restorative, not radical. Their ambition is to rescue and resuscitate a national treasure, rather than prepare for a fast and bumpy ride ahead. They were devised at a time of economic stability, when the Chancellor's coffers were brimming. They focus on technocratic fixes to enhance management and performance within the service, to clarify partnerships with other sectors, and to improve relationships between patients and clinicians. One thin chapter on 'improving health and reducing inequality' appears loosely connected with the rest of the Plan.

The Plan itself is only a stage in the restorative process and will doubtless be succeeded by other documents. The detail of it should concern us less than the overall approach of policy makers. Health is an essential component of citizenship. It can determine whether or how we participate in society – learning; working; moving from place to place; enjoying life with family, friends, neighbours; exercising our democratic rights. At the very least, therefore, the goals of a progressive politics must include an equal chance for all to live a healthy life within the limits of avoidable risk. The aim of this chapter is to consider how far health policy in 2001 is shaping up to the requirements of a progressive century. What is driving the agenda? What dangers and opportunities lie ahead? How should these be addressed?

At the turn of the century, health policy remains wedded to the post-war model of a powerful and protective state. The NHS is the most complete expression of that vision, having survived the Thatcher and Major years with just a few dents and scratches. It is a single institution, controlled from the centre, and expected to provide a universal, cradle-to-grave service financed wholly out of public funds. It looks after us when we are in need. It cures and cares and saves our lives. At least, that is the powerfully seductive idea that has won and sustained devoted support across the political spectrum for more than 50 years.

The strength of the idea has not been matched by strength of performance. From being a source of national pride, the NHS has become a perpetual headache – for patients, for health professionals and for policy makers. Wards are dirty, staff are demoralised, waiting lists are intractable, and management systems are paralysed by an apparently unstoppable flow of organisational change and ad hoc initiatives issued from the centre. The media revel in scandals and tragedies arising from clinical malpractice, managerial incompetence and variations in access to services and standards of care. In actual fact, many aspects of the service function well, and in some parts of the country there are far fewer problems than in others. But over the last ten years a new idea has taken root alongside the old one. Not only is the NHS an idealised source of cure and care; it is also in deep crisis. It is failing to meet the nation's needs and, at worst, it is even a threat to health.

Diagnoses abound and, broadly, there are three main lines of analysis. The first takes the view that the main problem afflicting the NHS is money, or lack of it. If only we can 'catch up' with health systems on the continent in terms of per capita expenditure, we can save the NHS. The second maintains that the problem is essentially managerial: money must be put to work wisely. What really matters is identifying and spreading effective management systems. The third diagnosis is that the system is buckling under the weight of demand and 'hard choices' must be made about what the NHS can and cannot provide. Services must be rationed, one way or another. All these arguments are familiar. They are not mutually exclusive and it is perfectly reasonable to suggest that the NHS needs more money, better systems for planning and delivery, and some means of setting priorities and allocating resources accordingly. However, all three 'solutions', like the NHS Plan itself, are trapped in the past. They imply that, with a bit of tweaking, the NHS can be saved for the nation and all will be well with the nation's health. Not so – for two reasons. One is that the model of health care that is supposedly being 'saved' is unsustainable in the medium and long term. The other is that the nation's health does not depend to any great extent on the NHS.

As citizens of an increasingly secular 'developed' world, we have come to expect that, if anything can be done to save us from injury or disease and lengthen our lives, then we have a right to it. We have also grown accustomed to a low tax burden. Our desire for longevity feeds the endeavours of science and business to find new ways of cheating death and disease – and there appear to be infinite possibilities, each with its own significant price tag. The more we get, the more we want. Demand follows an upward curve, but this is a public service, not a commercial enterprise. In the short term, pouring more money into the service and running it more intelligently should help to improve standards and restore public confidence. But that in turn is likely to stimulate rather than diminish expectations. When the economy falters (as it surely will) and Treasury funds are no longer in surplus, it will not be possible to keep supply in step with demand. Raising more taxes for the NHS carries high political risks, especially in times of recession, and requires a trade-off with other sectors – such as education, transport or policing – that may also be in dire need of more public funds. Further deep crises will ensue, and will prove just as intractable as the problems dogging the NHS at the turn of the century.

Various rationing formulae have been debated since the early 1990s. Some are already in use, more or less covertly. These include limiting what is available to older people, favouring patients most likely to benefit in terms of years and quality of life, and letting clinicians decide whose need is greatest, putting less urgent cases to the back of the queue. More radical options include defining a basic health care package to which everyone is entitled and charging for everything else, with new therapies subjected to rigorous appraisal before being admitted into the package. All are controversial and fraught with ethical and technical difficulties. Can age discrimination be justified? Can individuals' 'quality of life' be assessed by anyone other than themselves? How far should doctors be allowed to 'play god' by deciding whom to treat first, or who should be denied expensive new therapies? A basic package would penalise the poor, who would be unable to purchase the extras. Those who are better off – who are also healthier and more inclined towards elective treatments and complementary therapies that are likely to be excluded from the package – may start asking why they should pay taxes for a service that does not give them what they need, thereby unravelling the consensus on which support for the NHS is based.

However, the main difficulty with rationing, as with 'investment and reform', is that it remains within a charmed circle of assumptions about the nature and role of a national health service. Chiefly, these are that the government's main contribution to the health needs of the population is to provide a clinical service to deal with illness, and that the NHS – though periodically in crisis – is an enduring symbol of the nation's warm heart and good sense. Governments must give priority to showing that it is safe in their hands, since they are more likely to be judged by the health of the NHS than by the health of the population. Politicians meddle with its awesome identity at their peril. And its identity has certain, fixed component parts, welded into place by a compound of tradition and sentimental representations in the mass media: high-tech hospitals, tumultuous emergency services, heroic medics and (of course) an overriding mission to save lives.

Beyond the charmed circle there are vital questions that deserve to be central, rather than marginal, to health policy. What must be done to ensure that every individual has a fair chance of enjoying good health? And what might a truly modern health system look like – were it not weighed down by the concrete boots of its historic symbolism?

Over the years since the NHS was founded, two parallel and contradictory problems have emerged. One, which has been well aired, is the *inverse care law*, whereby better-off people expect more and get more from the NHS than those who are less well off. The other, which is less often discussed, may be described as the *inverse health law*, whereby people become healthier as their circumstances improve, for a range of reasons, and therefore need (as distinct from want) less health care than those who are relatively disadvantaged. If health is an essential component of citizenship and equity a basic principle underpinning progressive politics, then these two problems must be addressed as a matter of priority.

There is overwhelming evidence that avoidable risks to health are unevenly and unfairly distributed.[2] If you are poor, from a minority ethnic background or male, your chances of early death are far greater than if you are white, middle-class or female. And things have been getting worse. The average life expectancy of a man in the lowest social group is 9.5 years shorter than that of a man in the highest social group. In 1972, the gap was 5.5 years. The comparable figures for women are 6.4 and 5.3 years. These figures are just the tip of a very large iceberg.

The root causes of illness and premature death are by now widely understood and they have little to do with health services. They include levels of education and income; standards of nutrition and housing; opportunities for exercise; clean air and water; a minimum of hazards at work, at home and in the streets; freedom from fear, anxiety and stress; strong, affirming relationships and social networks, and a sense of control over one's own life and destiny. A government committed to equity in health must be prepared to tackle these 'upstream' issues to prevent the accumulation of risk.

There is well documented evidence that better-off, better-educated people living in more affluent areas have better access to the NHS and make more use of it.[3] But even striving for greater equality of access to health services will do relatively little to achieve equity in health, for those who are most disadvantaged in society not only get an unequal share of health services, they also get ill earlier and more often. The main goal must be to ensure that they have an equal chance of *not* needing to be treated for illness or injury.

One of New Labour's key aims, declared in 1999, is 'to improve the health of the worst off in society and to narrow the health gap'. The White Paper, *Saving Lives: Our Healthier Nation*, acknowledges that 'poverty, low wages and occupational stress, unemployment, poor housing, environmental pollution, poor education, limited access to transport and shops, crime and disorder, and a lack of recreational facilities all have had an impact on people's health'.[4] This is a dramatic improvement on the position of the Tories, who would not allow any mention of health inequalities in official circles. There are, however, aspects of New Labour politics that mitigate against a progressive approach to health.

The most obvious is the prevailing obsession with the NHS, already described. The Department of Health is effectively the Department of the NHS. Of the £45 billion it spends in a year, 98 per cent goes to the NHS.[5] The Secretary of State derives power and status from the size of the NHS budget, not from the formidable job of reducing health inequalities. His political future will depend on how far he can cut waiting lists and improve cardiac and cancer services, not on how far he can increase the life expectancy of the poor. The Minister responsible for public health is low in the departmental hierarchy, with a small share of the budget and commensurate power.

Preoccupation with the NHS is reinforced by the strong interests of the clinical professions, who bear the brunt of public and political expectations and are bound to want a bigger and better service. It is also embedded in a superficial view of public opinion, linked to New Labour's electioneering strategy: this focuses on swing voters in key marginal constituencies and what will make them support the party on polling day. It is a reductive and reactive strategy. By and large, the 'swing' voters are not those most at risk of ill-health, who tend to live in safe Labour seats and seldom vote anyway. But they are among those who care passionately about the state of the NHS and the length of its queues. This prompts government to promise it will pump more money into health services and cut waiting lists. It is then trapped by its pledges – there is one problem (the NHS) and one solution (invest-and-reform) – which determine priorities for funding and action. The point is not that queues should not be shortened, or that money should not be spent on improving services, but that the cart is being put before the horse. There is some evidence that the views of even the middle-class electorate are more sophisticated about the need to tackle the causes of ill health than routine polling suggests.[6] But there are no real incentives or opportunities to engage the public in informed discussion or negotiation, or to encourage voters to support a more complex and challenging agenda.

Another problem is New Labour's enduring preference for strong central control. An agenda for health that addresses the 'upstream' causes contains some elements that suit a top-down, *dirigiste* approach, and some that do not. For example, if poverty is part of the problem, as it surely is, a government can raise benefit levels and create jobs by pulling levers it directly controls. It would be fair to say that the Blair–Brown government has made a valiant effort on this front. The 'new deals' to get people off benefit and into paid work, the minimum wage, the Working Families and Childcare Tax Credits, the National Childcare Strategy, and the increases in child benefit, amount to an extensive programme to improve the life-chances of those who are poorest and most vulnerable to ill-health. Likewise, if crime and fear of crime are linked with poor physical and mental health (and evidence suggests they are), a strong government can ratchet up policing levels, spot-fine hooligans, impose curfews and imprison perpetrators of domestic violence. Law-abiding citizens may thus sleep more easily in their beds, and there may be fewer cases of injury and depression – although the knock-on effects on the health of young males subjected to this kind of treatment could be highly damaging.

A strong, centralising government will find it much harder to respond to evidence – which is persuasive – that people's sense of control over their lives has an important bearing on their health.[7] Powerlessness and low self-esteem are significant predictors of morbidity and premature death. A government that wants to improve health and reduce health inequalities will have to find ways of empowering individuals and communities, especially those who are poor and socially excluded. This is partly about giving people a greater say in how they are treated when they are ill. It is also about building the capacity of disadvantaged groups to decide and act for themselves, on their own turf and on their own terms.

New Labour is famously committed to tackling social exclusion and launched in 2000 a major strategy for neighbourhood renewal.[8] There is firm government support for building 'social capital' and the concept of 'community development' has been put back on the policy map, after two decades of being demonised as the work of long-haired subversives. Devolution to Scotland, Wales and Greater London has shifted some prerogatives away from Westminster. But at the same time, New Labour has no qualms about concentrating powers in Downing Street to control the development and implementation of its policies. Witness, for example, the growing battalions of special advisers and other appointees who have more leverage in decision making than all backbench MPs, most senior civil servants and many ministers.[9] There are fewer checks on the power of a British Prime Minister with a large majority in the House of Commons than in most Western democracies.

Central planning and nanny-statism may have become unfashionable, but they have been replaced by a fervent attachment to target setting, performance measurement and 'evidence-based' policy and practice. At one level this is to be welcomed: we all want to know 'what works', and how far the government's policies are delivering results. But a danger with this approach is that it discourages interventions whose outcomes cannot easily be pinned down and counted. Most efforts to develop and empower communities depend on grassroots activities that do not lend themselves to conventional forms of evaluation or measurement. They are messy and indeterminate; their impact on morbidity and mortality rates is often indirect, or too slight to be statistically significant, and may not be felt in any measurable way within a decade.[10] Furthermore, the focus on 'hard' evidence requires a considerable degree of central control over how targets are set as well as over the processes of monitoring, measurement and evaluation. This, in turn, limits the ways in which public funds are spent on health-related measures.

Can a party with entrenched centralising tendencies and a long attachment to state power live with the consequences of policies aimed at building strong and powerful communities? If you enable individuals and groups to shape their own destinies, you cannot be sure they will use their power to do as you wish. You cannot set out to give people more skills, confidence and agency, and yet expect to command and control their behaviour. A vibrant associational life is a sure sign of a 'strong community', but no guarantee that the government's policy goals will be faithfully pursued. Indeed, the stronger a community, the more likely it is to think and act for itself. A successful strategy of empowerment will bring more geographical variations and increasingly uncontrollable and unpredictable results. It is hard to see how this can be reconciled with the drive to measure outputs against specific targets, or with New Labour's attachment to a uniform service, or with its manifest urge to augment the authority of the centre and develop a presidential style of government.

All this makes it easier to understand New Labour's temptation to focus its reforming zeal and hefty resources on the NHS. It may be a big headache, but at least it can still be given orders from Whitehall, with some expectation of obedience. It is a large state-run machine, underpinned by universalist principles: comfortable territory for the party that ushered in the welfare state. Its core business is relatively susceptible to scientific methods of evaluation. And of course, the voters love it – or, at least, love to worry about it.

We should not have to choose between promoting health and improving health services. Both goals are necessary and should be achievable. Indeed, it is doubtful whether either can be reached independently of the other. But the latest plans for improving services are essentially conservative and greatly overshadow plans to improve health.

It makes no sense to go on shoring up an institution in ways that inhibit it from meeting the needs of the future. The NHS Plan talks robustly about 'modernisation', but really it is an old love song. More doctors, more nurses, more hospitals and clinics, more patient-centred health care, more autonomy to successful trusts. It conveys little sense of the rapidly shifting social, economic and environmental circumstances with which all health systems must engage. There is almost no mention of the ways in which genetic sciences and global communications are revolutionising lay and professional knowledge, and transforming the art of the possible. There is nothing about the implications for the NHS of an agenda for sustainable development. Or the possibility of an economic downturn that could lead, once again, to acute funding shortages. There are no intimations of the likelihood that, 25 years from now, an effective health care system will bear little resemblance to the one we know today.

There are several pointers to the kind of future that should be envisaged for the NHS. There will be more older people who are frail rather than sick, and have chronic conditions that need to be managed over long periods. Individuals will have far greater access to information and advice about their health from a range of sources, some more reliable than others. New ways of tracking and treating illness will almost certainly arise from developments in genetic science. More – and more expensive – wonder drugs will be developed. Communications technologies will increase the incidence of diagnosis and treatment being delivered from a distance, building on the approach pioneered by NHS Direct. There will be more unpredictable risks to health arising from industrial processes, climate change and other consequences of human endeavour and fecklessness. There will be periods of economic downturn when levels of unemployment and poverty rise as tax revenues decline. Concern about the environment and its impact on health will increase. And – last but not least – health inequalities are likely to persist.

What kind of health system would be best able to meet these eventualities? It should be one that gives priority to intermediate and long-term care, to supporting people who are living at home, and to complementing the work of lay experts and self-help groups, because these are sources of essential knowledge and experience. There should be more intensive use of telephony and the internet to inform and advise patients and carers as well as staff. Clinicians will have to learn to act as guides and facilitators for people seeking to understand more about their health and health care needs, rather than handing down diagnoses and prescriptions. This will require a radical change in the culture and training of the health professions. The doctor–patient relationship will have to be recast from what is essentially an adult–child relationship to one that is more egalitarian and co-operative; patients must be seen not as ignorant recipients of treatment, but as co-producers of their own health.

Such a service must also be prepared to deal with ethical dilemmas arising from the new capabilities of science and technology. Should people be able to 'design' their babies? Should those with a predisposition to illness identified through genetic testing be obliged to take out special insurance? Should each newly licensed pharmaceutical product be available free of charge to anyone who is thought likely to benefit from it, regardless of cost? Should governments try to protect citizens from bad advice on the world wide web – and, if so, how? Should citizens expect governments to protect them from every unpredictable risk to their health? These are questions that cannot be left to 'experts'. There are seldom 'right answers', just different ways of viewing evidence and weighing arguments. They need to be the subject of negotiation between health professionals and economists, politicians and the voting public. In other words, a health system fit for the future should be securely underpinned by open dialogue and participative decision making.

There are implications for the mix of skills that would be required by a future health system. For example, if more diagnosis and treatment can be done at a distance – by means of increasingly sophisticated interactive technologies – it may be that fewer specialist medics are needed, but more website managers, online counsellors and domiciliary carers. An effective system would include a much stronger civic and environmental role for the NHS – one that makes optimal use of health care resources to tackle the causes of ill-health and to minimise inequalities and risks to health. The NHS could do much more to contribute to area regeneration and sustainable development; for example, through recruitment and personnel policies, through planning and capital spending, and through the management of transport and waste.

It is almost impossible to predict what new therapies will become available over the next two decades, or how economic conditions will change. What is certain, however, is that an effective system will need to be as flexible and adaptable as possible, not pinned down by too many intractable commitments or trapped into fixed patterns of expenditure. Large new hospitals funded through the Private Finance Initiative may store up trouble because they commit the NHS to heavy charges over many years, during which time the types of service that are needed and the settings from which they are best delivered may change dramatically.[11]

To begin to shape a truly modern health system, it will be necessary to renegotiate public expectations about what the NHS stands for and what it can deliver. That means developing a greater sense of shared responsibility for health and health care, and respecting the capabilities of people who are not trained as health 'experts' but have accumulated expertise through their personal experience. It will involve learning to live with health services that are fallible, that cannot save every endangered life, and that will only ever work effectively in partnership with other sectors (education, housing, environment), and in close co-operation with voluntary organisations and with business. It will also involve opening up a public debate about priorities for health policy and spending, instead of responding to the desires of key voters. Just as the doctor–patient relationship must change, so must the relationship between citizens and policy makers – from one based on mutual ignorance and distrust to one based on mutual respect and mature deliberation.[12]

A system designed around democratised knowledge and decision making would have to accommodate local and regional variations, both in health needs and in the preferences of citizens and service users. But that need not be incompatible with the drive towards equity, provided that the latter were fully integrated with the process of modernisation. As we have seen, information can be empowering and health-enhancing, but access to it is seldom evenly distributed – so a progressive health system should make it its business to ensure that those who are poor, socially excluded and vulnerable to ill-health are able to benefit from the democratisation of knowledge. Likewise, if the system is to be underpinned by open dialogue and participative decision making, it is essential that these are genuinely inclusive processes.

Above all, a truly modern health system would be geared towards promoting opportunities for health rather than simply improving health care. It would, of course, seek to cut queues and raise professional standards, but these objectives would not take precedence over narrowing the 'health gap' between rich and poor. The idea of universal protection on which the NHS is based would give way to a different kind of egalitarianism: one that seeks to enable every individual to have an equal chance (within the limits of avoidable risk) to enjoy sound health and long life.

Notes

1. The NHS (2000) *The NHS Plan*, London: Stationery Office.
2. Acheson, D. (1998) *Independent Inquiry into Inequalities in Health*, London: Stationery Office.

3. For example, Payne, N. and Saul, C. (1997) 'Variations in use of cardiology services in a health authority: comparison of coronary artery revascularisation rates with prevalence of angina and coronary mortality', *British Medical Journal*, 314 (7076): 257–61 (25 January).
4. Department of Health (1999) *Saving Lives: Our Healthier Nation*, London: Stationery Office, p. 28; 3:13.
5. Department of Health (2000) *Expenditure Plans 2000–2001*, London: Stationery Office.
6. Davies, A. and Kendall, E. (1999) *Health and the London Mayor*, London: King's Fund, pp. 23–9.
7. Van Rossum, C.T.M., Shipley, M.J., van de Mheen, H., Grobbee, D.E. and Marmot, M.G. (2000) 'Employment grade differences in cause specific mortality. A 25 year follow up of civil servants from the first Whitehall study', *Journal of Epidemiology and Community Health*, 54, 178–84.
8. Social Exclusion Unit (2000) *National Strategy for Neighbourhood Renewal: A framework for consultation*, London: Cabinet Office.
9. Coote, A. (1999) 'The Helmsman and the Cattle Prod', in Gamble, A. and Wright, T., *The New Social Democracy*, Political Quarterly Publications, Oxford: Blackwell.
10. Gowman, N. and Coote, A. (2000) *Evidence and Public Health: Towards a common framework*, London: King's Fund.
11. Boyle, S. and Harrison, A. (2000) 'Private Finance and Service Development', in *Health Care UK*, London: Kings Fund.
12. Coote, A. and Franklin, J. (1999) 'Negotiating risks to public health: models for participation', in Bennett, P. and Calman, K., *Risk Communication and Public Health*, Oxford: Oxford University Press.

21

Europe and the New Politics

Robin Cook and Menzies Campbell

Since the last general election Labour and the Liberal Democrats have been engaged in a unique exercise in political co-operation. In the field of foreign affairs, this has led to constructive discussions on a number of issues and the publication of joint policy papers on European defence co-operation, objectives for EU institutional reform and the future of the United Nations.

Our starting point in this work has been the firm belief that a country is most likely to succeed abroad when its foreign policy is the product of a strong national consensus at home. In diplomacy, advantage goes to those countries able pursue a clear and consistent vision over the long term. Those who are most divided about what they want may end up getting least. It is important that our national political debate projects an image of maturity and self-confidence to the outside world.

In our view, politicians of all parties have a responsibility to maximise the areas of agreement and minimise the areas of disagreement in the conduct of Britain's external relations. That is not to say that important differences of principle should be submerged or political debate stifled. It is simply to point out that the national interest will be better served if foreign policy is spared an excess of partisan politics.

Our existing political culture is not conducive to the consensus-building that foreign policy needs. The adversarial approach to debate promotes polarisation of opinion. Our co-operation should not, therefore, be seen as an exercise in short-term political management, but as a continuing contribution towards the creation of a new style of politics in Britain.

For Labour and the Liberal Democrats, political co-operation in areas such as foreign affairs is a natural step. We represent different strands of a common progressive tradition with a shared commitment to internationalism and the pursuit of universal human values. This leads us to many similar conclusions about Britain's foreign policy priorities.

We agree that globalisation has significantly limited the capacity of nation-states to resolve problems unilaterally and that our prosperity, security and quality of life depend increasingly on our ability to influence events beyond our borders. We agree that the best way to defend our rights and liberties is to stand up for the rights and liberties of others, wherever they live. And we agree that international organisations must be modernised and strengthened to meet new challenges. Our desire to reform the United Nations, the European Union and the international financial architecture mirrors our commitment to radical constitutional reform at home.

The scope for further co-operation in foreign affairs is considerable, but it is in the conduct of Britain's affairs in Europe that the need to break out of the culture of adversarial politics is most acutely felt.

Britain has been a member of the European Union for 27 years. Almost 60 per cent of our exports in goods go to the European Single Market. Almost half a million British citizens take advantage of their right to free movement to live and work in other EU countries. Many citizens from the rest of the EU use the same right to live and work in Britain.

Almost every aspect of our lives, from prosperity to sport, is intimately tied to our relationship with our European neighbours. Yet Britain has rarely seemed at ease with its European destiny.

There are many reasons for this, not least the need to change the way the European Union works to make it more transparent and less remote. We take this problem seriously and regard successful reform of the EU's structures and systems as a fundamental priority.

But this is only part of the story. Scepticism certainly exists in other parts of the European Union, but in Britain the public debate is characterised by defensiveness, insecurity and, occasionally, paranoia.

This is encouraged by our political system and the attitudes it breeds. The parties excluded from government conduct a form of parliamentary warfare against anything the governing party attempts to do. Debates take the form of set-piece confrontations between opposing points of view. Politics in Britain is seen as a theatre of conflict in which one side advances its interests at the expense of the other.

International diplomacy, however, is conducted in an entirely different way. Any international agreement requires the consent of a number of different countries representing a diverse range of interests. Whereas politics in Britain is seen as a win–lose game, diplomacy consists of the search for win–win outcomes in which each of the parties involved make concessions in order to secure a greater good. And so it is with the European Union.

Our European partners understand this approach instinctively since in most cases their domestic political systems are based on coalition-building and power-sharing, both at a national level and between the centre and the regions. In Britain, we have only just started down this path.

It is little wonder that we often find the nature of European integration so difficult to grasp. This is clearly reflected in press coverage of European affairs which is littered with the language of conflict, such as 'threat', 'victory' or 'surrender'. The journalists attending every European summit pore over the conclusions to find out who 'won' and who 'lost'. Ministers who take part are often left wondering whether they attended the same event.

The picture that is presented is distorted. Negotiating concessions are described in the most lurid and hysterical terms while real achievements are ignored or taken for granted.

Take the example of Qualified Majority Voting (QMV). This is routinely portrayed by Eurosceptics as a threat and any move in that direction as a surrender on the part of Britain. The facts tell a different story. In 1998–99 there were 85 QMV votes in the Council of Ministers. Britain was outvoted or abstained on five occasions – fewer than either France or Germany. What is striking is that there were 80 occasions on which measures supported by Britain were agreed because of QMV, but would otherwise have been blocked by someone else's veto.

The political culture and the winner-takes-all electoral system on which it depends has another harmful effect on the British debate. It suppresses the natural cross-party consensus that has existed in favour of a positive engagement in Europe since the 1960s.

The partisan debate between government and Opposition conceals the truth that governments of all political persuasions have followed a broadly pro-European approach for almost four decades.

Today, government Ministers are condemned from the official Opposition benches for supporting steps of integration which are modest in comparison to those taken by their Conservative predecessors. Any suggestion of extending QMV in areas which would be in the British interest are rejected out of hand by some Conservatives who approved a much bigger extension of QMV in the Single European Act and the Maastricht Treaty.

Undoubted ideological shifts on left and right aside, the reason why this pattern has tended to replicate itself is built into the fabric of our political system. The governing party has to accept sole responsibility for discharging the national interest, and since the time when Harold Macmillan was Prime Minister, has invariably concluded that there is no workable alternative to Britain's engagement in Europe. The party of Opposition has no such responsibility and is driven by the imperative of winning the next election at all costs. It has no incentive to be honest with the British people about where its true interests lie.

Today's Conservative Party serves as a perfect illustration of this tendency. The further away from power it is, the more erratic it becomes and the more corrosive its effect on the public debate.

It is too easy for the demands of Opposition politics to take precedence over issues of principle. Why tell the truth when it is easier to score points by playing to the fears of the electorate? Those who disagree are silenced in the name of party unity rather than the national interest.

Adversarial politics has not yet given rise to the election of a government determined to engineer withdrawal from the European Union, but it has done enough to sour the national debate in a way that undermines our efforts to get the most out of our membership of it.

In the long term, maximising our interests in Europe will depend on our ability to break with that adversarial approach to the discussion of foreign policy. We both believe that when parties share a common view of the national interest, they should work together to secure it. We also believe that Britain needs a political system that encourages that approach. That is one of the reasons why we must continue to modernise and reform Britain's constitution in a way that promotes a political culture based on co-operation and consensus-building.

Part 4
Discussion and Endpiece

22
A Roundtable Discussion on the Prospects for a Progressive Century

Held on 29 September 2000 at the National Liberal Club

The group of men and women who came together for this roundtable discussion had different political affiliations but shared a commitment to a new approach to politics. They were invited because they believed, like us, in the need for a degree of pluralism and interparty co-operation. We wanted participants to explore whether Labour's statist tendencies would be improved with a dose of liberalism and whether Liberal Democrat individualism would benefit from a dose of collectivism. Participants were asked to define their visions of a new politics and identify which elements from each tradition they believed would help deliver the 'progressive century'.

The debate took place after the fuel blockades of September 2000 which had raised important questions concerning the politics of popular protest, and at the end of the week of the Labour Party Conference in Brighton, where the Prime Minister had made a landmark speech outlining his vision of Labour's 'core beliefs'.

The discussion is sometimes confused and contradictory. The tensions between the desire for equality and liberty at one and the same time are consistently evident. But this is the dialectic that will define a successful progressive politics. We should relish the struggle between these competing principles and look to a synthesis as a route map for the future.

There is an underlying sense of disappointment with the limited achievements of the first term of Labour's administration. But equally there is a sense of hope about what is still to be achieved. While there is little sense of a guiding philosophy of governance for New Labour, the long haul back from the margins of politics in the 1980s has now brought us to the point where such a vacuum is recognised as a fatal weakness that needs to be addressed. It is also interesting and encouraging that the participants discuss a 'critique of capitalism', another pointer that the centre-left has moved out of the shadow of Thatcherism. This is the seam that progressives must mine if they are to build on the electorate's apparent sustained rejection of neo-liberalism. It is another vacuum to be filled by creative and brave thinking.

From his comments below, David Marquand now at best seems sanguine about the prospects for a 'progressive century'. This is a pity because Marquand has offered the most coherent analysis of the failures of labourism in particular and the need for the link with liberalism to be re-forged. But what Marquand seems to be rejecting is not progressivism but modernisation. Here, New Labour has been guilty of not just sloppy but dangerous advocacy. 'Modernisation' has been hailed as unquestionably virtuous, and to be 'anti-modernisation' was to accept your place in the asylum of political Neanderthals. But we will do well to remember that Thatcher was a 'moderniser'. The question is, what form of 'modernisation', and who benefits? If Marquand is being critical of such lazy sloganeering, then he is right to be. A belief in progressive values, as defined throughout this book, is not akin to a belief in puerile modernisation.

Finally, this discussion, shaped and influenced as it is by the particular circumstances of the day, offers a refreshing and vibrant sense of hope in the prospects of the centre-left and its ambition for human fulfilment. It shows a group of centre-left thinkers and politicians ready to move from the back foot of defeatism that deadened our minds throughout the 1980s and 1990s to the front foot of a willingness to shape society in the image of the progressive values they hold.

Neal Lawson and Neil Sherlock

Neal Lawson (*Chair*)
Philip Dodd, *Director, ICA*
Will Hutton, *Director, Industrial Society*
Ruth Lister, *Professor of Social Policy, Loughborough University*
Calum Macdonald, *Labour MP for Western Isles*
David Marquand, *Principal, Mansfield College Oxford*
Mark Oaten MP, *Winchester, Lib-Dem spokesman on Foreign Affairs*
Matthew Taylor, *Director, Institute for Public Policy Research*
Polly Toynbee, *columnist on the* Guardian

NEAL LAWSON: Welcome ... the centre-left has failed for too long to outline a coherent political philosophy, so let's work out in intellectual terms what a progressive century would actually involve. I've got a series of questions that I'd like us to touch on if possible:

- What are the prospects for an ideologically driven form of politics in an age of instant protest?
- What defines progressive politics?
- What are the best elements of the social democratic and liberal tradition?
- What factors are critical to delivering the progressive century?
- What needs to change?

Let me elaborate on the first of these. What is the space for a more ideological form of politics, something that is driven by a definite view of the set of values that you stand for, the goals that you're trying to achieve? This is something in my party, the Labour Party, which the leadership has been less inclined to emphasise of late. What does that mean at a time when it seems that people are more volatile and fickle in their opinions? And does that narrow the scope for a more defined philosophy of political governance? We're here to examine these questions but don't feel limited or constrained by them. Say what you want. Will?

WILL HUTTON: I don't think that the centre-left will succeed if it's not clear about the meta-values that govern it. If by ideology we mean something with rigid constraints I would say that the chances of an ideologically driven party succeeding in the twenty-first century are poor, partly because the circumstances are changing so quickly. The left has to reorganise notions of equality, recognising equity and accountability as two driver values of the left.

I was struck at conference, and felt warm about it, that the Labour Party is a 'tribe', and on a bunch of things the tribe won't move: on things like vouchers for asylum-seekers, for example; and on the notion of the contributory principle underpinning social insurance, and that some level of taxation has to support quality public services. I thought Tony Blair picked that up cleverly in his speech. This is not ideology but the kind of values that a tribe can buy into. But I don't believe – I never did believe – in socialism, in that sense, and I think that's all gone.

POLLY TOYNBEE: Will's making a rather subtle distinction between tribal gut beliefs and core values and something called ideology. If you're defining ideology at some very high-flown, philosophical level, and saying that it has to be an '-ism' – socialism, for example – you might be right that that's all gone. But I profoundly believe that wherever you go in the world, within three minutes of meeting somebody, in whatever political context, there are 'them and us'; there are people who are – I'm with Gilbert and Sullivan on this – essentially conservative and there are people who are essentially liberal-progressive. This seems to be hard-wired into the human psyche, and it's one of the first things you want to know about people. You sit next to someone you don't know, and you might politely ask where they come from or what they do, but what you really want to know is which side of the line are they on. It's interesting that the numbers of people who shift from one to the other are still relatively small. Everybody talks about seismic changes, but actually not that many people change. Most people remain pretty much what their parents were. The essential values don't change.

You mentioned pensions; actually I don't think that is a tribal issue. There are some old people who still believe in the fraudulent mechanism of the National Insurance system, but everybody there [at the Labour Party Conference], the two-thirds on the floor of the hall who voted with the government, were voting just as passionately for more money for pensioners and redistribution. It was a technical question about whether you thought this was achieved the old-fashioned way or in the new way. Everybody was equally agreed that as much money as possible should be shoved towards pensioners.

Is the death of the National Insurance system really the death of an old ideology? Wasn't it more a sort of fix that Beveridge had for trying to get the rich to pay for the poor – a clever wheeze? I don't see that the new century's going to be fundamentally different. Underneath, there are the Bournemouth people [where the Conservatives held their conference in 2000] and there are the Brighton people [Labour's conference venue]. One way or another, you know pretty quickly where someone's sympathies lie, even if they vote uncharacteristically from time to time.

DAVID MARQUAND: Polly's notion that this divide is 'hard-wired' into the human psyche has no warrant in history. Which was the 'left' and which was the 'right' in the wars of religion? What I think is true is that there is a built-in tension between two facets of human nature. We are social animals but only weakly socialised. We need solidarity, community, fraternity if you like. We also need autonomy, individuality, freedom. These two drives inevitably collide.

The ideologies with which we have lived since the late nineteenth century, and which have, for better or worse, shaped the twentieth century, are now exhausted. Socialism, in any form that its founding parents would recognise, is clearly dead. I believe that the same is true of conservatism as traditionally understood – obviously in this country, but also on the continent. Liberalism is not exactly dead. In some ways it's the dominant ideology of the First World. But because of its dominance, it's become in practical terms vacuous.

The lesson of history is that we need ideology and I'm convinced that sooner or later new ideologies will arise to fill the current vacuum. But, almost by definition, we can't know what they'll be. It seems to me simplistic to believe that they are bound to fit the 'progressive'/'conservative' or 'left'/'right' divide that we have known since the French Revolution. They'll doubtless revolve around that inescapable polarity – but in ways that are utterly unpredictable.

NEAL: If the space for ideologically defined politics is diminishing, are we becoming fearful of the rule of the mob? Is there something happening to democracy – the 'consumerisation' of politics?

MARK OATEN: It's interesting to look at recent examples where the public has had to choose between a set of values and principles and a set of instant protests and the rule of the mob. For example, on paedophiles, or the case of Tony Martin [who shot a young man in defence of his property] or asylum-seekers, or on Section 28 and on gay rights. On these issues, William Hague and the Conservatives pressed what we assumed were all the right buttons in terms of what the man in the pub says. But it didn't actually do Hague any favours; and I'm still not sure why.

It may be because Hague is not popular, but I think there was also a sense in which the British public agreed with him – in terms of instant protest and quick fixes – but failed to identify with the overall sense of where the party was going. You might have expected the issues to springboard Hague way ahead of Blair in the run-up to the party conferences. But it didn't.

RUTH LISTER: I was on holiday in the States when the fuel crisis blew up and when I returned to Britain it was like coming back to another country; it was really, really strange. It seemed to me that a government with a clear political philosophy could have dealt with that much better than Labour appeared to have done.

If, for example, it had had a clearer philosophy around tax or been clearer about its green philosophy – part of the rationale for fuel taxes – then it would have had a coherent stance towards the protesters. But it's been so defensive on tax. It has been one of the words, along with redistribution, that you could not speak. Also I think Labour needs a clearer philosophy around protest. The fuel protests and the Portsmouth demonstrations around paedophilia make me shudder, but in one sense these people are doing things we think people should be doing. In other words, not just being deferential subjects but being active citizens. Portsmouth raised troubling issues, but what those women were doing was in one sense what I've written about as good citizenship. They were out there, empowering themselves in a way they probably never had before. Nonetheless, they were doing it at the expense of other citizens – paedophiles are still citizens and they still have civil rights.

I thought that raised enormously important issues. The government didn't cave in but nor did it respond with a coherent position. Without a clear political philosophy, government will get driven by the latest protest, or be left simply standing there saying 'we must be firm'.

NEAL: How should the government have responded to the paedophile demos?

RUTH: That's hard and I'm still grappling with the answer. I think it could have been clearer in trying to understand the position of those women while making clear the limits of citizen action. Those limits include not infringing the civil rights of others, however bad what they've done in the past is. It's not easy, but a clear political philosophy helps deal with such protests. Labour seems to have been similarly at sixes and sevens over the fuel protests and that is an easier one to answer. If they'd had a clear position on tax and a firm environmental philosophy, they might have been able to withstand the protest better without threatening to call in troops.

MATTHEW TAYLOR: It's clear to me that if you want to be an effective politician you need a strong set of values which you refer to and which should drive you on and save you from disappearing into pragmatism or cynicism. You should be very clever in order that you can understand what the consequences of policy are going to be. You need to have the capacity to win elections, which is another completely different set of skills. You do all this against the background of the media, which is trying to hack your legs away at every point. And watching Labour last week, I felt they were making quite a few mistakes.

It's easy to say what I think those mistakes were, but it's very difficult to imagine how we expect politicians to emerge who are up to the task, because in a sense the task of political leadership is becoming almost impossible.

PHILIP DODD: I have to say I find it difficult to have that melancholy sympathy with the political class or agree that their work is so hard. In the past 15 or 20 years every professional group has sat round a table saying that about themselves: doctors, lawyers, social workers, teachers. The twentieth century at one level belonged to the professional class.

Now politicians are under the kind of pressure that all other professional groups have been in the past two decades, and that includes arts administrators. I think there's a crisis in the relationship between professionals and others, which are unfortunately sometimes called the 'mob'.

That's one issue. The other is that the language of ideology, values, political philosophy could never become popular, because it's too abstract. What politicians have to do now is be able to tell stories. I don't say that simply because I come from a cultural institution; the point about stories is that a narrative is always about past, present and future. It's a way of rolling together political philosophy, values and ideology and the problem for New Labour, it seems to me, is they never quite got the story. Whatever else was wrong with Thatcher, she was able to tell a quite extraordinary story about Britain. And it seems to me the centre-left needs to find an adequate story.

Policy's not the problem; abstract values are not the problem; nor are political philosophy and ideology. What's needed is the idea that will turn into a narrative that helps families make sense of their lives.

So, of course you need a policy in relation to the exposure of paedophiles, but you also need a story about national life in which you can make sense of events like Portsmouth or the fuel protest. It's the absence of New Labour's story about the past of Britain, the present of Britain and the future that is its major difficulty. Thatcher did it. She had a foolish account of the Victorians, but it tapped into a way of thinking.

MATTHEW: I think you're right about the 'story'. It has to be a story that involves people. Labour has got a story – it's the Third Way – but it's a peculiarly unengaging story. It's not a story in which you see yourself as a character, really.

PHILIP: You felt you were a character in Thatcher's story, though.

CALUM MACDONALD: I think this is too pessimistic about the past two or three years. Matthew talks of the difficulty of political leadership, but we've had the most phenomenally popular – and therefore, in those terms, successful – government in polling history, a government that, despite the turbulent summer, is still leading in the polls. And that's not expected of governments at this stage in the political cycle.

The difficulty facing Labour is not lack of a story or a lack of values. I agree with Polly; these values are easily identified. You can identify values that you attach yourself to across societies, across cultures, across decades. Tony Blair's speech [to the Labour Conference], which talked about solidarity and mutual responsibility and things that brought him into the Labour Party addressed identifiable values.

If ideology means a set of policy prescriptions that are applied inflexibly for all socio-economic conditions, then I certainly don't think we have that. Policy prescriptions evolve over the decades, but we have identifiable values that have run throughout the history of the Labour Party and the centre-left.

The difficulty facing the Labour Party is that the 20 years leading to 1997, years of successive election defeats, followed a very problematic period for Labour in government. The legacy of that is that certain policy approaches became devalued. Big tax-and-spend programmes became deeply unpopular, and people thought it just didn't work. So Labour's difficulty was overturning that public mistrust. It tried to do this by being cautious in the way it projected itself and cautious in how it ran the first two or three years of government. It had to prove that it could run the economy. Now it's done that and the task is to move the argument on.

My sense is that we are making genuine progress and there is beginning to be a public appetite for a case to be made for necessary taxation to invest in public services.

MARK: But you've been making a big thing about cutting taxes. You've damaged that case. Labour has never gone around saying, 'We're increasing taxes because we want to invest in public services.' That's never been an argument.

CALUM: What we've tried to do is shift the debate from taxes that are particularly sensitive and thus to broaden the argument about the balance of taxation and investment. Income tax is obviously the most sensitive tax of the lot, but instead of fruitless debate over whether it should go up or down, Labour has tried to get people to see that investment in public services is a positive thing needing taxes to pay for it. I don't think Labour has abandoned the philosophical ground at all; there has been, instead, a tactical readjustment around various kinds of taxes.

NEAL: What then are the underlying values of a progressive politics? What are the best elements we can take from our separate traditions?

POLLY: There is ground which social democrats, New Labour and liberals hold in common, things which they would all agree with. These include a presumption in favour of the underdog; belief in progress, which is that things can always get better; a trust in reason; taxing as much as you dare; tolerating almost anything except intolerance; striving for a more equal society; siding with the consumer, not the producer; celebrating diversity; regarding sex and family life as no business of the state; and, above all, believing that all humans are redeemable.

Is there anything there that would divide Liberal Democrats from New Labour?

MARK: Individual freedom is something that separates me from New Labour. I think there is a still a bit of the nanny about New Labour. They want to tell people how to do things. I don't want to get bogged down in things like fox hunting, I guess, but that's one example where people might feel they are being told what to do. If you look at the way they've managed benefit reform, it's been very much a question of, 'It's a good idea that working mums get back to work and this is how it's going to happen, and unless you do it our way your benefit will be withdrawn because we know best.' I think the nanny state is an area of difference.

Labour policies also have a slightly anti-market feel to it, which as a former SDP person I feel uncomfortable with. I don't rule out the possibility that the private sector should be driving forward some issues. We could argue that there's an instinct in both our parties to believe government should run the NHS, schools, pensions. But I think some of us in the Liberal Democrats would say that some of these things could be provided by the private sector.

DAVID: I would say that the best elements of the social democratic tradition are a commitment to solidarity and justice, and the realisation of these values through democratic processes. In the liberal tradition I would identify a commitment to personal autonomy, pluralism, diversity and a resistance to the ever-present danger of populist demagogy and the 'tyranny of the majority'.

WILL: Can I take Polly's sheet of possible common values and try this on you: that what unites New Labour and the Liberal Democrats are the two values of equity and accountability. Let's go through the list. A presumption in favour of the underdog: I'd say that's an equity issue. Belief in progress: put that to one side. A trust in reason: I guess that's accountability. Taxing as much as you dare: equity. Tolerating almost anything except intolerance: equity. Striving for an equal society: definitely equity. Siding with the consumer, celebrating diversity, and regarding sex and family life as no business of the state: they're freedom, I guess. Belief in progress: I guess that's about science and rationality.

POLLY: No, it's about optimism and pessimism. Belief in progress is what distinguishes small 'l' liberals, or progressives, from the underlying state of mind of Conservatives. Conservatives think that change makes everything worse. Things were always better in the past; we're on the slippery slope downhill. Progressives throughout history have always thought that you can change things for the better and you don't have to keep looking back to the past for your inspiration.

DAVID: I have a lot of trouble with the term 'progressive politics'. I once wrote a book called *The Progressive Dilemma* and taught a course called 'The Progressive Tradition'. These experiences convinced me that the term was vacuous, a hangover from the days when the self-defined 'left' saw itself as the vehicle of preordained historical change. No one who broods for a second on the terrible history of the twentieth century can possibly accept that picture now. Surely we have learned that 'progress' can be destructive and even evil. This is not just academic nit-picking. When change is proceeding as rapidly and as confusingly as it is now, we need to be able to discriminate between desirable and undesirable changes. The implication that all change is good has disastrous consequences. Environmental catastrophe is perhaps the most obvious.

RUTH: I'd certainly sign up to Will's equity and accountability but I don't think you can put all the values mentioned by Polly into those two boxes. I want to question one of Polly's values and add two more. I think the notion that sex and family life is no business of the state risks recreating a very strong public/private split, because for a lot of things – domestic violence, rape in marriage, child abuse, and so forth – the state has to have a role. The two values I would add would be internationalism and democracy. I would put internationalism under equity in terms of thinking of equity issues in a global sense, including notions of global responsibility.

The other value is democracy. The debate about democracy is another way of talking about Will's notion of accountability and how we enable the voices of marginalised groups, those in poverty, for example, to be heard. This is partly what Tony Blair was talking about in his conference speech. We have to have mechanisms to ensure that it is not just the loudest voices that get heard, but that the voices of the most oppressed are heard as well.

MATTHEW: I don't think the lists we've had so far capture the democratic idea of human fulfilment, which is something at the heart of the progressive mission. I think what the Liberal heritage can bring to the social democratic debate is a richer account of human fulfilment which emphasises things such as participation, and a richer interest in culture, not necessarily the British version. What Conservatives tend to say to me is: 'All people want is to buy things and get on; why do you want to interfere with them? You're always interfering with people. Some people succeed, some people fail. People live in private boxes, watch television, go to the garden centre on Sunday and that's their life.' The left has always believed people want more than that. It matters to them what society's like around them; it's not just the little box, but the town they live in and how people get on.

I think the left should always be fighting for a broader definition of human fulfilment, both in terms of the individual's needs but also in terms of the individual's place in society. The modern right has a more atomised and narrower account.

PHILIP: I'm glad someone other than me has mentioned culture. I'm worried about Ruth Lister's term 'internationalism', although I think the impulse is right. Internationalism as a concept has a problem because it leaves the nation as a kind of unproblematic entity, so it's an awful word. I prefer the idea of 'routedness'; in other words, the way we're routed across the world. What distinguished Britain historically and presently is that it's extraordinarily routed. It's routed to the old Empire, to the States, to Europe. None of these will motivate you into any particular position vis-à-vis Europe, for instance, because the issue of belonging is not addressed by any of these. What motivates people profoundly is the sense of belonging.

WILL: Belonging may be very important in the next ten or twenty years. I take globalisation seriously. I think that a lot of the direct action movements, whether they are in Prague or outside an oil refinery in Cheshire, are about disempowerment, wanting a voice, resentment about inequality. Not resentment about inequality as the left would see it but resentment about other groups getting ahead in a hierarchy of where they think they stand. Farmers and road hauliers find themselves sinking down the hierarchy.

Then there's the attempt to respond to globalisation by developing supranational institutions such as the European Union. Equity and accountability, or notions of liberty, don't provide any compass in the big question about who you might belong to. Maybe Margaret Thatcher's talent as a politician was to hook her ideology to a story of where you belong.

CALUM: Polly's list is more a set of attitudes that typify the left personality and the left outlook. I don't think they're values as such. They typify the left because of a deeper underlying set of values, and I think these are much closer to what Matthew was saying. To me, the core value of the left over the ages has been the notion of universal human potential and our duty to fulfil that potential, I don't think equality is best understood as a value but as a means to unlock human potential. We all have a responsibility to develop our own potential but also to help others realise theirs. This is why progress and optimism are left-wing attitudes. We have this metabelief in human potential and the desire to remove impediments to its development.

WILL: That is so wrong. Conservatives have this same belief in human potential. It's a conceit and it's a disastrous mistake. Conservatives believe that all you need to realise it is to be unlocked from the control of the state.

CALUM: No, I disagree. Right-wingers, not just Conservatives but libertarians, have no substantive notion of human potential. However people develop and whatever they want to do, whatever pulp they want to watch on television, for example, then that's right for them. Individual choice is paramount. Whereas on the left we have a deeper sense of human potential regarding culture, education, art, etc., which is not just confined to an elite. From the left point of view it's not good enough to have an endless number of channels which people can surf through which is why we are so deeply and instinctively committed to the educational mission which underlies public service broadcasting.

POLLY: There's a way of talking about this that is pure Thatcher and there is a way of talking about it that's essentially left. Potential and opportunity are devious words.

CALUM: The notion of getting better is not just about the acquisition of material goods and so on, it's fundamentally about the development of the self, the belief that everyone has that potential and a duty to do everything possible to develop it.

WILL: I think this is a serious blind alley. I repeat, I think it's wrong to think that people who hold different values from us don't also believe in the possibility of self-improvement, don't believe in culture, don't believe in art. It's such a mistake to traduce what your opponents are. The appeal of market liberalism in the 1980s was that it bound together the wealth-creating prospects of capitalism with individual empowerment and some sense that if you gave individuals a break by lifting burdens and regulations and so on, then they would arrive at some notion of fulfilment. Of course Conservatives believe in self-fulfilment. It's a calamity to mis-describe your opponents, because you get your own story wrong. It's a calamity also to ask the left to define itself in terms of virtues rather than values. Self-fulfilment is a virtue; economic efficiency is a virtue; a sunny day is a virtue. We're all for that. It doesn't actually give you a compass for political action or coalition building.

RUTH: I'm concerned at this idea of dismissing equality as a tactic. Yes, both right and left take the idea of the development of human potential seriously. But isn't the difference between the two, as Tawney wrote, that without equality – not literal equality of income, but without some degree of equality – the development of human potential is not possible? So to simply define it as a tactic is misguided.

CALUM: It is not an end in itself but a means.

RUTH: But it's a crucial one.

MATTHEW: I think the real differences between left and right concern collective responsibility. In terms of what I'd junk from social democracy, I'd want people on the social democratic left to be suspicious of various things. I'd want them to be suspicious of the capacity of governments to do things, for example. It's an area where I think we could learn from the right.

POLLY: Because it helps governments do things better by constantly worrying or because they shouldn't be doing it? The right would say that they shouldn't be doing it. We would say, we must remember we often get it wrong. Therefore we must find other ways or improve our delivery systems.

MATTHEW: It's partly that, but it's partly saying that you are unlikely to succeed unless you engage people and give them a sense of ownership or involvement. Government should recognise that you might have to sacrifice some notions of equality, some notions of equity of outcome, in order to gain the effectiveness that comes from giving people more choice.

I also think there's an economism on the left, which I'd want to minimise. I'd want to counsel against a view that work and money is all it's about. I'd also want to say, how are you changing people? The notion of changing people is one that people get worried about because it sounds totalitarian. I think the left in Britain has tended to be weak on what it's trying to do for people. Thatcher had a story about liberating people's selfishness, liberating them to express themselves. I'm not sure what we're trying to liberate people to do. What is a New Labour citizen? I think that's an interesting question.

MARK: I would like to think that among the things Lib Dems bring to the party is a sense of individualism and a liberal tradition of strong communities and trying to empower those communities to take decisions for themselves. And less central control, less belief in government setting the parameters by which things are defined. God knows how you empower people. It's very difficult, but there are examples such as neighbourhood school trusts in Liverpool.

WILL: There are occasions when citizens actually don't want to give up lots of time for grassroots participation. They just want the school to work, because part of their individualism is living their lives, going to clubs, reading books, watching TV, going to the movies, building their family life, and not sacrificing time at the margin for grassroots participation in endeavours which, they think, should simply be there. One of the arguments about the state pension is partly about that. Citizens, particularly as they get over 50, want a basic income in retirement that they know politicians can't fiddle with. It's a curious expression of your individualism and a distrust of the state; you just want it to be there and to rise in line with earnings.

MATTHEW: I think Labour has tended to be statist, although New Labour, set out explicitly to challenge an obsession with public ownership and public control, has found itself being pulled back into this. We have seen Gordon Brown saying that the National Health Service would be run 'by public servants', with Alan Milburn proudly announcing, no more competitive tendering, as if we've rediscovered that one of the really important things to the left is that the state must grow.

POLLY: Well, I'm going to pick that up, because you've just said the opposite to what you said about democratisation of the NHS. People were angry about the postcode lottery in the NHS, or that this school is better than that school and I can't get into the good school. Of all inequalities, these things make people far angrier than anything else, even angrier than financial inequalities.

MATTHEW: The reason people are obsessed by postcode lotteries and inequalities is because public services in Britain continue to be so poor. If there's only one good school in London, then people are obsessed with inequalities. We'd be less obsessed about wanting everything to be the same if fewer hospitals and schools weren't failing. User involvement is not an abstract notion. One of the reasons schools underachieve is lack of parental involvement. You particularly want to get poorer parents involved, because then education is more likely to succeed. Likewise, the Health Service is more likely to succeed if people have some sense of owning it.

PHILIP: Polly's mentioned 'a trust in reason' as a defining principle of the centre-left. I keep thinking of that great seventeenth-century Catholic, Pascal, who said 'the heart has reasons reason knows not of'. In other words, one of the things that Tories are better at is appealing to things that occupy our daily lives in a way other than reason. One of the things that seems to me extraordinarily important in resisting the right is to understand that people don't live life in a rational seminar.

For instance, on asylum-seekers: you can go down the line of toleration, but you need to make it part of a larger argument – that to belong in Britain is to belong to a centuries-old import and export culture. In other words, you need to be able to describe a belonging that appeals to something other than reason.

Secondly, I think there has to be a more wholehearted embrace of the democratic impulse. The fuel crisis showed this wonderfully well. Remember that famous short poem of Brecht where he said, 'the people have disappointed the government; let us elect a new people'. The centre-left is very fond of proclaiming its love for the people until the people do something it doesn't like.

Thirdly, the centre-left is appallingly puritan and suspicious of pleasure. The right has a better time. I sense there is a deep anxiety in this government about the pleasure principle. Culture is one of those sites of pleasure, which is why the government never quite knows what to do about it. I think Conservatives have traditionally understood these three principles better.

NEAL: Is Philip Gould [polling adviser to Tony Blair] right that this is a profoundly conservative country?

WILL: I used to agree with the Gould view that you mustn't talk about sustaining taxes to increase public provision and all the rest. Now I take a different view of the past decade, and I think it's one of the rather comforting things for the left at the moment. I think the country has moved away from the Conservative position. It's much more tolerant about sex and what used to be called deviancy, which I think is lost vocabulary. I think it's more tolerant about drugs; much more tolerant about lifestyle. I think it's losing its attachment to organised religion and is prepared to experiment with all kinds of lifestyles and beliefs. A lot of the Conservative shibboleths – the Union Jack, 'Rule Britannia', 'Jerusalem', the hunt, the village green, the big country house – have all become much weaker.

I think there are Conservative residues. There is a lot of populist prejudice that can be exploited, but the right can't put together a coherent story in the way that Hague believes they can. That's why he will lose and why the Tories will be in the wilderness for a long time.

RUTH: The right really does think the past is a better place, and actually the past was a bloody awful place if you were gay, black or disabled. It may not be a great place now but it's a darn sight better than it was. New Labour's big, big failure is not to have used the kind of spirit with which they were elected to develop a story about tax and solidarity. Politicians can assume that people are basically selfish and are in for themselves and therefore that you can't give them a story about why tax is a positive thing, but actually we do need a story on why we tax people. I think all of us have an individualist, selfish side – I certainly have; but I'd also like to think I've got a side that is concerned about others and the wider community. Most of us are a mix. If politicians constantly talk to the selfish, individualistic side of people, then that's how they will respond. If politicians develop a wider story, then I think they could carry people with them and make a case for progressive taxation as part of our responsibility to each other.

POLLY: Philip's point about pleasure was very good. The Tories always seem to be the devil-may-care, let's-have-fun party. There's something very dull and mechanistic about the dour Gordon Brown view – you get a stable economy, and then we put more money out there, and there you are – that's the end. It's a low vision, or no vision. Labour has to make its statism more inspirational, not just 'the state's going to take your money and tell you what to have'.

MATTHEW: Both the right and the left in Britain have had to abandon the language of paternalism. People do not respect the old hierarchies. They don't exhibit the old deference. But the left understands better than the right that there are some choices which you can have in the short term or long term, but not both. The environment's a classic example of this. One of the reasons the fuel tax revolt was depressing was because it highlighted how weakly the argument about transport and environment for the long term had been made.

We should also be making the case more strongly that poor people still don't have choices. The left should be able to say that the sorts of choices offered by the market are shallow choices, and that we want to encourage people to view the real choices they have about their lives and relationships.

NEAL: What are the issues and policies that have to change to begin to make a difference?

DAVID: Culture and structure both need to change dramatically. The Labour tradition is not monolithic. It contains a pluralist, decentralist, civic-activist strand and a centralist, statist, Big-Brother-Knows-Best strand. The first strand was quite strong in the early days of the party but it was overwhelmed by the second strand once Labour became a major player in the 1920s. It remained dormant until the Thatcher Revolution of the 1980s led sections of the labour movement to question the centralism of the preceding 50 years. Now centralist statism has had a new lease of life. The crunch question for the future is whether the Labour leadership has the courage and imagination to retrieve the pluralistic, decentralist elements in its heritage. The omens are not encouraging.

MARK: I agree entirely with Will that we are living in a more tolerant society. I'm not quite sure why it is more tolerant, but we can't take credit for it, and that troubles me slightly! I think society has changed but I'm acutely aware that there is an establishment out there and that as MP for Winchester I'm attending certain things where, because I am not a Conservative, I am an outsider. And that will exist for a long time. However, I buy the view that we've become more tolerant, though I'm not sure why it's happened.

CALUM: I think we can take a bit of credit for it. It has been people on the left who have articulated pluralism and tolerance. We're working against the background of 100 years in which the Conservatives have been politically successful. That is why we have to try to take on board some of the fears and doubts that people have about the left and Labour. If the income tax rate is a psychologically sensitive point for people, then we should shift the argument on to another tax where we can make progress.

WILL: I think capitalism generates inequalities, concentrations of unaccountable private power. It is unstable, oscillates between boom and bust. But it's all the things that New Labour has discovered as well: it's wealth-generating, it's dynamic; it's often very creative and all the rest. Part of the left has been about trying to correct the deficiencies in some way – at the extreme trying to socialise it, and at the more moderate end trying to regulate, manage and superintend it. That's where I remain. And I think globalisation has now made that even more urgent.

I also think part of the story is stakeholding – trying to embed in capitalism new responsibilities that it won't adopt of its own accord. My great influences are Keynes, and all the left school economists of the twentieth century who were on the left because they mounted a critique about the operation of capitalism. I'm still there. I believe in alliance with the Liberal Democrats. I've never subscribed to a formal view of socialism, even as a 15-year-old. I never sang 'The Red Flag'. But if a left story or social democratic or progressive story doesn't include checks and balances in how contemporary capitalism affects ordinary people, then it's not doing the business. One of the disappointments about New Labour is that in its desire to be business-friendly, it has not gone near any of that.

MATTHEW: I'd want to add to what Will said about capitalism that we have to become involved with the cultural critique of capitalism, because capitalism is amoral. It's not immoral; it's amoral. It's equally happy with apartheid or with black majority rule in South Africa; and it was the same with fascism. It will go wherever profit is to be made.

Young people are growing up in a society where the non-values of capitalism are a huge part of the noise around them, and there is a mouse-like squeak of political ethics and religious beliefs to counter this cacophony. This government has treated politics and democracy as a means to achieve the ends of a better society. I think that's wrong. You can't degrade the political process as we saw over the election of the London mayor or in Wales, or over freedom of information, and then say, 'we're doing this to keep control to make a better society'. That's missing the point that the left has to restore people's faith in the process.

RUTH: If I were to draw up a policy wish list, I'd put it under the rubric of what I would call progressive and inclusive citizenship. In no particular order – first, a raft of issues around equality, welfare, tax. Actually the government has done some very good things, and what is so extraordinary is that few people know that it has increased the real value of benefits for young children on income support by 72 per cent, because it goes exactly against what the government said it would do. So people are going round saying, the government is cutting benefits. But actually it has redistributed, but it has to make the case, tell the story.

Secondly, I'd like to see development in the area of global citizenship. If there's one thing I feel ashamed of as a member of the Labour Party, it's our treatment of asylum-seekers.

There are critical issues around work, in particular the value we give to different kinds of work and work–life balance. There are critical issues around gender and the division of responsibilities between women and men. We should be looking to Scandinavian countries and the kind of policies they've introduced to try and encourage men to take on greater responsibilities in the home. We can also learn a lot from the liberal tradition about issues around discrimination and the recognition of diversity. This is a very white government and gays and lesbians still do not have full citizenship because they are discriminated against. Finally, would be policies to promote democracy and the voices of marginalised groups.

MARK: Ruth's list was really good. I would add the environment. It feels an embarrassment to say it, and it shouldn't be. We've got to engage in some fairly fundamental issues about the environment, and

God knows how we do it. Low turnouts are also deeply troubling. We haven't addressed how we engage the public in any of the things we have been discussing.

And if we talk about a progressive century, the way we run our parties and Westminster are in dire need of reform. We're not going to get the right decisions coming out of politicians unless we rip up the whole system, the kind of people who get involved in politics and the way we structure politics.

23
Endpiece

Peter Mandelson

Introduction

I regard the debate about 'the Progressive Century' as important for New Labour. This book is therefore significant. It provokes us. I do not agree with all of its premises or conclusions. But it is a genuinely original contribution to the dialogue on the British centre-left.

My gut instinct as a proud and lifelong member of the Labour tribe is to revel in the party's huge Commons majority. And I will work night and day to retain it.

Yet four historic landslides in a hundred years (1906, 1945, 1966 and 1997) leading to temporary spurts of reforming zeal cannot make up for a sustained period of progressive government in Britain.

Look at the legacy we inherited in 1997: a country with lower material living standards, weaker public services, lower educational attainment and greater social divisions than the majority of our partners in the European Union. This is a society where millions are still denied a basic personal freedom – the chance to fulfil the potential that it is their right to do. This is the legacy of the Conservative century, overwhelmingly shaping the Britain that New Labour strives to rebuild today.

No progressive person would dispute this analysis of the problems facing Britain, nor I suspect the priorities the Government has chosen.

For this reason alone, it is important that dialogue on the centre-left continues. A genuine exchange of ideas about the challenges our country faces in the next 25 years is necessary if we are to create a model twenty-first-century Britain.

The progressive values

With an effective political appeal based on the progressive values of fairness, efficiency and social justice, Labour should go all out to maximise its popular vote. And this approach works. We need look no further than the New Labour platform enabling Tony Blair to mobilise a stunningly diverse constituency of support in the 1997 election.

The strength of the progressive ideal lies in its potential to bind together disparate regions, classes and interests in a broad coalition sympathetic to political change. So not only did Labour maximise its own appeal in 1997 but people from across the progressive spectrum converged to vote out the Conservatives, focusing on the most credible anti-Tory alternative, constituency by constituency.

There is no doubt that some people voted tactically in 1997. And there is no point in politicians speaking in favour or against tactical voting. Voters will make up their own minds and cannot be mobilised like an army, led by a political deal or arrangement manufactured by Westminster politicians.

Of course, my instinct is that I would prefer Labour to absorb like-minded Liberal Democrats and leave the rest to history. But head should prevail over heart. In a small number of straight Labour–Liberal contests there is of course no alternative to a fight to the finish. In every one of these cases I want to see Labour candidates elected. But in most of the country mutual self-destruction would be disastrous. It would make it far easier for the Conservatives to prevail over both parties, electorally and politically. They would win against a divided centre-left opposition as they did for so much of the last century.

One alternative solution to 'the progressive dilemma' is the miraculous emergence of a hegemonic 'big tent party of the centre-left' modelled on the US Democrats. Apart from the fact that I have no idea how in practice this miracle could be brought about, it would destroy the character of the Labour Party, and this is not a direction for New Labour that I would support.

The trade union link evolved a long way in the 1990s. I supported reform. But the creation of a US Democrat-style party would involve the inevitable severing of Labour's constitutional link with the unions.

New Labour has now demonstrated conclusively that we govern in the interests of the country as a whole and that there is no question of reverting to the practices of the 1970s. As a result, my view today is that retaining the trade union link in its reformed state strengthens the Labour Party.

But maintaining the umbilical cord does not preclude us from talking to other political parties about our policy agenda. This is especially so if it makes that programme more sustainable, ensuring that the Conservatives do not prevail in this century as they did in the last.

The progressive principle

So the progressive principle is about values. Bringing together social justice and economic efficiency to deliver the priorities that led to the creation of the Labour Party in 1900. An end to poverty, the maintenance of full employment, and providing the highest quality public services so that, together, we provide a ladder of opportunity to all in our society.

Progressive values also provide us with a clear-sighted agenda. One of the most important explanations for the failure of the British left in the twentieth century was the confusion about the purpose of its politics. For much of the period the Labour Party gave the impression of being obsessed with a particular means of implementing policies, rather than the best tools to hand to pursue its ethical objectives.

For most of the last century, planning and nationalisation defined Labour's socialism. This negated the importance of a widely shared vision for society based on the values of fairness and social justice, stronger community and a wider distribution of opportunity.

As a result, when its immediate programme was fulfilled, and the electorate grew disenchanted with austerity, the 1945–51 Labour Government ended its period of office appearing aimless and lacking direction. Labour's confusion and the internal divisions surrounding it, consequently lost it the support of many who shared the ideals of social democracy.

Progressive values help to address this by offering Labour a clearer, more meaningful conception of its political objectives. If we are to break the unhappy sequence of Conservative domination in our country, Labour must replace ideological dogma with a dialogue about ideas. A framework for constant intellectual revitalisation and political renewal is a necessary prerequisite for Labour's long-term electoral success.

The new style of politics

Nowhere is the need for change and renewal more apparent than in the modernisation of the British constitution. But the editors of this book are more downbeat than they ought to be about New Labour's achievements in creating a new style of politics in Britain.

The present government has pursued a bold agenda of constitutional reform. We have rightly been cautious about trumpeting the radicalism of the programme until the new institutions have proved themselves.

Yet by the standards of the great reforming governments of the nineteenth century our programme has been remarkable in winning consent and moving with speed.

In creating the new devolved institutions and ending the monopoly of Westminster power, progressive politics based on power sharing and co-operation now flourishes in Scotland and Wales, and is taking root in Northern Ireland. At last, political institutions have been created enabling people to be Scottish, Welsh and Irish as well as British, without being forced to choose between these identities.

Constitutional reform will take many years to complete. It is important that the dialogue across the political parties continues, so that the momentum is sustained for further political reform where a majority support it. This could include the House of Lords, a referendum on the electoral system for the House of Commons, and local government reform in England and Wales.

Yet the discussion between Labour and the Liberal Democrats should not end merely with constitutional issues. For example, a central theme of domestic politics over the next ten years will be whether we can transform the quality of our public services in Britain.

Since this book is intended to be a constructive dialogue, I must say I find Liberal Democrat claims that they could somehow go further and faster on public service reform perplexing.

Of course, party representatives are entitled to argue that they would increase income tax and spend more heavily than the present government. What is illegitimate is the pretence that there is a magic solution to the genuine supply-side constraints that exist in the public services. For example, it will take years of investment to overcome the severe shortage of highly trained teachers, nurses and doctors.

The Liberal Democrats must also acknowledge that the real enemy of progress in Britain is the Conservative Party. The dogmatic Tory impulse to roll back further the parameters of the British state is expressive of an ideological crisis on the right similar to that once experienced by Labour over nationalisation. That impulse is the great political threat to the progressive values we hold dear. The British centre-left must act from a sense of moral duty to protect public institutions from the Conservative assault.

On Britain's future relationship with the European Union progressives can similarly make common cause. The European issue provides an important platform on which politicians can articulate their progressive values. In this case, standing up to xenophobia and intolerance and making the argument for a strengthened European commitment as a means of protecting and advancing British national interests. This is not only a political necessity but also a patriotic duty.

Conclusion

There is also a more fundamental reason why a broader progressive dialogue should continue.

For the cause of the progressive century can only be won if our values are perceived by the general public to be in the interests of the country, and not simply those of political parties. It is my dearest wish as a Labour politician to destroy the electoral prospects of the Conservative Party and dominate this century just as they did the last against a divided centre-left opposition.

But our cause is the historic mission to create a fairer society in which individuals can fulfil the potential that is uniquely theirs. It is the centre-left's greatest insight that a commonwealth of talents is the strongest form of community.

The achievement of this goal necessarily requires sustained progressive government. It will take years of reform and careful policy implementation, as well as the widest possible commitment for our programme of change to endure.

I desperately want today's Labour Party to triumph long in to the future. But this should never preclude closer working with others if it means we can more readily create a society in Britain that uniquely combines economic dynamism, personal freedom and social justice. That is why I believe the ideas outlined in *The Progressive Century* are important to reflect on.

Index

Compiled by Sue Carlton